# EXPERIENCE
### AND
# ITS MODES

# EXPERIENCE
## AND
## ITS MODES

by

MICHAEL OAKESHOTT

❋

CAMBRIDGE
AT THE UNIVERSITY PRESS

PUBLISHED BY

THE SYNDICS OF THE CAMBRIDGE UNIVERSITY PRESS

Bentley House, 200 Euston Road, London, N.W.1
American Branch: 32 East 57th Street, New York, N.Y. 10022

*First printed in Great Britain at the University Press, Cambridge*
*Library of Congress Catalogue Card Number: 34–16688*
*Reprinted in the United States of America*

*First published* 1933
*Reprinted* 1966
1978

# PREFACE

In the composition of this book I owe much to the kindness and encouragement of Professor W. R. Sorley, Professor H. H. Joachim and Mr J. S. Boys-Smith, and their copious criticisms have enabled me to avoid many pitfalls and to correct many blunders. They are not, of course, responsible for the mistakes and imperfections which remain, but without their generous help the defects would have been even greater.

M.O.

*August,* 1933

# CONTENTS

V. Practical Experience (*cont.*)

VI. Conclusion                                            322

# I

## INTRODUCTION

An interest in philosophy is often first aroused by an irrelevant impulse to see the world and ourselves better than we find them. We seek in philosophy what wiser men would look for in a gospel, some guidance as to *le prix des choses*, some convincing proof that there is nothing degrading in one's being alive, something to make the mystery of human existence less incomprehensible. Thinking is at first associated with an extraneous desire for action. And it is some time, perhaps, before we discern that philosophy is without any direct bearing upon the practical conduct of life, and that it has certainly never offered its true followers anything which could be mistaken for a gospel. Of course, some so-called philosophers afford pretext enough for this particular misunderstanding. Nearly always a philosopher hides a secret ambition, foreign to philosophy, and often it is that of the preacher. But we must learn not to follow the philosophers upon these holiday excursions.

Nor is this the only error to be avoided. The impulse of mere curiosity is no less foreign to philosophy. When we are consumed with a greed for information, philosophy appears as universal knowledge. Nothing, it seems, should be alien to the philosopher, who must hate ignorance more than he loves discrimination. But this indiscriminate pursuit of universal knowledge is scarcely better than a romantic obsession. And it is foreign to the character of philosophy, because when we are intent upon what is a whole and complete we must resign what is merely encyclopaedic. The *savant* as such is not a philosopher; there is little or nothing in common between the philosopher and the *philosophe*. It is only in the childhood of thought, when knowledge appears undifferentiated and each fresh piece of information seems significant just because it is fresh, that universal knowledge can appear to satisfy the philosophic passion. At all events, in these days when we are more conscious of the futility of knowledge than its blessing, it is not to be expected that an encyclopaedia will attract him who is looking for a philosophy.

But when universal knowledge has been rejected in favour of valid knowledge as the end in philosophy, there are still more paths than one for us to choose from. And it is scarcely to be expected, in these days, that we should not be tempted to take up with the idea of philosophy as, in some sense, 'the fusion of the sciences', 'the synthesis of the sciences' or the *scientia scientiarum*. Yet, what are the sciences that they must be accepted as the datum, and as a datum not to be changed, of valid knowledge? And if we begin with the sciences, can our conclusion be other or more than merely scientific? These and other questions like them are what any-one must consider who, in search of a complete and satis-factory world of experience, is tempted by science. Never-theless, whatever defect we may discover in, for example, the world of scientific experience, it is impossible to dismiss such a world of experience as merely invalid and look for a philo-sophy beyond it in some other, different world; that is too easy an escape. Even if truth is difficult to come at, nothing can be dismissed as mere error. Rather, what is required is a point of view from which the relative validity of any world of experience can be determined; what is required is a criterion. And in seeking this point of view, we seek a philo-sophy; and could we find it we should have found, if not a philosophy, at least a foundation upon which to build one.

Philosophical experience, then, I take to be experience without presupposition, reservation, arrest or modification. Philosophical knowledge is knowledge which carries with it the evidence of its own completeness. The philosopher is simply the victim of thought. And again, philosophy seems to be a mood; for we cannot always be engaged upon this pursuit of what is finally satisfactory in experience. A man cannot be a philosopher and nothing else; to be so were either more or less than human. Such a life would, indeed, be at once febrile and insipid and not to be endured. But in philosophy (seldom desired and less often achieved), what is satisfactory is only what is positive and complete. And when philosophy is sought, it must be sought for its own sake. It depends for its existence upon maintaining its independence from all extraneous interests, and in particular from the practical interest. To popularize philosophy is at once to debase it: a general demand for philosophy is a general demand for its degradation. Few, perhaps, will be found willing to surrender the green for the grey, but only those few are on the way to a philosophy. And instead of a gospel, the most philosophy can offer us (in respect of practical life) is an escape, perhaps the only complete escape open to us.

The purpose of this book is to discover the main implications of this conception of philosophy. And in it I shall do no more than present a general point of view. It is an attempt, not to formulate a system, but to see clearly and to grasp firmly a single idea—the notion of philosophy as experience without reservation or arrest, experience which is critical throughout, unhindered and undistracted by what is subsidiary, partial or abstract. Such an idea is necessarily fleeting and elusive. And anyone moderately acquainted with the difficulties will not need to be told how often I have seen the day confuse what in the night had seemed clear. But, at the end, I am still not without hope that I have managed to convey the general point of view which lies at the back of my mind. It is a personal point of view in so far as it is mine and because philosophy consists, not in persuading others, but in making our own minds clear. But, in so far as I have been able to present the grounds upon which it rests, it is more than merely personal. Nor in saying that it is mine do I wish to claim any personal originality. Whatever element of truth it may contain has probably been advanced by others before me, even if I am not myself aware of the occasion.

But philosophy, when it is taken to be experience without reservation or arrest, cannot disclaim the responsibility of accounting for the arrests which occur in experience, or at least the responsibility of determining their character. Indeed, this might be considered the main business of a philosophy conceived in this way. For ordinarily our experience is not clear and unclouded by abstract categories and postulates, but confused and distracted by a thousand extraneous purposes. And unless we are exceptionally fortunate, a clear and unclouded experience is to be realized only by a process of criticism and rejection. In philosophy, then, it is not less necessary to be unwearied in rejection than in invention, and it is certainly more difficult. But further, in philosophy nothing may be merely rejected. A form of experience is fallacious and to be rejected in so far as it fails to provide what is satisfactory in experience. But its refutation is not to be accomplished merely by ignoring or dismissing it. To refute is to exhibit the principle of the fallacy or error in virtue of which a form of experience falls short of complete coherence; it is to discover both the half-truth in the error, and the error in the half-truth.

Thus, what I have undertaken is, first, a study of the relationship which subsists between experience as a whole and for its own sake and the various arrests which experience suffers; and, secondly, a study of the relationship of these arrests to one another. It is, as I hope to show, an investigation of the relation of what is concrete to what is abstract, and of the relation of any one abstract world to any other. Of the first of these topics I will say no more now; it has frequently been considered and from many different standpoints. The second, however, has less frequently been discussed; and since it has about it an air of unreality, some apology may be required for considering it. To many, the question whether or not a certain way of thinking belongs (for example) to history, to science or to practice will appear to introduce into the concrete whole of experience a principle of sterile purism; at best it will be considered merely 'academic', at worst an opportunity for pedantry. Indeed, those whose interest lies in the elucidation of one or other of these worlds of experience will naturally think it an insignificant question whether or not what they study is a science; and when we consider the way in which this question is usually formulated and discussed nothing, it would appear, could exceed its futility. To bother about a *confusion des genres* is the sign of decadent thought. But this is not the view of the matter I have come to take. For, as I considered the problem, it became increasingly clear that unless these forms of experience were separated and kept separate, our experience would be unprotected against the most insidious and crippling of all forms of error—irrelevance. And when we consider further the errors and confusion, the irrelevance and cross-purpose, which follow from a failure to determine the exact character and significance of (for example) scientific or historical experience, it becomes possible to suppose that those who offer us their opinions upon these topics may have something to say of which we should take notice. To dismiss the whole affair as a matter of mere words is the first impulse only of those who are ignorant of the chaos into which experience degenerates when this kind of question is answered perfunctorily or is left altogether without an answer. "Truth", says Bacon, "comes more easily out of error than of confusion": but the view which I have to recommend is that confusion, *ignoratio elenchi*, is itself the most fatal of all errors, and that it occurs whenever argument or inference passes from one world of experience to another, from what is abstracted upon one principle to what is abstracted upon another, from what is abstract to what is concrete, and from what is concrete to what is abstract. And if this be so, the importance of a criterion for determining this confusion is extreme. So far, then, as this part of my subject is concerned, it may be considered as an investigation of the character of irrelevance or *ignoratio elenchi*.

My purpose, then, is to defend a general view—to defend it by elucidating it. And consequently whatever detail I have admitted to my argument has been subordinated. I should, indeed, have preferred to have divested it even more thoroughly than I have been able of extraneous and obscuring detail. And that I have not been able to achieve this improvement is due, at least in part, to the present state of thought on the subjects I have been obliged to discuss. Where the field is encumbered with so many and elementary fallacies, a writer can scarcely avoid the task of weeding them out. Nevertheless, what I have to offer is not a complete account of my view, an account in which every alternative is considered, but an imperfect sketch, a mere outline. And further, I ought perhaps to say that it is a view which derives all that is valuable in it from its affinity to what is known by the somewhat ambiguous name of Idealism, and that the works from which I am conscious of having learnt most are Hegel's *Phänomenologie des Geistes* and Bradley's *Appearance and Reality*. I am aware that in these days many readers will require no other evidence than this confession to condemn my view out of hand. For the abuse which was formerly the lot of philosophy in general is now reserved for philosophical Idealism, which (it is the common opinion) is decadent, if not already dead. Its doctrines are held to comprise a mixture of fallacies and truisms, and the 'intellectualism' in philosophy of which it is the chief representative is counted a spent force needing no other evidence of its falsity than its own decay. So far as I can ascertain, however, these opinions are founded upon no firmer basis than one of confused reasoning and irrelevant anecdote. Idealism is in these days dismissed, it seems, because it has presumed to raise difficulties and question postulates which it were wiser to have left hidden and undisputed. There was, indeed, a time when a kind of Idealism was the orthodoxy of philosophy, but this fortunately is no longer the case. A received philosophy is one already dead. And if by calling it decadent, the opponents of Idealism mean nothing more than that it is out of fashion, its friends will ask nothing better than the dispassionate criticism which a philosophy without a reputation to be feared may reasonably expect. In these circumstances, then, what seems to be required is not so much an apology for Idealism as a restatement of its first principles, and in so far as my view is Idealistic (and how far it is, I do not myself know), this is what I have attempted.

Anyone who has had a glimpse of the range and subtlety of the thought of Plato or of Hegel will long ago have despaired of becoming a philosopher. And most who have reflected upon the vigour and reach which enable these writers to afford place for what, to the lesser thinkers who preceded and followed them, is merely contradictory and irreconcilable, must have considered whether it were not better that they should give up the attempt. For there is less place for what is second-class in the field of philosophy than in any other field of intellectual interest. And moreover, the character of philosophy forbids us to console ourselves with the notion that, if we fail to achieve a coherent view of the whole field, we can at least do honest work in the cultivation of one of its corners. Philosophy has no such corners; whatever we say is said, if not explicitly, then ignorantly and implicitly, of the whole.

Thinking, however, is not a professional matter; if it were it would be something much less important than I take it to be. It is something we may engage in without putting ourselves in competition; it is something independent of the futile attempt to convince or persuade. Philosophy, the effort in thought to begin at the beginning and to press to the end, stands to lose more by professionalism and its impedimenta than any other study. And it is perhaps more important that we should keep ourselves unencumbered with merely parasitic opinion than that we should be aware of all, or even the best, that has been thought and said. For a philosophy, if it is to stand at all, must stand absolutely upon its own feet, and anything which tends to obscure this fact must be regarded with suspicion.

My debts, however, are many. And if I have often omitted to acknowledge the source of my arguments, it is for the double reason that in most cases I have forgotten it and that, since there are no 'authorities' in philosophy, references of this kind would but promote a groundless trust in books and a false attitude of mind. A philosopher is not, as such, a scholar; and philosophy, more often than not, has foundered in learning. There is no book which is indispensable for the study of philosophy. And to speak of a philosopher as ignorant is to commit an *ignoratio elenchi*; an historian or a scientist may be ignorant, philosophers merely stupid. But if, in an attempt to sail as free as possible from ballast, I have occasionally endangered my ship, I must plead that all I have desired is to achieve a general point of view, neither complete nor final, but systematic as far as it goes and presented as a reasoned whole.

# II

## EXPERIENCE AND ITS MODES

The purpose of this chapter is to consider the general character of experience. And here, as elsewhere, what I have to offer is merely a point of view, defended briefly and as best I can. I shall consider first experience in its most general character, secondly experience and truth, thirdly experience and reality, and lastly the modes of experience.

### § 1

'Experience', of all the words in the philosophic vocabulary, is the most difficult to manage; and it must be the ambition of every writer reckless enough to use the word to escape the ambiguities it contains. I will begin, then, by indicating what I take it to denote. 'Experience' stands for the concrete whole which analysis divides into 'experiencing' and 'what is experienced'. Experiencing and what is experienced are, taken separately, meaningless abstractions; they cannot, in fact, be separated. Perceiving, for example, involves a something perceived, willing a something willed. The one side does not determine the other; the relationship is certainly not that of cause and consequent. The character of what is experienced is, in the strictest sense, correlative to the manner in which it is experienced. These two abstractions stand to one another in the most complete interdependence; they compose a single whole. It would, then, be possible to build up one's view of the character of experience either from the side of experiencing, or from the side of what is experienced; and it would be superfluous to do both, for whatever is true of the one side will be true also of the other. But, since it is our business in philosophy to avoid abstractions, this concrete whole, experience, is what calls for attention. And what I am concerned with primarily is not experiencing severed from what is experienced, or what is experienced severed from experiencing, but with experience itself, the concrete whole.

Reflection on the character of experience finds in most men a mind filled with prejudice and confusion; and not uncommonly these prejudices and this confusion will be found to spring from distinctions elevated into differences. One such distinction is that which divides experience into the part which may properly be called thought, that which (because it is more elementary or immediate) falls short of the condition of thought, and that which passes beyond the condition of thought. Thought, we have been told, is a particular mode of experience, which must be distinguished at once from mere consciousness, from sensation, from perception, from volition, from intuition, and from feeling. And we shall perhaps find ourselves to have inherited also beliefs about the order and relative validity of such modes of experience.

Now, it need not be denied that, for some purposes, such an analysis of experience may be relevant and useful. These names certainly stand for what can be distinguished. Nevertheless, it is difficult to understand how, if it be pressed to its conclusion, the issue can be anything but one of error. For, in the end, a consciousness which is mere consciousness (and not a thinking consciousness) turns out to be a mere contradiction; sensation, when it is isolated, turns out a meaningless abstraction; and intuition achieves independence only to discover that the price of it is nonentity. And the view I propose to maintain is that experience is a single whole, within which modifications may be distinguished, but which admits of no final or absolute division; and that experience everywhere, not merely is inseparable from thought, but is itself a form of thought. It is not, of course, wrong to attempt an analysis of experience, to distinguish (for example) sensation, reflection, volition, feeling and intuition; the error lies in supposing that in so doing we are considering activities which are different in principle and can be separated from one another finally and absolutely. They are the products of analysis, lifeless abstractions which (like all such) call out to be joined to the concrete whole to which they belong and whence they derive their nature. All abstract and incomplete experience is a modification of what is complete, individual and concrete, and to this it must be referred if we are to ascertain its character. And thought or judgment, as I see it, is not one form of experience, but is itself the concrete whole of experience.

This view of the character of experience is not so well established as to require no argument in its support; indeed, no view of experience can ever be, in that sense, established. And, although the possibility of presenting an altogether satisfactory defence of my view is somewhat remote, I must give what account I can of the grounds on which I conceive it to rest. I will consider first the experience which claims to fall short of the condition of thought, and secondly that which claims to pass beyond it. And I need scarcely remark that I shall consider these claims in their logical form only; for, if they prove groundless in this form, there can no longer be any meaning in the suggestion that we may seek in the past a pre-thinking stage of experience or in the future a supra-thinking stage.

A distinction, which goes back to the beginning of reflection upon the character of experience, has been maintained between the senses and the mind, between sensation and thought or judgment. And among those who maintain this distinction there are some who believe that sensation is a mode of experience independent of thought or judgment. And it is this opinion which we are to examine. The questions of the priority and the validity of this mode of experience may, for the present, be left on one side; our business is with the belief that sensation exists as a mode of experience entirely independent of thought or judgment.

There is, I think, little doubt about the character of the difference which is asserted between sensation and judgment.

The first is direct, immediate experience, unqualified by inference, relieved from the interference of reflection: the second implies interpretation and reflection; it is mediated experience, qualified and modified by whatever knowledge or opinion the experient may happen already to possess. Of course, the preciseness of the distinction may, in particular instances, be blurred so that it seems almost to disappear. Sensation may be so complex and sophisticated that it approaches the condition of judgment, and judgment so simple and direct that it appears almost to assume the character of sensation. But, in the main and in general, the distinction holds and is absolute; sensation is not thought, thought is not sensation, and both are forms of experience. And examples of what is meant by this purely sensual experience are ready to hand. "I am, let us say, lying in bed and dropping asleep. Suddenly I am startled by a loud and prolonged sound resembling that which might be produced by the whistle of a passing train. In the whole previously acquired system of my knowledge there may be nothing from which I could by any logical manipulation have elicited the cognition that this sensation would emerge in my consciousness at this moment; even if I could have found grounds for anticipating it, I may not have attended to them; finally, if I did actually anticipate the occurrence of the sound at that moment, yet the actual hearing of it is not included in and does not issue out of the anticipation of it. It obtrudes itself on consciousness whether I anticipate it or not. I need no ground for asserting its presence because it directly asserts itself."[1]  Briefly then, what we have in sensation is direct experience, immediate, unmodified, complete and neither pointing to, nor involving any experience whatever beyond itself. And the question for us is, Is this a possible form of experience?

Now, setting on one side examples from which we shall learn little, let us suppose that sensation is all that it is said to be, that in it experience is separated entirely from the influence of judgment, and ask what (in that case) must be

[1] G. F. Stout, *Studies in Philosophy and Psychology*, p. 309.

its character. The separation of sensation from judgment implies, in the first place, that the given in sensation must be isolated, simple, exclusive, and wholly unrelated; transient, inexpressible, unsharable and impossible of repetition. In sensation (thus conceived) there can be nothing more than a bare 'this is', in which the 'this' is utterly indeterminate, without name or character, and the 'is' is limited to merely 'here' and 'now'. That there can be as much as this, is perhaps doubtful; but certainly there can be no more. And I think those who believe that sensation is an independent form of experience will not be found to contest this. It is true that we are accustomed to speak of a sensation of yellow, but in doing so we use the word sensation with a meaning different from that before us. In experience, yellow is never isolated and unrelated, unmodified by previous experience. Yellow is, of course, a general concept, and what is experienced in terms of this concept is certainly not inexpressible, without name or character. On the contrary, yellow, as it is in actual experience, is characterized by connexion with previous experiences recognized as different or similar either in kind or in degree. It is recognized. But it is exactly this freedom from recognition which is claimed for what is given in sensation. And secondly, the subject in sensation must be correlative with its object. Sensation, because what is given in it is singular, unrelated and indeterminate, a mere 'this', implies the absence of any continuous or unified experiencing agent. The self in sensation is, like the object, a mere abstraction, now to be identified with sight, now with hearing, and always devoid of continuity and individuality. The subject in a given sensation is the momentary state of an isolated sense. Sensation, then, when it is separated from judgment, is without either determinate object or determinate subject; it is immediate experience.

To turn from this to actual experience involves us, I think, in a contrast. Experience, I take it, even in its most elementary form, implies, at least, consciousness. And it is impossible to be conscious of a mere and indeterminate 'this' or of a bare

'here'. However simple it be, in experience there is always
something not entirely indeterminate, and whatever has passed
beyond the condition of sheer indeterminacy has passed, also,
beyond the condition of isolation, singularity and unrelated-
ness. To be conscious of something is, in some degree, to
recognize it; and recognition involves us at once in judgment,
in inference, in reflection, in thought. Consciousness, moreover, requires a subject which stands above mere momentary
states of sensation; it requires, at least, a body of related
experiences in some degree organized and harmonious.
Nothing, in short, can maintain its claim to be in experience
which presents itself in utter isolation, alone, without world,
generation or relevance. Experience is always and everywhere
significant.

Sensation, then, as a form of experience independent of
thought or judgment, must be pronounced self-contradictory.
This absolute separation of sensation and thought is false:
to claim release from the despotism of thought is to claim
a place altogether outside possible experience. On the one
side, the given in experience cannot be of the character
attributed to the given in sensation. And on the other side,
whatever can be known cannot come and go in isolation
(as the given in sensation was believed to come and go); it
comes and goes for a coherent, continuous self. The self in
sensation (thus conceived), this abstract, indeterminate,
momentary self, without memory and incapable of reflection
is, also, a contradiction. A self, replete with opinion, prejudice, habit, knowledge is implied in every actual experience;
and to exclude this self from any experience whatever
is an absolute impossibility. There are, of course, occasions
when it is less fully present, there are many occasions when
we are not conscious of its presence; nevertheless, it remains
a *conditio sine qua non* of experience. And sensation severed
from judgment, because such a self is unknown to it, pro-
claims its own alienation from experience.

If sensation is unable to sustain the character of a form of
experience untouched by thought or judgment, it would

appear unlikely that this character will be found to belong to any experience whatever. Nevertheless, the claim made on behalf of sensation is made, also, in respect of perception. And this claim must be considered. Perception, I take it, is distinguished from mere sensation by reason of its complexity. Sensation is always simple, singular and isolated; but perception, though it must be singular and isolated, is not simple, for it is often composed of more than one sensation. In perception, sensations lose their characteristic simplicity and enter a world in which they are related to one another so as to form a determinate whole. And, it is contended, this complex experience is itself independent of judgment. Perception, then, in so far as it advances upon the condition of sensation, must say something more determinate than merely, 'This is here and now'; nevertheless, if it is to preserve its independence of thought and judgment, it must say less than, e.g., 'This is a tree'. But what vague utterance remains for it in this dim interspace between sensation and judgment, and how in any case it can fail to be judgment of some sort, is not clear to me. And I cannot conceive of perception succeeding where sensation has failed.

There is, however, one argument in favour of the belief that perception is a form of experience independent of thought or judgment which ought to be considered if only because it is relied upon by so many writers. It is suggested that the obvious and undeniable difference between actual perception and any judgment which may follow upon it involves the separation of perception from thought. There is a difference between seeing a green leaf and judging "that the leaf is green", and this difference implies that perception is not judgment. And, indeed, a similar argument is used to support the claim of sensation. There is a difference between the sensation blackness and the judgment "that this is black", and this difference can be accounted for only upon the assumption that sensation does not involve judgment. Nevertheless, though it appears to me difficult (though not impossible) to deny this difference with regard both to sensation and to perception, I am unable to conclude from it that actual sensation and perception do not themselves involve judgment. By securing their independence of certain specific judgments, sensation and perception cannot hope to secure themselves absolute independence of all judgment. To have made clear that *this* sensation or *this* perception is not identical with *this* judgment, can scarcely be taken as equivalent to a demonstration that it is not identical with *any* judgment. And it is this demonstration which I believe to be impossible. Nor, I think, will the familiar contrast between perception and conception afford us grounds for any other opinion. For this contrast, like others, can be usefully insisted upon only while we see that the difference it expresses is a difference of degree and a difference within the world of judgment. If conception means taking several elementary experiences and understanding them in such a way that they become elements of a connected and intelligible whole (and I know of no other meaning for it), then perception can differ from it only by reason of the kind of experiences it comprehends and not because it comprehends them in a wholly different manner. In short, neither sensation nor perception can maintain itself as a form of experience which does not involve judgment. We perceive only that which we, in some sense, recognize, that which has some meaning or significance for us; and where there is meaning or significance there is judgment, and perhaps also memory. And experience less than thought is a contradiction and nowhere to be found.

It cannot, however, be denied that this is an important and difficult question, and on that account I propose to reconsider it from a fresh standpoint. The contrast between thought or judgment and a form of experience which does not involve thought is sometimes conceived as a distinction between mediate and immediate experience. And sensation, it is asserted, is immediate experience. Our question, then, may be formulated thus: Are there any valid grounds upon which a form of experience claiming to be genuinely immediate can maintain at once its claim and its character as a form of experience? And, for our purpose we may leave on one side the view that in so-called self-evident propositions we have an immediate experience, and concentrate our attention upon the claim of sensation to be this form of experience. Now, as we have already seen, there cannot be any doubt about the general character of what is given in 'immediate experience'. What is given in such an experience would be confined to what is given in the exact moment of reception. It would be isolated, without meaning or relevance and wholly unrelated to any other experience, immediate or mediate. What is given in 'immediate experience' is limited to a 'this', a 'here' and a 'now'. Immediacy cannot be separated from indeterminateness and inexpressibility. But when we turn to what is given in actual sensation, it is not merely difficult, but impossible to recognize there any of the characteristics of genuine immediacy. Everything given in sensation is determinate; sensation is always sensation of something. Everything has some meaning and relevance for us, and nothing is confined merely and absolutely to what is given in the exact moment of reception. There is no sensation unmodified by apperception; for everything in sensation is presented, not in utter isolation, but as part of a system of experience, as part of ourselves. And separated from this system it loses its character as experience. In short, if we take immediacy seriously, nothing in experience can be said to be immediate; for immediacy and experience are mutually exclusive. Judgment and experience are inseparable; wherever there is judgment there is inference, and immediacy has given place to mediation. And the claim of sensation to be, on account of its immediacy, a form of experience exclusive of thought, must be said to have failed. Indeed, the whole contrast between mediate and immediate experience is vicious and misleading. In one sense it might be said that all experience whatever is immediate, because (as we shall see) experience is reality. And in another sense, all experience may be said to be mediate, because of its character as a coherent system. But a more profound view of the nature of experience would, I think, be obliged to reject both these terms as misleading.

Nevertheless, although neither sensation nor perception can maintain themselves as immediate experience, it is not, I think, difficult to understand why the attempt to discover such experience somewhere should have been considered so important. Experience, it is said, must begin somewhere, and if thought involves mediation, it cannot begin with thought. "It is as if one should say that in building a wall every brick must be laid on the top of another brick and none directly on the ground." The necessity of a form of immediate experience, a form of experience independent of thought or judgment, seems to be involved in the fact of experience. Any conception of experience seems to require something prior to thought, and what is prior is, for that reason, independent. And a distinction between sensation and thought has been maintained in which sensation is a form of experience which, because the given in it is the manifold and the nonsensical, precedes judgment and provides judgment with its material. Experience, it is said, begins with disconnected, simple, immediate sensations, the product of particular physical activities. And thought, interpreting these data, replaces sensation by judgment. The principle of the priority of sensation to judgment is not so much the formula of a particular doctrine as an unavoidable observation, the neglect of which can involve us in nothing but error and confusion. Nevertheless, I can discover in this view nothing but the distorting influence of a false analogy. This so-called necessity of finding a beginning for thought outside the region of judgment is no necessity at all: and further, what is given in 'immediate experience', this manifold and nonsensical, because it could never actually be in experience, offers nothing which could be even mistaken for an intelligible starting place for thought. And could this false conception of experience be exposed and destroyed we should, I think, be troubled no longer with the fallacies it involves. The notion that thought requires raw material, a datum which is not itself judgment, and the consequent eagerness to discover its character, may be traced to the fact that in experience, so far as we can recollect, we find ourselves always manipulating some material independent of the actual process of manipulation. But it is false to infer from this that what is manipulated is not itself judgment. In thought there is nothing analogous to the painter's colours or the builder's bricks—raw material existing apart from the use made of it. Sensation implies consciousness, consciousness implies judgment, and judgment is thought. These do not follow one another, there is no process here, and to postulate a process is to be under the influence of a false analogy. That there is a process somewhere cannot be denied; but it takes place within the world of thought, and is a process by which one mode of thought supersedes another.

And yet, a denial of the need for, or the existence of any data for thought outside the world of thought is not likely to shake our confidence in there being data of some kind, or at least something which may be called a beginning. If one professes to be 'thinking', the enquiry may be made, "Thinking about what?" Thinking we assume is about something, and about something other than itself. If, then, the analogies of the builder and his bricks and of the painter and his colours are false and misleading, are there no others to take their place? Thinking, according to the analogy of the *Theaetetus*, is a process of catching not wild birds, not what is outside experience (such as the objects in mere sensation), but tame birds already within the cage of the mind. It is a process of recognition in which we reconsider judgments already in some degree affirmed. But, although this frees us in some measure from the errors of the more naïve analogy of the builder and his bricks, it is not without its difficulties. When pressed to its conclusion it is found to postulate birds once wild, judgments once less than judgments, and so falls back upon the notion of an original datum outside thought. And, in any case, a clear view of the character of thought does not depend upon finding an analogy for it; it depends, rather, upon a refusal to be deceived by analogies. Thinking begins neither from sense-data, nor from given feelings or perceptions; it begins neither with what is immediate, nor with the manifold, the contradictory and the nonsensical. What is at first given in experience is single and significant, a One and not a Many. The given in thought is the complex situation in which we find ourselves in the first moments of consciousness. There is nothing immediate or 'natural' in contrast to what is mediate or sophisticated; there are only degrees of sophistication. And the process in experience is the continuous modification and extension of this datum, which is given everywhere in order to be changed and never merely to be preserved. The relation of this given in experience to what is achieved is, however, another question which I must consider in its place. My business here is merely to establish the general character of the given; and my view is that in experience we begin and end with judgment.

I take it, then, that the common view of sensation and perception as forms of experience which fall below the condition of thought, is a prejudice which we can no longer allow. Indeed the claim of any form of experience to be more elementary than judgment, in whatever form it is preferred, turns out to be contradictory. For, were this claim substantiated, it would not merely distinguish sensation and perception from thought, but it would at the same time deprive them of their character as forms of experience. What is given in experience and at the same time escapes the despotism of significance is a mere contradiction. What is given in experience, it is true, appears more immediate on some occasions than on others, appears to depend less upon a conscious process of comprehension within an individual world of experience, but this psychological reflection upon the speed, degree or manner of that process has no bearing whatever upon the fact that to be given in experience at all means to have a place within such a world. Nor should it be supposed that, in asserting that sensation and perception are modes of thought, I am asserting that they are not distinguishable within thought and are nothing at all. Sensation, it appears to me, is a mode of judgment, differing only in degree from our more precisely formulated judgments. And when judgment supervenes on sense-perception, it is judgment supervening on less coherent judgment. My purpose, however, does not require me to consider the actual and detailed structure of sensation, to consider what differentiates sensation as a mode of thought, or even to consider the part played by memory in sensation: my business is merely to point out that these differentiae cannot, in any circumstances whatever, be supposed to carry sensation outside thought.

The result of the preceding argument would seem to be that it is impossible to discover a form of experience which is *less* than judgment. The assertion that such a form of experience exists, involves us at once in contradiction. If, however, this conclusion were taken to imply that all experience whatever necessarily takes the form of judgment, there would be room for objection. For, even had it not been claimed for certain forms of experience that they are other than thought because they are *more* than thought, it might be expected that I ought to consider the possibility of such a form of experience. And I propose now to discuss briefly the claim of a form of experience, which I will call intuition, to be something other and more than judgment.

There are two senses in which intuition has been taken in this connexion; a psychological sense, and a logical sense. The psychological sense need not, however, detain us. It is sometimes suggested that in mathematics, in the sciences and in practical life, either after reflection or without any previous consideration, the factors of a number or the solution of a problem or difficulty will suddenly flash upon the mind, apparently without the mediation of any process of thought; and these flashes of insight, in order to distinguish them from pedestrian thinking, are called intuitive. But it is not difficult to see that intuition, in this purely psychological sense, must fail to establish a home for itself outside judgment, and that when it submits to the implications of judgment, its claim to independence will become contradictory. The validity of this form of experience (which certainly exists) is admitted to rest upon the ability of what is given in it to sustain the test of reflection (the given in intuition, that is, is not as such self-evident), and what is not proved is not known. To call an experience intuitive, in this sense, no more establishes it outside the world of thought than calling it subjective would establish it outside the world of phenomena. The speed with which an element of the world of consciousness finds its implications is not a relevant category in the logic of experience.

Intuition in the logical sense, however, is a more complex conception and less easily disposed of. It is suggested that there is a form of experience in which judgment is superseded by direct experience. Sensation, it is said, has the elementary immediacy of a simple consciousness; in thought there is the consciousness of a subject and a predicate held together, but not identified, in judgment; and in intuition there is a direct subject-predicate experience in which relations have been superseded. Now, the force of the contention that direct experience of this kind exists and that it goes beyond judgment, lies in the implication that this direct experience is, in some sense, truer or more complete than the mediate experience in judgment. The assertion, in the logical sense, of the existence of an intuitive form of experience, carrying us beyond thought, involves the assertion that such a form of experience is a closer or more accurate experience than thought. Judgment is a defective, incomplete form of experience; we must look to intuition for a form of experience which bears the mark of completeness. An absolute can be given only in intuition. There are, then, two contentions for us to consider: first, the belief that judgment is inherently defective experience; secondly, the belief that in intuition the defects of judgment have disappeared.

Thinking, it is said, is the qualification of existence by an idea. Without an idea there can be no thinking; and an idea involves the separation of predicate from subject. Thus, thinking is always a relational, never a direct experience: the predicate is always the adjective of existence, never existence itself. Judgment implies a disruption of the single whole of existence and can remain only so long as that disruption is maintained. And again, less precise writers contend that thinking is a process of analysis and classification which, though it may tell us something about the object in thought, prevents any direct knowledge of it. It is a systematic process of falsification.

In intuition, on the other hand, there is no judgment and consequently none of the separations which judgment entails. It is a non-relational experience. In it we are no longer conscious of subject and predicate as separate and as held together; our consciousness includes both subject and predicate, but, as such, they disappear. It implies a direct knowledge of the whole, freed from the distortion of analysis and the artificial distinctions of judgment. Relation gives place to identity, I place myself within and become what I know, and the adjectival predicate becomes its subject. Intuition is, therefore, a fuller experience; it is a form of experience from which the defects of judgment have been banished. And because intuition is a more complete experience than judgment it lies beyond thought and is independent of it.

Now, were we to follow out to the end the various implications of this view of experience, we should be obliged to travel far afield and to anticipate much that will be more fittingly considered later. This view implies, among much else, an absolute distinction between what is called 'knowledge *of*' and 'knowledge *about*', it implies that the object in thought is never reality but a mere being-for-thought, it implies that the so-called categories of thought stand between the subject and reality, and it implies that a direct and immediate experience, because it is direct and immediate, is a complete experience—and all this I take to be false and misleading. Instead therefore of pressing at once these more radical objections, I intend to suggest here that, since this view rests upon a misconception of the nature of thought or judgment, the claim it prefers on behalf of intuition must be disallowed.

Thinking, the view I am considering maintains, is the explicit and conscious qualification of existence by an idea: the subject in judgment is existence, of which something less than the whole of existence is predicated. This, no doubt, is true of many of our judgments; but that it is the unavoidable character of all judgment whatever is not so clear. Indeed, we have already observed that judgment and explicit, conscious inference and proposition are not identical: perception is certainly judgment, and equally certainly in perception there is frequently no explicit inference or proposition. Thinking is not the mere qualification of existence by an idea; it is a qualification of existence by itself, which extends, in the end, to a qualification of the whole of existence by its whole character. Judgments, in the sense of propositions in which predicate and subject are separate and remain separated from beginning to end, are the mere deposits of the current of concrete experience. And in order to find this continuous experience it is not necessary to go outside thought. A form of experience beyond thought appears necessary only if thought is identified with one of its least developed forms. In its full character thought is not the explicit qualification of existence by an idea, but the self-revelation of existence. Or again, it is impossible to sustain the assertion that all thought is merely relational experience and consequently incomplete, unless the whole scope of thought is restricted to the manipulation of explicit relations. From one standpoint, indeed, it might be said that a non-relational experience is a contradiction and that whatever claims this character claims nonentity; but from another, thought or judgment is seen to pass beyond the assertion of explicit relations without ceasing to be thought. And once more, it is necessary to identify thought with the most barren 'rationalism' if the view that judgment is merely analysis and classification is to be sustained—rationalism with its "passwords of 'Either—Or'", as Hegel says. Of course there are forms of thought which fall below the full character of thought; but nothing but misconception can result from a determination to confine thought to conscious and explicit judgment. And intuition can maintain its claim to pass beyond the condition of thought only when thought at its furthest reach is imagined to turn into something foreign to itself.

I do not propose to consider here the character of this so-called intuitional experience in greater detail, but it may be remarked in passing that, in so far as intuition relies upon the abandonment of judgment, the immediateness of what is given in it must be barren, a merely abstract universal. And further, since few would be so foolish as to claim not only that intuition is a form of experience beyond thought, but also that this claim is self-evident, the independence of intuition must be less absolute than was suggested. A form of experience which is unable to establish its own validity is clearly less complete than that to which it must appeal for this purpose. Indeed, such a form of experience must, in virtue of the necessity of appealing outside itself for its justification, at once be counted subsidiary, abstract and dependent. What is unable to maintain itself without the aid of judgment can scarcely be considered independent of judgment and to pass beyond it.

Two further examples of the assertion that there are forms of experience independent of thought and judgment may be noticed briefly. First, this character is attributed to volition. But, since this view suffers, in the main, from all the old difficulties and raises no new ones, I do not propose to consider it in detail. To see the assertion clearly is, I think, to see its shortcomings. It has been suggested that volition is a form of experience which falls short of the condition of thought. But we have observed already that no experience can escape the despotism of significance, and that recognition certainly involves judgment. The will for nothing in particular, or for something isolated, independent, and unrecognized, are not possible states of consciousness. The same arguments which obliged us to consider sensation and perception as forms of thought, oblige us also to conclude that wherever there is volition there is judgment. And it has been suggested that volition is a form of experience which passes beyond thought, in the same way as intuition was conceived to pass beyond thought. But here again, the objections we discovered to this claim on behalf of intuition are relevant and insurmountable. Volition cannot carry us beyond thought, because there is no beyond. And every form of experience which claims this character makes a home for itself only by an arbitrary limitation of the conception of thought.

And secondly, this character of being independent of judgment is claimed for feeling. Feeling, in this sense, means, I suppose, pleasurable or painful feeling; and it is suggested that in pleasure and pain we have immediate experience, unmodified by judgment. The suggestion, however, is misleading. What we saw to be true of sensation is true also of feeling. The given in feeling is never isolated, unrelated, without name or character. Pain as it is actually felt is characterized by connexion with previous experience, recognized as different or similar either in kind or degree. And where what is given in experience is recognized and significant it has ceased to be immediate and has taken its place within the world of thought.

It will be recollected that the purpose of the preceding argument was to show experience as a single homogeneous whole, to show it as thought or judgment. There are, of course, different forms of thought, and judgment is not everywhere realized in its full character; but nowhere is there to be found a form of experience which is not a form of thought. There is, in my view, no experiencing which is not thinking, nothing experienced which is not thought, and consequently no experience which is not a world of ideas.

§ 2

The general character of experience I have taken to be thought or judgment. And experience is, consequently, a homogeneous whole within which distinctions and modifications may appear, but which knows no absolute division. Experience is a world of ideas. And it remains now to consider its character more in detail. I wish, however, at this point to confine my attention to a single, abstract aspect of experience, to consider it solely *as* a world of ideas; to consider it, that is, from the standpoint of truth. Ordinarily we believe that ideas are about something, that they refer to a world of things or realities, but this is a belief which I do not wish to consider at present; I am concerned now with experience as a world of mere ideas. A pure or mere idea is, of course, an abstraction, and a world of mere ideas is an abstract world, and consequently this view of experience cannot stand by itself; it is incomplete and calls out for completion. But, for the present, I propose to neglect this demand. And I wish also to treat experience as a single, undivided whole, and to postpone the consideration of such modifications as may on occasion appear within it. In short, I intend to consider experience as a totality of facts, not of things; as truth, not reality.

Writers are to be found who adopt the somewhat venturesome course of building up a conception of the character of experience from materials supplied by a particular view of the nature of truth. But, for myself, I wish to choose the more modest plan of constructing a view of truth from an examination of the character of experience. For truth, I take it, is inseparable from experience. It is a condition of the world of experience, a condition which, although it may never be fully established, is never wholly absent. Truth is the condition of the world of experience in which that world is satisfactory to itself. This assertion of the inseparableness of truth and experience appears to me the point from which any satisfactory conception of truth must begin. And it involves the rejection of the view that truth, because it lies somehow outside experience, is an unknowable or inscrutable sum of knowledge, an Absolute not inherent in the character of experience itself but dictated *ab extra*, a prize, extraneous to the race itself, and (when the race is finished) more frequently withheld than awarded.

Truth, then, is correlative to experience. It is the world of experience itself in so far as that world is satisfactory in itself. Let us consider what this means.

Experience, I have suggested, begins with ideas. The character of what is given depends, of course, upon the character of what can be accepted, and in the view I have been presenting, the given in experience can be nothing but ideas. But further, the given in experience is always a world or system. What we begin with is the situation in which we discover ourselves in the first moments of consciousness, and this situation is complex and a whole. The given in experience is, then, a world of ideas. And by a world I mean a complex, integral whole or system; wherever there is a world there is unity. This view, as we have observed already, must be taken to deny first, that the given in experience is immediate, unrelated or without significance in the sense of being other than ideas; and secondly, that the given is particular ideas, whether these ideas are conceived to be self-evident or merely to be inherently isolated and without relations. Particular ideas, in this extreme sense, are, indeed, nowhere to be found in experience: whatever is absolutely isolated and without relations must be devoid of significance and consequently falls outside experience. In a modified sense particular ideas may perhaps be said to be known in experience as the products of analysis and abstraction. They are the creatures of designation, and designation is experience arrested at a point short of that which can satisfy it. Whenever attention is centred upon mere uniqueness experience falls below its full character. These relatively particular ideas are single observations the limits of which are accidental. They are abstracted moments in a continuous process: they are neither necessary stages through which experience must pass, nor self-sufficient elements in the totality of experience, but merely the arbitrary points with which analysis has broken the unity of experience and which abstraction has fixed. But, whatever be the character of these particular ideas, they are certainly not what is given in experience. The given and the isolated, so far from being synonymous, are contradictory: to be given means to be, to that extent, recognized and understood, while the isolated, as such, is what is unrecognizable, meaningless and incapable of being understood. The manifold, the unique, the nonsensical, whatever else they are, are not what is given in experience. We begin, then, with a world of ideas; the given is neither a collection, nor a series of ideas, but a complex, significant whole. Behind this there is nothing at all.

Furthermore, the given in experience is given always in order to be transformed. The primary datum in experience, as such, is never solid, fixed and inviolable, never merely to be accepted, never absolute or capable of maintaining itself, never satisfactory. The condition of the given world of ideas is never such that it may merely be acquiesced in. And consequently our attitude in experience towards what is given is always positive and always critical. From the given as such, we turn to what is to be achieved; from the unstable and defective, we turn to what is complete and can maintain itself. What is achieved is, then, first, a world which differs from the given world only by being more of a world; the given and the achieved are both worlds, but not equally worlds: and secondly, it is a world of ideas. Experience, that is, nowhere deserts either its character as a world, or its character as a world of ideas. And this view of the character of what is achieved in experience must be taken to exclude the views that what is achieved is a world, but not a world of ideas; a mere collection of ideas; or a mere series of ideas. In experience a given world of ideas is never transformed into a world of anything save ideas. And when the notion of the given in experience as particular ideas has been rejected, it is no longer possible to hold that the achieved is a mere collection or series of ideas. In suggesting that the achieved in experience is a world I mean, then, that it is a whole as opposed to a mere series, and a system as opposed to a mere collection. In a system each constituent rests upon the whole, not merely upon its nearest neighbour; and our reading of it may be retrospective or prospective from whatever point we care to take it up. And at whatever point we take it up, we take up the whole, for the so-called constituents of a system are no more than the accidental creations of the circumstances in which we came to apprehend it. And again, these constituents have no individuality or character of their own in isolation from the whole which they constitute; their character is their place in the system. To modify the system as a whole is to cause every constituent to take on a new character; to modify any of the constituents is to alter the system as a whole. In experience, then, a given world of ideas is transformed into a world of ideas which is more of a world.

A world devoid of unity is a contradiction; to enhance a world is to enhance its unity. And in experience a given world of ideas is raised above its given condition by endowing it with a greater degree of unity. In experience we begin, consequently, with the negation of the presented unity wherever that is seen to be false or inadequate. The first step in experience is a denial of the confusion and lack of unity which it finds in its given world—a confusion, however, which (in so far as it is presented) can never be absolute. In experience, given ideas are never merely combined and integrated into a unity; a given world or unity of ideas is reorganized into a closer unity. No constituent, either of this given world or of the world achieved, can be said to have an independent place within the unity of its world, nor is this unity a world constituted of separate yet related ideas; each idea, in so far as it is distinguishable, expresses the unity of its world, and the world (in turn) is presented as a whole in each constituent.

Now, in experience, as the development of a given world or system of ideas, we proceed always by way of implication. We never look *away from* a given world to another world, but always *at* a given world to discover the unity it implies. And consequently what is achieved is contained seminally or implicitly in what is given. And whether it is said that in experience we begin by knowing nothing, or that we begin by knowing, confusedly and implicitly, everything, is of little consequence, so long as it is not supposed either that 'nothing' implies a mere blank, or that 'everything' leaves nothing to be achieved. Implication, moreover, is possible only within a system, and there it is inherent and unavoidable. For it involves a whole in which explicit relationship has given place to a system of complete and mutual dependence; and experience is everywhere a whole of this character. And here again we may notice what is excluded by this view of the character of experience. The view, for example, that in experience the world achieved is an interpretation of the world given, implies a fixed and persisting datum distinguished from and set over against an interpretation or translation of it; and consequently I take it to be excluded by the view I have recommended. And it is excluded even where it is not taken to imply a given which is *not* itself an idea and an interpretation which *is* an idea corresponding to whatever was given. For, setting aside these more elementary errors, the notion that in experience there are two completely separate worlds of ideas, the given and that which is achieved, and that these remain permanently separate, seems to be incompatible with the view of it I have suggested. Generically the achieved world may be said to follow the given world, but since what is achieved is the given endowed with a greater degree of unity, at no time are they separate or even distinct. Interpretation requires something to interpret, but when we speak of *it* our language slips under our feet, for there is never in experience an *it*, an original, distinguishable from the interpretation, and consequently there can be no interpretation. And similarly, in experience there is neither an association of ideas, nor the construction of a chain of ideas. With these notions we find ourselves back again with separate and particular ideas and with the conception of linear inference which they involve; and for that reason they must be rejected.

Unity, then, is what differentiates a world; and a greater degree of unity is what differentiates the world of ideas achieved from the world of ideas given in experience. But when we come to consider in detail the character of this unity it will be found necessary to distinguish it from the unity which belongs to a class, from that which involves mere essences, and from that which has its seat in a 'principle', called for this purpose a unifying principle. The notion of a class is that of a collection of ideas made by selecting an element or factor common to a number of ideas and holding those ideas together as examples or instances of that element or factor. The element selected requires merely to be common to all the members of the class. But such a conglomeration of ideas as this affords clearly falls short of the unity which belongs to experience. It is an abstract unity because it is a unity of abstractions. The common element is never the whole idea and the collection which is built up around it is as limited as it is arbitrary. Classification is a modification of experience and not the concrete whole; it is an arrest in experience. Further, the abstraction of the essence of presented ideas and the achievement of a world of essences should not be mistaken for the concrete whole of experience. And the unity which belongs to a world of essences should not be mistaken for that of experience. Essences, if they appear less arbitrary, are no less abstract than the common elements postulated in collection and classification, and the unity to be achieved by holding together these essences falls short of the unity satisfactory to experience. Nor, again, should the unity of experience be confused with that which arises from conformity to some fixed and central principle;

indeed, it is impossible to find place for such a principle in the world of experience. In experience separate and independent ideas are never gathered together round a given principle or nucleus; a given world of ideas is always amplified by the elucidation of its implications.

The unity of experience, we must conclude, is neither a unity which revolves round some fixed point, nor one derived from conformity to some original datum, nor one which involves mere abstractions, whether these be essences or common elements. It is a unity congenial to a world or system in which every element is indispensable, in which no one is more important than any other and none is immune from change and rearrangement. The unity of a world of ideas lies in its coherence, not in its conformity to or agreement with any one fixed idea. It is neither 'in' nor 'outside' its constituents, but is the character of its constituents in so far as they are satisfactory in experience. Pluralism or dualism are not, as we are frequently invited to believe, the final achievement in experience with regard to some ideas; they are characteristic of any world when insufficiently known. A diversity judged to be ultimate and unconditional is the form of all that fails to be satisfactory in experience.

The idea of unity remains, however, abstract and imperfect while it is divorced from that of completeness. What is satisfactory in experience is achieved only when what is achieved is a world of ideas both single and complete. For the unity which is characteristic of a system is a necessary unity, and there is no necessity apart from completeness. In experience what is established is the necessary character of a world of ideas; and no judgment is satisfactory until it is an assertion, the grounds of which are both complete and seen to be complete. The notion of a system demands the inclusion of all relevant material and demands, at the same time, its unification. A unity achieved without regard to completeness is both arbitrary and precarious; and a whole which is all-inclusive and yet not a unity is a contradiction. The incomplete is, as such, internally discrepant; disunity is the characteristic of a world which has failed to realize itself as a complete whole. What is achieved in experience is, then, a world of ideas which, because it is a system, is unified, and because it is unified, is complete. Unity and completeness are not separate qualities of a world of ideas in so far as it is satisfactory in experience; separated they are meaningless. A world of ideas which is unified because it is complete and complete because it is unified is a coherent world of ideas, and such a world alone is satisfactory in experience. To experience little is to experience incoherently; to know in part is at once to know something less than the whole and to know it imperfectly.

Briefly, then, what is achieved in experience is a coherent world of ideas. This world is itself the arbiter of fact, for to be a fact means to have a necessary place within it. And the acceptance or rejection of an idea is always a question of the result to the world of ideas in which it is intended to be comprehended. Thus the character of an idea is its significance, and its significance is its place in its world. And experience remains incomplete until the world of ideas is so far coherent as not to suggest or oblige another way of conceiving it.

This view of the character of experience is not, of course, new, and there are objections ready to hand. And to consider a few of them may perhaps make my position clearer. It will be suggested that this absolutely coherent world of ideas, which I have spoken of as what is achieved in experience, is discontinuous with the actual process in experience. If what is satisfactory in experience is only a fully coherent world of ideas, then there is no satisfaction: nothing more than partial and momentary coherence can be achieved. And in experience, so far from there being an uninterrupted process, there is only a series of partial achievements. But this objection rests, I think, upon a misconception of the view I am recommending. Experience, as I see it, is nowhere less than a partially coherent world of ideas, but in so far as it falls short of absolute coherence it is temporary and unstable. It would, no doubt, be encouraging could it be shown that each of the momentary states of partial coherence was a step on the way to an absolutely coherent world, but such a view should not be confused with that which I am suggesting. While retaining the notion of a continuous process in experience, we must divest ourselves of the ideas that, should it be arrested at any point, the moment thus created is anything more than a barren abstraction, and that the process itself is a series of such moments. For, so long as we retain these notions, there can be in experience only the fruitless pursuit of satisfaction in a world other than its world. What is achieved in experience is an absolutely coherent world of ideas, not in the sense that it is ever actually achieved, but in the more important sense that it is the criterion of whatever satisfaction is achieved. Absolute coherence as the end in experience is implicit in the character of experience because, where partial coherence is achieved and found to be momentarily satisfactory, the criterion is always coherence itself, that is, absolute coherence. It is because partially and deficiently coherent worlds resemble and can be mistaken for absolutely coherent worlds that they ever enter experience. The full obligations of experience are, no doubt, frequently avoided, but they are always avoided in some mistaken attempt to achieve a positive and coherent world of ideas. In experience, then, in the view I am suggesting, there is not a uniform process in which that which comes later is necessarily nearer the end than that which came earlier. To separate the process into moments is to destroy it, and to imagine it as pursuing some already fixed and determined end is to misconceive it.

But there are other difficulties to consider. It will be said, perhaps, that coherence is a mere disguise for conceivability, and that this view of experience says no more than that the criterion in experience is what is conceivable. How far this objection is valid depends, of course, upon the meaning we attach to 'conceive'; and since there are at least two meanings to confuse us, we must distinguish them. On the one hand, 'to conceive' may be taken to represent the merely psychological aspect of an experience; and 'the conceivable' may mean merely that which has been or can be pictured or brought together in the mind. But it is clear that what is conceivable in this sense cannot, as such, be satisfactory in experience. And it would be a piece of folly to associate the view that the end in experience is a coherent world of ideas with the view that in experience what is satisfactory is whatever can, in this sense, be conceived. On the other hand, however, 'to conceive' may mean to hold together as a consistent whole; and 'the conceivable' may signify that which can be maintained as a coherent unity. And when this view is held, there appears to me no difference between it and that which I have recommended. And the only objection to formulating our view of experience in terms of conceivability is the not remote danger of this being understood in its merely psychological meaning.

A third objection to the view of experience I have presented suggests that this view is defective because it fails to attend to the most insistent (and, to the philosopher, the most embarrassing) element in experience—the irrational— and therefore stands self-convicted of pretentious rationalism. The rational is the coherent, so far at least there is agreement; and the irrational is the incoherent. In what sense, then, does the view I have recommended fail to recognize and do justice to the irrational? Wherever in experience there is at any point an arrest, the world of ideas is to some extent incoherent or irrational; experience has fallen short of its full character. And on the other hand, wherever a world of ideas is presented in experience it must possess the semblance of coherence; that is the meaning and least condition of presentation. A world of ideas is coherent because it is a world given in experience; it is incoherent because experience is not completed in it. Any given world of ideas is, consequently, in a measure irrational; but no given world of ideas can be presented and recognized as irrational. And my view of the character of experience may be said, in this sense, to recognize and to account for irrationality; and had it failed to do so it would, I conceive, have failed in its business. But the misologist requires more, he requires a view of experience which not merely accounts for irrationality but also preserves it. Because irrationality or incoherence is in some sense present (though not as such presented) in every given world of ideas, he conceives that it should be retained. But such a view could be admitted only on the ground (which I take to be false and have already rejected) that whatever is given is fixed and that what is original is permanent and must not be lost. Experience, says Plato, is dialectic; the true form of experience is argument. And argument everywhere is based upon the belief that in experience ideas are not merely collected or associated, but belong to a world or coherent system. And in such a system there is no permanent place for what is incoherent or irrational. For the rest, my view neither involves nor tolerates the rationalism which denies that there is, or should be, any mode of experience less coherent than that which is absolutely coherent, nor the intellectualism which mistakes the arbitrary and abstract intellect for the experiencing mind as a whole.

What is given in experience is, then, a world of ideas and, by pursuing the implications of what is given, a world of ideas, which is satisfactory because it is complete and can maintain itself, is achieved. Nothing, in the view I have suggested, may be merely ejected; but nothing also is beyond criticism and transformation. In experience the given is simultaneously conserved and transformed; and the principle everywhere is that of coherence. And it remains only to observe that, in my view, coherence is the sole criterion; it requires neither modification nor supplement, and is operative always and everywhere. It does not stand at the head of a series or hierarchy of criteria; it is alone and complete in itself.

Now, I am aware that there are other views than this of the criterion of experience, and I wish here to consider one of these. In experience, it is said, a given world of ideas is made to agree with an already fixed and determined world of ideas. The criterion of experience is not the coherence of the world of experience but its correspondence with another world of ideas. And this view may take either of two forms. The criterion may be agreement with either the world of ideas originally given in experience, or an already determined and perfectly satisfactory world of ideas. And it must be considered in both these forms. The first suggestion is that a satisfactory condition of experience is achieved where the world of experience is seen to correspond with the world of ideas originally given in experience, and it is satisfactory on account of this correspondence. It is a dismal doctrine. The given in experience, I have argued, is always a world of ideas; that is, there is no given which is not experience. And, if this be true, the chief difficulty the suggestion I am considering must face is the lack of a world with which agreement may be established. For, unless *per impossibile* the originally given world be a genuinely immediate world, there is no reason for selecting it (rather than any other world of ideas) as the world to which all others must correspond, the absolute in experience. And if it be a genuinely immediate world, it could never enter experience, and consequently agreement with it could never be established. Everything actually in experience is already infected with the possibility of being unsatisfactory, and yet nothing save what is in experience can serve as a criterion for experience. If, then, in experience satisfaction were to lie in making a world of ideas correspond with what we have seen is actually given in experience, the process is one of self-deception and we are left without any stable criterion of satisfaction at all. While, if the criterion of experience be agreement with what is genuinely immediate, satisfaction is not merely difficult but impossible, for such an immediate is a contradiction.

The second suggestion is that a satisfactory condition of experience is achieved when the world of experience is seen to correspond with an already determined and perfectly satisfactory world of ideas. But here the self-contradiction lies unconcealed. By what criterion are we to judge the satisfactoriness of this already determined world? It cannot be a criterion of agreement with any other world, for there is none superior to it with which it might agree. And if the criterion here is coherence, for what reason is this criterion judged unsatisfactory in the case of an actual world of experience? That in experience the given world is pressed forward to a condition of coherence is, of course, the view I have been maintaining, but to set this condition up as an independent world beyond experience, to suppose, moreover, as must be supposed, that it is a known world, and then to define the achievement in experience as a state of correspondence with that world, is a scheme which involves us in too many contradictions to be convincing. Briefly, then, the defect of every view of satisfaction in experience which selects agreement or correspondence as the criterion of satisfaction lies in the impossibility of finding anything with which agreement could be established.

Yet it would be foolish to deny the plausibility and attractiveness of the view that in experience what is satisfactory is achieved only when the correspondence of a given world of ideas with some other world of ideas has been established. Memory is significant only in so far as it is faithful to a past which has not altered, perception only when it does not add fantasy to fact, history recognizes an obligation to what actually happened or it becomes indistinguishable from fiction, and the savour is gone out of science when it neglects what has been observed. Impugn this view, and the whole notion of experience is down about our ears. Nevertheless, I believe this view to be attractive only because it is plausible, and plausible only because it hides the elementary confusion of thought upon which it rests: I mean the confusion of a genetic standpoint with the standpoint of logic. It is true enough that genetically my world of experience has been built upon a foundation which, at times, I have taken to be absolute. But it does not follow that this is its logical as well as its genetic basis. What is hitherto unquestioned is not therefore unquestionable, and what (for certain purposes) has been assumed absolute is not therefore always and everywhere infallible. Neither perception, nor memory, nor history knows of any observation or incident beyond the reach of doubt, any self-evident absolute which does not derive its significance from the world of ideas to which it belongs. And science acknowledges no fact or body of facts with which all subsequent observations have merely to agree in order to win acceptance. Correspondence, then, certainly exists, but it does not afford an adequate representation of the unity of the world of experience. It is a genetical, and consequently a partial, defective, abstract representation of the character of experience. It tells us something of the genesis of satisfaction, but nothing of the criterion of satisfaction in experience. In the process in experience there are countless correspondents, ideas taken for the moment to be fixed, and there is no idea which may not, in this sense, be a correspondent. But, since none of these can ever be absolute, since none is infallible, none established or fixed for more than a limited time or a specific purpose, the final satisfaction in experience can never lie in mere correspondence. The only absolute in experience is a complete and unified world of ideas, and for experience to correspond with that is but to correspond with itself; and that is what I mean by coherence.

How this view of the character of experience will affect our conception of other aspects of experience, I need not stay to enquire in detail. I will notice only the conception of knowledge it implies. We ordinarily think of knowledge as the transformation into experience of something which is not itself experience, the conversion of 'things' into ideas or facts, and this is a view I must consider in a moment. From our present standpoint, however, knowledge is always a coherent system of ideas, and we can be said to know only a system of ideas which is, or appears to be, coherent. Again, knowledge consists in whatever in experience we are obliged to accept, whatever in experience we are led to and find satisfaction in. Wherever this necessity prevails in our world of ideas, there is knowledge; and wherever it appears, there is the appearance of knowledge. Whatever we know, we know as a whole and in its place in our whole world of experience. And knowledge as something apart from that which affords satisfaction in experience is an idle fancy. Consequently, the process of knowledge is not a process of mere accretion. To speak of 'adding to knowledge' is misleading. For a gain in knowledge is always the transformation and the recreation of an entire world of ideas. It is the creation of a new world by transforming a given world. If knowledge consisted in a mere series of ideas, an addition to it could touch only the raw end. If it were a mere collection of ideas, increase could affect only the circumference. But, since it is a system, each advance affects retrospectively the entire whole, and is the creation of a new world. Knowledge, in the view I have suggested, is not the extension of a mere series, or the enlargement of a mere collection of ideas; it is the achievement of the coherence of a given world or system of ideas by the pursuit of the implications of that world.

This view of the character of experience is, of course, susceptible of explanation in terms other than those I have hitherto employed. And I wish now to consider it again from some fresh points of view. Experience, we have seen, is everywhere a world of ideas; and in experience a given world of ideas is transformed into a world which is more of a world, the criterion of achievement everywhere being one of coherence. It is my intention now to show the achievement in experience as (i) fact, (ii) individual ideas, (iii) universal ideas, (iv) a world of absolute ideas.

(i) 'Fact is the material of experience; it is the solid datum which experience must accept and may come to understand. In experience facts are accepted, analysed and co-ordinated, but they may not be tampered with. Facts are observed, remembered and combined; they are the material, not the result of judgment. Fact is coercive because it cannot be questioned, infallible because from it there is no appeal, and both because it is given. The furthest reach of experience is the collection and reflective consideration of unalterable facts.'

This melancholy doctrine, as common as it is crude, suffers from obvious disabilities. Fact, whatever else it may be, is experience; without thought there can be no fact. Even a view which separates ideas from things must recognize that facts are ideas. Fact is what has been made or achieved; it is the product of judgment. And if there be an unalterable datum in experience, it certainly cannot consist of fact. Fact, then, is not what is given, it is what is achieved in experience. Facts are never merely observed, remembered or combined; they are always made. We cannot 'take' facts, because there are none to take until we have constructed them. And until a fact is established, that is, until it has achieved a place in a coherent world, it is no more than an hypothesis or a fiction.

In experience, as I see it, fact is what is achieved. And fact consequently is achieved only with a coherence of the world of experience. Only a perfectly coherent world of ideas is a world of fact. The so-called 'clash of facts' in experience is in reality a clash of imperfectly coherent ideas. Again, fact is coercive, not because it is given (for the given and the questionable stand ever close together), but because it is complete. Fact is what we are obliged to think, not because it corresponds with some outside world of existence, but because it is required for the coherence of the world of experience. And in experience satisfaction is achieved when the level of fact is reached.

In experience or thought, it is sometimes suggested, what is achieved is theory, and theory must be based upon, or derived from, facts. Science, for example, has its facts, and the way in which they are related, connected and explained is a theory. This view, however, involves a rigid distinction between fact and theory and a belief that facts are and remain independent of the theory which is said to connect them, and for these reasons I take it to be false. If fact were the datum in experience, and theory the achievement, it would appear that the naïve opinion that all theories are false (as compared with 'the actual facts') and that thinking about facts serves only to carry us further from the truth, is correct; and it would be difficult to clear thought from the charge of universal corruption. But facts, we have seen, are what is achieved in experience, they are ideas which we are obliged to think; and theories similarly are what is achieved, ideas which (in so far as we accept them) we are obliged to think. The difference between them is a difference of degree. A theory does not correspond to a number of facts, it is those facts seen as they are when held together in a unified whole. Theories become facts by becoming more certain and established; facts become theories by being seen in a wider relationship which exhibits their implications more fully. That which is fact under one aspect is theory under another. All facts imply a theory; that is, they imply a wider relationship than that in which they are first or frequently conceived. And when that wider relationship is elucidated the result is equally a theory and a fact; a theory because it relates hitherto separate facts, a fact because these relations are not external but necessary.

Briefly, then, the view of experience which sees it as a world of fact, is merely another form of the view I have already suggested—that in experience what is elucidated is the implications of a given world of ideas under the guidance of the criterion of coherence.

(ii) 'In so far as an idea is satisfactory in experience it is individual. Individuality is the criterion of experience.'

From one standpoint an individual idea might be taken to mean an idea which is separated and held separate from its world or environment. Frequently in experience we find ourselves with ideas which we have abstracted and divorced from their implications. We think of time as distinct and separable from space, of unity as independent of completeness, of body disjoined from mind, and truth sundered from reality. These separate units we call individual ideas, and by calling them individual we mean that we have managed to separate them from others and to hold them 'individually' before our minds. And it is suggested that in experience the confused and relatively incoherent mass of presented ideas is unravelled and separated into its constituents: the process is one of dissociation. To recognize is to determine limits, to know is to apprehend what is separate and particular, to experience is to individualize. And the criterion of individuality here is explicitness: whatever is distinct is an individual.

Nevertheless, it may perhaps be questioned whether this view of experience has followed out to its conclusion the criterion of individuality it has proposed. For, in the first place, it must be observed that if what is individual is what is specific and distinct, individuality is a matter of degree and circumstance. Nothing distinguishable is altogether without it. And secondly, if in experience the process be one establishing individuality, it must be supposed that what possesses the highest degree of this quality will be preferred. Satisfaction does not lie, as this view suggests, in whatever presents itself with any degree of distinctness, in that which is merely distinguishable as such, but only in what is permanently distinct and able to maintain its explicitness without qualification. In short, satisfaction in experience lies only in that which is separate and self-contained. And when this suggestion is pressed to the end, it becomes clear that individuality is the reverse of particularity, that it must be sought ahead and not behind, in what is self-complete and not in what is merely isolated, in what is a whole in itself and not in mere solitariness. It must be sought in the world of ideas which an isolated idea implies. For, whenever an idea points beyond itself, however distinct it may appear, it has demonstrated its own lack of individuality, and is powerless to resist inclusion in what is more individual than itself. In the end, individuality is inseparable from independence and self-existence, which (in turn) can substantiate them-

selves, not by asserting mere separateness, but by demon-
strating their completeness. *Die Individualität ist was ihre
Welt ist*. And in experience, an idea seen to be incomplete
in itself, a merely abstract individual, is an idea seen to be
incoherent and unsatisfactory.

It appears, then, that the view of experience I have recommended may be restated in this form: In experience what
is pursued is individuality; given some, more is sought for;
and satisfaction is achieved only with the achievement of an
unlimitedly individual idea. The criterion of experience is
always independence and self-completeness. And an arrest
in experience indicates that, for the moment at least, what
has been achieved is an idea which appears to be complete
in itself. Experience is not mere designation, which is satisfied with what is separate because it appears to be complete;
it is definition, which is characterised by the unremitting
pursuit of concrete individuality. And individuality is, in
the world of experience, but another name for the point at
which experience is obliged to stop; it is the world of experience as a coherent whole.

(iii) 'In experience, what is achieved is a world of universal
ideas. To experience is to make universal.'

The truth or falsehood of this view depends, of course,
upon the meaning we attribute to universality. And I will
begin by dismissing some views of universality which in this
connexion I take to be false. The universal has been taken
to mean that which is common to a number of particular
ideas; but so long as it is understood in this abstract sense,
it cannot be considered as what is achieved in experience.
That which is common is merely what remains over when
the particularity of particular ideas has been removed, and
it cannot pretend to be anything but an abstraction. Secondly,
the universal has been understood as the essence of particular
ideas; but this also provides us with only an abstraction. An
essence, in the sense of something separable from, and opposed to, other properties of ideas is inherently unstable,
changing its character with every change of circumstance

(what is essential, from one standpoint, will be negligible from another), and consequently it cannot be supposed to be satisfactory in experience. And thirdly, the universal is said to contain or include particular ideas: it is a collection of units, a sum of particulars. But, here again, the assumption of particular ideas as the datum in experience renders this view untenable.

These abstract views of universality have, for the most part, been engendered in opposition to equally abstract views of individuality: the abstract individual, that which is merely separate however fortuitous its limits, calls forth the abstract universal. And in experience satisfaction can be found in neither the one nor the other. The particulars of nominalism and the universals of realism are equally foreign to the character of experience.

Nevertheless, experience (as we have observed) is always a coherent world of ideas, and it is in this respect that it may be said to be universal. The universality of experience is implied in, and belongs to its unity. Thus, universality and individuality, so far from being contradictory notions of what is achieved in experience, depend for their significance upon being held together. Either without the other is a vicious abstraction. There is no individual, in the end, which is not the complete whole; and universality, when pressed from abstraction to abstraction, can find rest nowhere but in unity and completeness. In experience, what is individual is also universal; and where individuality and universality are achieved there is also achieved a coherent world of ideas.

(iv) 'A world of absolute ideas', to a greater extent perhaps than the other descriptions of what is achieved in experience which I have considered, has been the victim of dogma and the subject of a jargon which none but initiates pretend to understand. It, more than anything else, has been identified with this supernatural prize which in experience is supposed to be striven for, but which is never attained. Nevertheless, if the misunderstandings to which this conception has been subject are set on one side, it will not,

I think, be found improper to speak of the achievement in experience as a world of absolute ideas. The end in experience, we have seen, is a coherent world of ideas, a world or system of ideas which is at once unitary and complete; and it is difficult to know to what, if not to this, the word absolute might be appropriate. What is absolute means here that which is absolved or emancipated from the necessity of finding its significance in relations with what is outside itself. It means that which is self-complete, whole, individual, and removed from change. What is absolute, in this sense, is no inscrutable Absolute, beyond conception and outside the world of experience, it is the world of experience as a coherent unity, for that alone *is* absolute. And every idea, in proportion as it is individual and complete, in proportion as it approaches the condition of being a world itself, approaches the condition of absoluteness. In this sense, then, and in no other, we are forced by the nature of experience to what is absolute, and there is no point at which an arrest in the process can be justified, no other point which offers final satisfaction in experience.

I come now to consider truth, *proprio nomine*. But what I have to offer is not an independent treatment of a new subject, scarcely even a fresh aspect, but merely another way of saying what I have said already. Nor is it in any sense a conclusion, for (as I have tried to show) conclusions in the sense of propositions of unique importance, independent of the world of ideas to which they belong, are foreign to the character of experience.

Wherever the character of truth is discussed there will be found one at least ready to doubt whether it can be known; but this is what I have been most anxious to avoid. The moment truth is separated from knowledge and placed in another and independent world of its own, there is no way in which they can be united again. And until they are recognized as inseparable, truth remains the arbitrary creation of an irresponsible fancy and knowledge the aimless acquisition of insignificant trifles. A truth which is or may be outside knowledge is no less arbitrary and has no more meaning than an unknowable which is inside reality. It is, then, for the view I am recommending, meaningless to ask whether truth can be known. Whatever is satisfactory in experience is true, and it is true because it is satisfactory. Nothing save what is true can, in the full sense, be known. Truth is a correlative of experience. Without experience there can be no truth; without truth there can be no experience.

Now experience, we have seen, is always a world or system of ideas. What is given is not particular ideas, nor a collection, nor a series of ideas, but a world. And what is achieved is a world, but more of a world; a system which is more systematic; a whole which is more unified and more complete. In experience, moreover, what is pursued is the coherence of a given world of ideas. And the criterion of experience is the coherence of the world of experience. It follows, then, that truth can concern only a world of ideas; it is conceivable only as a totality of experience. No particular idea can be true, for particular ideas are abstractions such as cannot be supposed to afford satisfaction in experience. Further, truth does not belong to the given world in experience as such, but only to what is achieved in experience. Truth is a result, and it is true because it is a result. Truth, that is, is concrete and belongs only to what is a whole. And again, the criterion of truth is the coherence of the world of experience; a world of ideas is true when it is coherent and because it is coherent. Consequently, there is no external means by which truth can be established; the only evidence of truth is self-evidence. *Veritas nullo eget signo*. And finally, truth is not another world; it is always the truth *of* a given world of ideas.

## § 3

Experience is always and everywhere a world of ideas. What is given in experience is a world of ideas. But the given is given always to be transformed; it is, as such, inherently

unsatisfactory. Given a world of ideas, the end and achievement in experience is that world made more of a world, made
coherent. And since truth is what is satisfactory in experience,
the criterion of truth is coherence. What is true and all that
is true is a coherent world of ideas.

I come now to consider experience from a less abstract
standpoint; for it cannot be supposed that this coherent world
of mere ideas which constitutes truth and fact is, as such,
more than an abstraction. If we do not believe that our
ideas are about something, that they refer to existences in
an external world, we believe at least that there are 'things'
as well as facts and that there may be some relation between
them; and it is my business now to consider these beliefs.
But here, once more, nothing save an imperfect sketch, the
statement of a point of view, should be expected.

It seems that philosophers (and others) have considered
reality so important that to conceive of it as situated within
experience appeared to offer it an affront. Consequently
it has become almost a tradition to begin by postulating
a gulf between experience and reality, a gulf which many
have declared impassable, but which some have believed
themselves to have bridged. Such a point of departure,
however, appears to me misconceived, and I must beg
to be allowed another from which to consider this subject.
Instead of constructing a view of experience on the basis
of a conception of reality, I propose to derive my view
of the character of reality from what I conceive to be the
character of experience. And what I have first to suggest
is that reality is experience.

The view, of course, is well known. In experience, knowledge and reality are elements given in connexion; they are
correlatives. When we analyse experience we make distinctions and harden them into divisions, with the result that
knowledge becomes one unit and reality another, and we are
puzzled how to relate them. For, the moment knowledge and
reality are separated there seems to be no way in which they
can be brought together again; and left apart they perish

without hope of resurrection. Knowledge, if we are to avoid contradiction, must be seen to have its place in the universe of the real; and reality must lie within the universe of knowledge. For, if experience be not, in some sense, real, then nothing can be real, and consequently nothing unreal. And if reality be separated from knowledge, it must resign itself to the condition of nonentity, an empty concept, an idea without meaning or significance. Reality is experience, not because it is made real by being known, but because it cannot without contradiction be separated from knowledge. To insist upon the separation of knowledge and reality is, then, to commit ourselves to an absurdity which will serve only to throw open the door to more of its kind.

And I have no doubt that the first to enter will be the view that reality is that which is independent of experience, and is real because it is independent of experience. Reality, whatever else it is, is what is unmodified by experience. Now, against this view I have no new argument to raise, and none is required. When we see what it implies, the objections to it scarcely need urging. It implies, of course, that reality is unknowable, and that it is real because it is unknowable. Whatever can be known cannot, for that reason, be real. And the objection to it is twofold; it is an attempt to define reality as that which is not something else, and it involves a *petitio principii*. To define a thing as not something else may solve some riddles, but it is clearly ineffective in the case of reality. For reality, whatever else it is, cannot be a thing among things; it must be everything, and has not even the alternative of being nothing. Reality cannot be set over against anything else without ceasing to be the whole of reality: and it cannot be separated from experience and defined as that which is not knowable, not because the real is merely what is experienced, but because experience is real. But further, it is a strange perversion of the idea of knowledge to assert that anything is unknowable, and it is difficult to understand why reality should form an exception. To assert the impossibility of knowledge is always to assert a piece of knowledge, and is therefore self-contradictory. In short, if this view were true, it would be self-contradictory. And consequently it has no meaning. In a misguided attempt to establish the absolute integrity of reality, its complete independence of experience, this view has degraded it to the position of a nonentity. The unknowableness of reality is, in the end, conditional upon there being nothing to know.

No doubt it will be suggested that this argument relies upon a confused use of the word knowledge, and is consequently no argument at all and worthless. And I must do what I can to remove this misunderstanding. Knowledge, I shall be told, is of two kinds, neither of which involves the other. There is knowledge by actual acquaintance with things, and there is knowledge about things. And it will be said that while showing that we must believe ourselves to have knowledge of the second kind about reality (unless we wish to be involved in a contradiction), I have taken myself to have shown that we must have knowledge of the first kind also. And what I have to consider is how far and in what sense this distinction can be maintained. Some European languages distinguish these kinds of knowledge, and we may assume that the distinction arises from some logical instinct in the languages and not from mere caprice. But we ought not to assume that the distinction is necessarily valid in the exact form in which it is asserted. What, then, is the true distinction between the knowledge of direct acquaintance and knowledge about things? I must dismiss at once (because I have already considered it at length) the superstition that the knowledge of direct acquaintance, unlike any other kind of knowledge, is immediate, in the sense of being not in the form of concepts. There is no knowledge of 'things' apart from concepts. Mere physical acquaintance and nothing more is not a possible form of experience. To see, to touch, to taste, to hear, to smell is, always and everywhere, to judge and to infer. And I must dismiss also the view that although concepts are necessary to both forms of knowledge, no kind or degree of conceptual knowledge amounts to real acquaintance. A kind of knowledge which is in the form of concepts and something other than concepts is as monstrous as one which is believed to be not in the form of concepts at all. On the view I have taken any distinction within knowledge must be rejected which relies upon the existence of a thing which is not a fact, or of two independent sources of knowledge.

Now, knowledge about things is usually taken to mean knowledge which falls short of direct experience. Our knowledge of the earth leads us to believe that it is whirling through space at a high velocity; but we do not experience this directly. Is it, *qua* knowledge, defective by reason of this limitation? It is not obvious that this fact is less true, less obligatory, because we do not feel it, or that it would be more true and more difficult to avoid were we able to feel it in addition to knowing about it. Direct acquaintance, in this sense, wrongly appears to add something to our certainty, but, as such, it certainly adds nothing to our knowledge. We ought not to confuse intensity of sensitive affection with adequacy of experience. Knowledge about a thing cannot properly be said to be defective because it falls short of direct acquaintance. But there is another sense in which mere knowledge about things may be considered inadequate. It may mean knowledge which falls short of definition, and in that case it is certainly defective. But it is not an independent kind of knowledge; it is merely defective knowledge. And to make good its defects it does not require to become more direct or immediate, but more complete. Knowledge about things is, then, taken by itself, defective knowledge, but it is not defective because it fails to be direct knowledge. The knowledge of direct acquaintance, on the other hand, because it cannot mean immediate knowledge, seems to mean such knowledge as comes nearest to being immediate. But the peculiarity of this knowledge is the isolation and incoherence of its contents. Not that they are absolutely isolated or incoherent, for that is impossible. They are merely as isolated and incoherent as elements in a world of experience can be without falling outside that world. Direct knowledge is not an independent kind of knowledge, it is a certain degree of knowledge. It is knowledge presented in the form of a world of ideas expressly characterized as *mine*. And I need scarcely urge that it is also a defective form of knowledge. And it is defective for the same reason as mere knowledge about things is defective; it is knowledge which falls short of definition. It seems, then, that this distinction within knowledge means something (it means perhaps that judgment may be either implicit or explicit in knowledge), but that it does not mean that in experience an absolute division can be maintained or that knowledge is of two kinds. There is only one kind of experience, and reality is inseparable from it. And an unknowable reality, a reality which is real because it is independent of experience, is the contradiction I have maintained it to be.[1]

But the notion that experience and reality are given in separation and that it is the business of philosophy to determine the relations between them, may bring with it other views than that which sees reality as what is inherently independent of experience. In place of the assertion of the independence of reality and experience, we shall be reminded of the limits of human understanding and the presumption involved in any intellectual attempt to penetrate to reality. At least, it will be said, we must not claim for experience the competence to apprehend reality completely. But, if reality be that which is independent of experience, any move to get

[1] The position may perhaps be restated in this manner. All knowledge whatever is "knowledge that..." in the sense that (a) all knowledge is judgment, and (b) all judgment is of the real. Judgment in knowledge by acquaintance is, perhaps, not explicit because the particular content is relatively isolated from the complete world to which it belongs, but were the isolation absolute there would be no knowledge at all because there would be no judgment. To know a green leaf is to know that the real contains it; it is knowledge *about* the real. To know *that* the leaf is green is to know that the real (of which this leaf is the special focus) is, in this special respect, green. Thus, once more, there is but one kind of knowledge and reality is inseparable from it.

acquainted with it must be stupid rather than presumptuous, and to restrain a man from the undertaking would be not less foolish than to prohibit his drinking the sea. While, if it be inseparable from experience, and consequently knowable, it seems nonsense to speak of it as beyond the limits of human knowledge. Nor is it easy to see how we could be aware of those limits were they not abstract, arbitrary and in fact exceeded. Whatever can be known, can be known completely. The doctrine, then, that the real is what is independent of experience should be distinguished from the doctrine that the weakness and imperfection of our human faculties place a permanent barrier between knowledge and reality; but it is difficult to say which is the more ridiculous.

In short, the view which takes reality to be separate from experience, and the conception of reality as that which is independent of experience, involve us in fictitious difficulties and distressing contradictions. It is, indeed, nonsensical to speak of reality as if it belonged to a separate world of its own. Either it is a character of the world of experience, or it must confess itself a nonentity. It is not a unique substance, but a predicative conception appropriate only to a world of experience. And the thinker who demands a reality beyond experience is certain of disappointment. Thus, in throwing overboard, at this early stage, these common but self-contradictory views, we shall not, I think, be rejecting anything we are likely to stand in need of later.

No separation is possible between reality and experience; reality is experience and is nothing but experience. And, since experience is always a world of ideas, reality is a world of ideas. This conclusion, however, is open to a misconception, which I must make haste to remove. In asserting that reality is experience and is a world of ideas, I do not intend to assert that reality is either a world of mere mental events or a world of mere ideas. Both these views have, indeed, been advanced, but it is now too late in the day to undertake their defence, even were I inclined to attempt it. Nevertheless,

I propose now to consider them in order to make clear, not so much their defects (which are obvious enough), but rather the impossibility of holding them together with the view I am recommending.

The first suggestion is that reality, because it is experience, is a world of mere mental events. Experience is always somebody's experience; we can know only our own states of consciousness, and these (if reality be experience) are the only reality. There is only psychical existence, for nothing other or beyond this is possible in experience. Now, the defects of this position, which I take to be fatal to it, are that it is self-contradictory and abstract or incomplete. It is self-contradictory because it is impossible to hold, at once, that experience is a world and that it is mere mental events or states of consciousness as such. Any view which understands experience as a world of ideas I take to have avoided already the mistake of conceiving it as mental events and nothing more, for so soon as ideas are recognized as belonging to a world they have ceased to be mere psychical states. Certainly my experience is always mine, is always my psychical state, but it does not follow that it is merely mine. Indeed, the fact that my experience is mine is never more than a single abstract aspect of my experience, an aspect which can never stand alone. My experience (for example) must be coherent or incoherent, but it is never this by reason of its being merely mine, by reason of its being my psychical state. To be coherent and to be mine are equally aspects of my experience, and neither can take the place of the other. If my experience were my psychical states as such and nothing more, I should be obliged to take every experience at its face value; to question would be contradictory, to doubt impossible. But this is not so. And when I doubt and attempt to resolve the doubt, what I appeal to is not my experience as mine, but to my experience as a world, to the coherence of my experience. Thus, if I am determined to confine myself to the world of my personal experience and assert that this alone is what is real, so far from being obliged to believe that what is real is a world of experience known only as mine, a world of mere mental events as such, I am unable to do so without contradicting myself and representing as reality what I know to be a mere abstraction.

The second view, though different in character, involves similar considerations. Reality, it suggests, because it is experience, is a world of mere ideas, is mere being-for-experience. It is admitted that reality is experience and that experience is always a world of ideas, and therefore cannot be mere mental events as such; but this view goes forward to assert that reality is a world of ideas and nothing more. But here again, the defect is that abstractions are admitted in place of what is concrete and complete. Reality is certainly experience and is consequently a world of ideas, but it does not follow that it is a world of mere ideas and nothing more. Indeed, if experience is a world of ideas it cannot be a world of mere ideas. Mere ideas, ideas (that is) which are not asserted, are abstractions and never, as such and separately, to be found in experience. They are an aspect of every experience, but the concrete whole of no experience whatever. A merely conceptual reality is impossible because what is lacking is a merely conceptual experience.

It appears, then, that we must assert first, that reality is experience and nothing but experience; there is no reality which is not a world of ideas. And secondly, that what is real is neither a world of mere mental events, nor a world of mere ideas, for these are abstractions and nowhere, as such, found in experience. If reality be experience and be nothing but experience, it cannot be my experience as such, my state of mind merely as mine, and it cannot be a world of mere ideas, ideas which are not asserted.

There is, however, another view which ought to be considered, no less contradictory than these of the position I am recommending, and contradictory for much the same reasons. It is suggested that what we have in actual experience is a world of ideas, but that reality lies somewhere beyond this. Experience, we are told, is confined to ideas, whereas reality belongs to things. Experience is subjective from end to end, but, since what is real is objective, it lies outside what is actually in experience. What is in experience and what we know directly is not what is real, but only our experience or knowledge of what is real. Now, the defects of this view of experience and reality lie, of course, upon the surface, and it is instructive to notice them only because they afford an example of the kind of errors involved in any rejection of the position that reality is nothing but experience. First, it will be observed that this view recognizes experience as a world of ideas, but it fails to recognize that, if it be this, it cannot be a world of mere ideas. What this view requires is a world of ideas which, though it lies outside reality, yet exists and has a being of its own in experience, and such a world is nowhere to be found in experience. For mere ideas, ideas which are not asserted, are, so far as experience is concerned, mere abstractions. Ideas have no separate existence; they do not intervene between reality, and ourselves. To have an idea of a thing is simply to have it in experience. And that a thing enters my experience is merely another way of saying that it is my idea. And secondly, according to this view, reality has an existence separate from ideas; things exist and are real by themselves, and outside experience. Indeed, they never enter experience at all; for, to enter experience is to cease to be a thing. Reality, consequently, is what is unknowable, it is what is independent of experience. And the difficulties of this view have already been considered. A gulf is fixed between experience and reality and there is no way in which it can be bridged, and yet, until it is bridged, reality must remain a nonentity and experience a contradiction. And the necessity of finding some starting place for our conception of reality, other than this antithesis between experience and reality, is once more pressed upon us.

Reality, we have seen, is a world of ideas; it is experience and nothing save experience. And because it is this, it is neither a world of mere ideas, nor an existence which lies beyond a world of ideas. It is time now to take our third and final step: Reality is what is achieved and is satisfactory in experience. But, since we have seen already what it is that is satisfactory in experience, it will be unnecessary for me to do more than recapitulate the argument by which I attempted to establish this view when discussing experience from the abstract standpoint of mere truth as such. What is achieved and is satisfactory in experience is a coherent world of ideas, and this is satisfactory solely on account of its coherence, that is, its unity and completeness. And again, what is satisfactory in experience is what is individual and therefore a whole in itself. And once more, what is satisfactory is what is universal and absolute. And these are the characteristics of what is real. Reality is a coherent world of ideas, and it is real because it is coherent. This world is not a world of mere ideas, because the world of experience is not such a world. In experience, that is, there is always a reference beyond what is merely true to what is real, because what is merely true—a coherent world of mere ideas—is, in the end, neither complete nor absolute, but an abstraction. Reality is a coherent world of concrete ideas, that is of things. Consequently, it is one, a single system, and it is real only as a whole. My view is, then, that reality and experience are inseparable; that reality is experience, a world of ideas and therefore not a world of mere ideas; that experience is reality (that is, everything is real so long as we do not take it for more than it is); that reality is what is satisfactory in experience; and that reality is, consequently, a coherent world of concrete ideas. This alone is real because this alone is independent, absolute, complete and able to maintain itself. Reality, in short, is what we are obliged to think; and, since to think is to experience, and to experience is to experience meaning, the real is always what has meaning, or is rational. Whatever has a meaning, if we give it its full meaning, is real; and whatever is real has a meaning.

This view of experience and reality might, of course, be presented from other standpoints. To speak, for example, of the real world as an objective world or a world of objects is merely to say again what I have already said. But, for me at least, it seems to emphasize a characteristic of what is real which might otherwise fall into the background. And for that reason it may be useful to consider it for a moment. The world of reality is the world of experience. But it is not our world of experience as such, not a world of mere ideas. It is, on the contrary, a world of coherent or necessary ideas. Reality is not whatever I happen to think; it is what I am obliged to think. And to say that it is objective, a world of things, serves to distinguish it from this world of mere ideas, from the world of *denken als denken*. Nevertheless, if the view that what is real is what is objective is to be distinguished from error, it is clear that our conception of objectivity must be distinguished from that with which some writers are satisfied. The view that objectivity signifies independence of experience must be rejected because the notion (which it implies) of a world of existence outside experience is self-contradictory. If what is real is what is objective, what is objective must stand for something other than merely what is not subjective—that which is untouched by consciousness, that from which experience has been withdrawn. For, in the first place, what is objective must, it would appear, be an object, and an object is always an object of consciousness. And secondly, a reality distinguished merely as what is uninterfered with by experience, must be unknowable and therefore a contradiction. Objectivity, then, if it is to be a characteristic of reality, must imply, and not deny, experience. But it is not to be supposed that reality is fully given in every item or moment of experience. We have seen that reality is given in every experience, but we have not seen that in every experience reality is given equally. And the question for us is not, How can we get outside our purely personal experience to a world of objective, real existence? but, Where is the experience in which reality is given fully? (The common terms of philosophic debate—What do we know of the external world? How are objects related to mind?—are not merely misleading, but, to me, nonsensical.) And in saying that reality is given in experience in so far as it is an objective experience, I mean that reality is given in experience in so far as that experience is obligatory, unavoidable and therefore complete. The objective is what cannot be denied, what is absolute, and consequently what is real. And it stands over against a world of mere ideas, a merely subjective world, not because it is absolved from the so-called interference of experience, but because it is a complete experience. Subject and object are not independent elements or portions of experience; they are aspects of experience which, when separated from one another, degenerate into abstractions. Every experience does not merely involve the holding together of a subject and an object, but is the unity of these, a unity which may be analysed into these two sides but which can never be reduced to a mere relation between them. There is, then, no object apart from a subject; no subject independent of an object. For again, an object is not something independent of experience, but merely what I am obliged to think, and for that reason it is real. And the subject, the I, which belongs to this object, is not my body, nor a merely psychological subject, not (that is) an element or portion of my world, but is my world as a whole. And my world is a world of objects. The subject does not belong to my world, it is my world. Thus, to speak of reality as what is objective, should not withdraw our attention from the view of reality as experience, a world of ideas, but serves to direct it towards the more concrete conception of reality as what we are obliged to think, as a complete experience.

The view I wish to present is, then, that the real world is the world of experience, and it is real because and in so far as it is satisfactory in experience. Everything is real so long as we do not take it for something other than it is. Every judgment we make asserts this or that to be a characteristic of reality. But reality itself belongs only to the whole; no item of experience is real in isolation. And this implies, among much else, the rejection of all views which tolerate a divorce, either at the beginning or at the end, between experience and reality. It is, however, one thing to renounce a doctrine and another to rid oneself of its influence. The notion of reality as separate from experience is so ingrained in our way of thinking that it is not easily thrown off: and our way of talking serves only to emphasize this vicious and negligent dualism. Indeed, so great is the difficulty that I think any philosophy which wishes to assert the futility of separating reality and experience, the futility of attempting to reach a conception of reality except by considering the character of experience, can go forward now only by devising a means of expressing its belief which does not involve the use of words and phrases designed to convey the opposite view. 'Reality', for example, has somehow got itself separated from 'existence'; 'to be real' has acquired an esoteric meaning different from 'to be'; 'subject' and 'object', 'subjective' and 'objective' have escaped from their own world of psychology and have invaded that of philosophy; and the current ways of indicating that a 'fact' or an 'idea' or a 'thing' which is less than the whole is neither true nor real, and consequently not properly a fact, an idea or a thing at all, are (to say the least) clumsy and involved. And if we could do without speaking of what we believe to be abstractions, our manner of expressing what we believe to be real might be less ambiguous. Perhaps the only satisfactory view would be one which grasped, even more thoroughly than Hegel's, the fact that what we have, and all we have, is a world of 'meanings', and constructed its philosophy without recourse to extraneous conceptions which belong to other views. But in whatever direction a satisfactory view may lie, the task of constructing it is beyond me. I wish, however, before leaving this topic, to present my view of reality and experience from another standpoint. I wish to consider what we mean when we say that such-and-such is a 'thing'.

It is not easy to determine exactly what we mean when we use the word 'thing'; and it will not make it easier for us to clear up our ideas on the subject if we fall into the error of Theaetetus and substitute a list of things for a definition of a thing. Indeed, a great part of the ordinary obscurity of our minds on this point arises, I believe, from this habit of confusing what should be separate judgments.[1] But I suppose any discussion of the nature of a thing must begin with the proposition that "it is not in virtue of a substance contained in them that things are; they are, when they are qualified to produce an appearance of there being a substance in them".[2] To speak of a thing indicates a mode of behaviour, and not the presence of a mere essential substance which is supposed to make the thing what it is. And, for the justification of this starting point, I must point to what has already been said. A thing, then, is whatever behaves (and can sustain such behaviour) as a single whole or unity. Whatever shows some kind or degree of independence and competence to exist in its own right, we call a thing. And whatever appears to be constructed wholly of relations and is without power to be on its own, is not a thing. But the notion of unity is, we have seen, barren and abstract so long as it is divorced from that of completeness. And whatever would demonstrate its unity and maintain itself as a single whole must do so by proving its completeness in itself. A thing is a unity, and therefore a totality. Or again, whatever we are obliged to think of as one, whatever is fully known without reference to something outside itself, we call a thing. The character of being a thing is the attribute of unity and totality; and to whatever we attribute this character we do so because we believe it (perhaps mistakenly) to be single and a whole, and for no other reason.

It will be observed that the first step in considering the

[1] So-called materialism frequently makes this mistake. Instead of saying, "The nature of reality is such-and-such, that of matter is such-and-such, therefore matter is real, or reality is material", materialism sometimes passes at once to the confused judgment, "Material things are real", which usually means no more than, "When I say 'reality', I mean 'materiality'". It is as if we said, "Peter is a good swimmer" without having any notion of what we meant by 'good swimmer' beyond what the word Peter contained.

[2] Lotze, *Metaphysic*, Bk I, ch. iv (E.T. I, p. 100).

character of a thing has led us back to the problem of individuality. For the integrity, unity and totality which belong to a thing are the already noticed characteristics of what is individual. A thing is simply what is individual. It will be remembered also that it was found impossible to separate the notion of degree from that of individuality. And just as individuality was seen to lie in the view we take of it and is always a matter of more or less, so the character of being a thing is a question of degree. It is a character which cannot be denied absolutely to whatever is in any way distinguishable from its environment; but it is a character, the mere assertion or denial of which is meaningless. And this presents us with fresh difficulties.

If we choose the lower end of the scale, and say that whatever can be designated is a thing, we shall be saying what, in a sense, is true, but what is nevertheless misleading. Where the character of a thing is discovered in its separateness, its unity will be found to lie in its exclusiveness, and such a unity we know is merely abstract. And further, it is far from being the case that the separation of the thing from its environment is a matter of no difficulty. For, beyond the bare assertion that the thing begins where the environment ends, lies a jungle of difficulties. It is, in fact, impossible to say, in detail, where the environment ends and the thing begins. Whatever terms we choose with which to indicate the environment, the same must be applied to the thing. A thing surrounded by mere space is itself a mere particle of space; or if the environment be what presses upon and confines the thing, then the thing is mere pressure. But this lets us into no secrets and answers no questions. The result of mere designation stands always connected with an environment necessary to it and from which it cannot be finally distinguished. It is dependent and incomplete, and in the end a bare abstraction. A thing opposed to its environment is as abstract as an environment opposed to its thing; what we know of each depends upon our knowledge of the other, and in spite of our various attempts to distinguish them, they remain inseparable. We are faced, then, with the alternative of asserting that a thing is whatever is barely designable and is consequently an abstract unit which must look for totality in what lies outside itself, or of seeking elsewhere some other view. And we shall not, I think, remain long in doubt as to which side we must choose. For the notion of the thing as a unit and a totality itself is contradicted by this idea of the thing as what is somehow distinguishable from its environment. And if we are to adhere to our original notion, it is impossible to understand how the character of being a thing can rest upon mere designation.

We are obliged, it seems, to turn to the upper end of the scale. If the character of being a thing be a matter of degree, a thing must, in the end, be whatever shows the greatest degree of this character. Whatever is most a unit and most complete in itself will be most a thing. No result of designation can, as such, sustain an absolutely individual existence, and yet we may not assert that it lacks altogether the character of a thing. Nevertheless, in the end, the thing must be the whole thing; and if we choose to distinguish thing and environment, the whole thing will always be a union of these. The thing is inclusive, not exclusive; whatever reaches furthest and contains most of what (in another view) is its environment, is most a thing. It must be concluded, then, that a 'thing' which falls short of singleness and totality is an abstraction and is incomplete, and that it has no power to resist incorporation in, or transformation into, what is less abstract and consequently more of a thing. The character of thing cannot be denied absolutely to whatever can be thought of as a single whole (however ill-distinguished from its environment), but neither can it be asserted unlimitedly of anything which is not seen to contain all that might otherwise appear as its environment.

But there is another and more familiar direction from which this question may be approached. The difficulty, it is said, is not to distinguish the thing from its environment, but to distinguish it from itself. Experience introduces us, not to bare, static units, but to what changes and yet remains some-how the same. On the subject of identity I shall, however, confine myself to a few remarks. A thing, we are told, must preserve an identity: if it change, it must do so, not spora-dically, but according to some regular plan. What merely changes, is careless of continuity and gives no evidence of permanence as well as change, has no identity and con-sequently cannot be thought of as a thing. Wherever a thing goes beyond a static unity with itself (as, it will be said, is always the case), if it is to remain a thing, it must maintain an identity. Now, whatever else the notion of identity may imply, I take it, first, to signify a mode of behaviour, and secondly, to be a matter of degree. That is to say, all identity is qualitative, consists in the maintenance of a certain character, and not in the mere retention of a fixed and original substance. For, such a core or centre of existence, whether it is conceived in terms of content, shape, size, purpose, or 'spirit', so long as it is imagined to be exclusive of states and differences, is a mere abstraction, untouched and unaltered for no other reason than that it is too insignificant to suffer change. Identity, if it belong to the character of a thing, must be sought in its differences and changes, and not beyond them: so far from denying them, it implies and unifies them. And if identity be this, it must be a matter of degree whether or not it is maintained.

And with this we are brought to an unavoidable conclusion. Whatever view of identity we favour, the so-called thing the identity of which can be questioned or asserted, is not the whole thing, but an abstraction, the result of mere designa-tion. For identity reintroduces the distinction of thing and environment in another form, and gives us consequently, in place of the whole thing, two abstractions. It takes at least two to make an identity, but, so soon as there is a whole thing, there is no longer two, but one. It is absurd to speak of, because it is absurd to question, the identity of a complete individual or thing.

A thing, then, implies a certain mode of behaviour

which may exist in various degrees. In experience what is given is, not particular, isolated things, but a world of things; for things, because they are ideas, cannot be bare and unconnected. And the end of this given world of things is to become more of a world. For it is not a world of fixed data: the reason, indeed, for calling it a world (and not a collection or a series) is that the elements into which it may be analysed have no finality in themselves. What is given is a world of things, but in so far as this world is seen to be incoherent, we are obliged to take its elements to be things in a merely limited sense, abstractions which must look for their totality outside themselves. These incomplete 'things' fall short of their full character because they are unable to resist transformation into what is more complete. And when once what is given has submitted itself to this process, there is no point at which it can be arrested short of some thing which is a totality in itself. Thus every 'thing', everything given in observation and designation, is a thing in some sense; but no thing is complete until we have ceased to take it for less than it is. And every thing is less than it is, in so far as it is not itself the concrete world of things as a whole. The character of what we ordinarily call a thing forces it to lose itself in the whole from which it has been abstracted.

And should it be asked, What has this to do with reality? I must answer that it is reality. When we say that such-and-such is a thing we mean that it is real and that it is real in so far as it is a thing. Real is a title belonging in some degree to whatever in some manner behaves as a thing, but belonging unlimitedly only to the concrete world of things as a whole, into which no single 'thing' can resist being transformed. A 'thing' is real in so far as it is a unit and a totality, and it is a thing for the same reason as it is real. Reality, then, is a datum and a result. We cannot escape from it or get outside it, but it is scarcely less difficult to achieve it. No single thing can be utterly foreign to reality. But equally no single thing, short of the concrete world of things as a whole, is unlimitedly real. The abstract, where it is taken to be concrete and a whole, is certainly unreal, but to take it so is to take it for less than it is, for, by its character, it is unable to resist transformation into what is less abstract—what it is abstracted from. That which is a whole and complete is implied in that which is abstract; that which falls short of complete reality belongs nevertheless to the world of reality.

Briefly, then, the view of the character of reality which I am suggesting is this. When we say that something 'is', we imply that it is self-existent, and we do not distinguish this from reality. To be real is to be; and to be is to be self-existent. The real world is, therefore, not a world apart from and independent of experience, it is the world of experience. It is consequently a world of ideas; yet not a world of mere ideas, for that is an abstraction. Also, it is a world of things; yet not a world of mere things, things independent of experience, for that is an abstraction. And again, reality, because it is experience, is a world, and because it is a world it is fully itself only when it is coherent. And if coherence be our criterion, the given world in experience may be more or less real, though it cannot fall altogether outside reality. The concrete world of reality, as such, can, of course, have no degrees; it is perfect and complete. To speak of degrees of reality means only that whatever belongs to experience, however incomplete it be, cannot be wholly foreign to reality, and that the process in experience, when unimpeded by extraneous motives, is a movement from what is abstract to what is concrete, from what is real incompletely to what is completely real. It means that everything is real if we do not take it for more or for less than it is.

Before passing to other matters I must notice a difficult subject which the preceding argument has suggested, but which it cannot be said to have considered. I mean the relation of truth and reality, of what is true and what is real. I cannot, however, do more than state the view of that relation which seems to me to be implied in what has gone before.

There are, it appears, three standpoints from which my world of experience may be viewed. In the first place, it may be seen as my world of experience and not yours. From this standpoint my experience is neither true nor false; it is merely mine. Its specific content, its reference, its coherence are ignored, and it is seen only as a world of ideas which belongs exclusively to me. And this is certainly a distinguishable aspect of my world of experience. Nevertheless, it is an abstraction. My world of experience is certainly mine, but it is never merely mine, and it is never known as merely mine. This aspect of my experience cannot, therefore, stand alone. To take my experience as merely mine is to take it as less than it is, and so as other than it is. Secondly, my world of experience may be seen as a world of concepts, mere ideas, or ideas as such. And from this standpoint my experience is seen to have specific content and is seen to be satisfactory or relatively unsatisfactory, coherent or relatively incoherent, true or relatively false. It is never, of course, seen to be wholly false, for that would imply that it was meaningless, and wherever there is experience there is meaning. And it may never be seen to be absolutely true, not because this is an impossible condition, but because it is a highly improbable condition. To see my world of experience as a world of concepts as such, is to go beyond it as merely mine and involves a judgment about its relative coherence. And this, too, is a distinguishable aspect of my experience. Nevertheless, it also is an abstraction. My world of experience is certainly a world of concepts, and the end in experience is certainly that world made coherent or true; but it is never a world of mere concepts. This also is an aspect of all experience, distinguishable, but nevertheless abstract and incomplete and unable to stand alone. To take my experience as merely true or false is to take it as less than it is, and so as other than it is. The third standpoint from which my experience may be seen is the standpoint of reality. My experience may be seen as a world of concrete ideas. And from this point of view it is coherent or relatively incoherent, real or relatively abstract. To see it thus is to judge its degree of reality. But this, so far from being an abstract aspect of experience, is recognized as experience as a whole. It is the totality from which the former views were abstracted. For my experience seen as real, seen in terms of its reality, comprehends its character as merely mine and as merely true, and supersedes them. All experience is somebody's experience, all experience is a world of concepts, and all experience belongs to the real world; yet, though no experience is merely mine, and none is merely true, all experience is experience (and therefore is mine and is true) only in so far as reality is given in it. In short, my experience is mine and it is true because it is real. It is mine because I have accepted it, and I accept it only because it appears coherent. It is true because it is a coherent world of ideas, and its coherence rests, in the end, upon its reality. Experience to be experience must be reality; truth to be true must be true of reality. Experience, truth and reality are inseparable.

## § 4

Experience is a world of ideas. And the condition of a world of ideas satisfactory in experience is a condition of coherence, of unity and completeness. Further, the world of experience is the real world; there is no reality outside experience. Reality is the world of experience in so far as it is satisfactory, in so far as it is coherent. These, such as they are, seem to be our conclusions; but they seem also to be unsatisfactory. And they appear likely to remain so until I have faced what writers are now in the habit of calling 'the fact of diversity'. I cannot, of course, admit that this so-called fact has been left altogether on one side; it has already been remarked, and it remains now to consider it.

Whatever assent to the view that in experience there is the continuous modification of a given world of ideas in the attempt to make it coherent, must be taken to exclude (and it excludes much), it is not necessary to suppose that it denies any kind of diversity or arrest in experience. Indeed, the notion of degrees, which we have seen to be inseparable from that of experience as a coherent world of ideas, actually implies diversity and admits arrest. If my view obliged me to assert that what is incomplete does not belong to the same world as what is complete, that what is not wholly true is wholly false, then it would be difficult to understand how experience could be at once single and diverse. But it places me in no such predicament. Diversity no less than unity appears in experience, and some explanation of it must be offered by any theory which expects a hearing. I must make clear, however, that I do not propose to consider the question *why* there is diversity; that lies beyond my purpose. I wish to consider here, (i) What is the character of this diversity? (ii) How, in general, are the differences, which together constitute the total fact of diversity, related to one another? (iii) How, in general, are these differences related to the totality of experience or experience as a single whole?

(i) The view I have been suggesting is that experience is single and a whole, and that when it is regarded as a concrete totality no degrees or divergencies appear in it. Nevertheless it is possible, in some measure, to break up this concrete totality; the single whole of experience may suffer disruption. Or, from another standpoint, in experience, I have maintained, there is a movement directed towards the achievement of a coherent world of experience. Nevertheless this movement not infrequently falls short of its end. This may happen because, in spite of genuine attempt to reach the end, it fails. But more often the shortcoming is due to a failure to take seriously the criterion of satisfaction implied in the process. The easily approachable is preferred to what, in the end, can alone afford complete satisfaction. In experience there is the alternative of pressing forward towards the perfectly coherent world of concrete ideas or of turning aside from the main current in order to construct and explore a restricted world of abstract ideas. The full obligations of the character of experience are avoided when (as so often) the attempt to define, the attempt to see clearly and as a whole, is surrendered for the abstract satisfaction of designation. To be satisfied with what a singular judgment, in which the subject is a proper name, can tell us, is to have diverged from the concrete purpose in experience and to have taken up with a purpose which is satisfactory because it appears to be what is required in experience, and unsatisfying when this appearance reveals itself as mere appearance. These divergencies, these arrests in experience are, then, not an invention of my own; they are recognizable by all who reflect upon the character of experience. And to assert that in experience there is a continuous elucidation of the implications of a given world of ideas and that the criterion of satisfaction is always coherence, implies that, if at any point short of complete coherence there is an arrest, a modification of the full character of experience ensues. And it is the nature of these modes which is to engage our attention.

Now, in the first place, whatever else a mode of experience, a divergence from the concrete purpose in experience, may escape, it cannot escape from the world of experience itself. A mode of experience is defective, not because it has ceased to be experience or has abandoned the proper criterion of experience, but because it no longer attempts to satisfy that criterion in full. Secondly, modes of experience are not specific kinds of experience. In this sense, we have seen, there are no kinds of experience. There is only one kind of experience, and what falls short of that is not a separate kind of experience, but a defective mode of experience. Thirdly, a mode of experience is not a separable part of reality, but the whole from a limited standpoint. It is not an island in the sea of experience, but a limited view of the totality of experience. It is not partial (in the literal sense), but abstract. There are indeed no 'parts' in experience, no separable 'tracts' of experience. And further, in speaking of these divergencies from the concrete purpose of experience as *modes* of experience, I intend to exclude two current conceptions of their character; I intend to exclude the notion of them as the products of diverse faculties, and the notion of them as stages or phases in a development of experience.

The view that these modes of experience are adequately explained by attributing them to appropriate faculties is open to various objections. We might, following Hegel and others, observe that such faculties are no more than possibilities masquerading as things, that they are hypostatized abstractions. Moral action implies the possibility of morality, motion the possibility of movement; but to speak of these possibilities as faculties gives a name to the unknown without adding to our knowledge. It covers up truth with a phrase. Or again, we might say that, when pressed to its conclusion, this view leaves no place for the self or for experience as a whole. It explains each activity separately by attributing it to a faculty invented *ad hoc*. Volition springs from the will, religion from the religious consciousness, morality from the moral sense. And variety is explained merely by dismissing unity.[1] These objections appear to me conclusive, but I propose to adopt another and shorter line of attack. The view of faculties fails as a full explanation of the character of the diversity in experience, not because it turns out to be bad psychology, but merely because it is psychological. Psychology is itself a divergence from the concrete purpose in experience, and its conclusions therefore cannot be taken to afford an explanation of the character of experience. The totality cannot be explained in terms of a mode.

The view of the modifications of experience as stages in the development of experience has outlived the view which accounts for them in terms of faculties, but it is scarcely more satisfactory. Experience is regarded as a development in which certain stages emerge and are distinguishable, and they are explained by placing them in the order of their appearance.

---

[1] It is true, of course, that (for example) 'the will' by bringing together and uniting different acts of volition, 'explains' them and gives them unity. But since, at the same time, each particular set of experiences is referred to a different faculty, the unity of the self is disrupted.

These stages supersede one another, they are phases in the partial and progressive knowledge of the real world. Sensation, for example, is not so much a defective form of experience as a phase in the development of experience. And the movement in experience is represented as a movement which, in pursuit of what is perfectly coherent, passes through a number of imperfect and subsidiary phases. Now, I am not disposed to deny that this is a possible view of the character of experience, but I do not think it affords us the full explanation we are looking for. And its defect lies, not so much in its doubtfulness as a genetic account, but rather in its being genetic at all. To say that the diversities of experience are stages or phases in the history of an individual or racial consciousness, and to say nothing more, is merely to assert the diversity without offering any explanation of it. The presupposition that first in time implies first in reason imprisons us within an abstract world, and without this pre-supposition it is difficult to understand how the character of these modes of experience is likely to be made clearer by arranging them in the empirical order in which they seem to emerge in the life of the individual or the race.

These modes of experience are to be explained, then, neither as the products of distinctive faculties, nor as mere stages in a development of experience. The explanation I con-ceive to be required, and that which I have to offer, is in terms of the character of experience itself as a whole. In experience what is ultimately satisfactory is a completely coherent world of ideas, and whatever falls short of this can be explained fully only in terms of modification or abstrac-tion, in terms, that is, of the whole from which it diverges. And since abstraction (because it is thinking) is not merely selective omission, not merely a process in which experience falls short of its end, but also and always the construction of a separate world of ideas at the point of the arrest, since it is not merely separative, but also synthetic and integrative, a mode of experience is not merely an arrest in experience, but also the construction of a world of ideas at the point of the arrest. Any falling short of the achievement of what is completely satisfactory in experience may, then, be considered from two standpoints. It may be considered, first, as an arrest in experience; and, we have seen, from this point of view it is not a separable kind of experience, but the whole from a limited standpoint; it is a partial experience. And secondly, it may be considered as a specific world of ideas which stands in contrast to every other world of ideas and to the world of ideas which, by reason of its perfect coherence, would be completely satisfactory. And, from this point of view also, a mode of experience is not a part of reality, but the whole from a limited standpoint. The significance of the arrest lies, however, in the character of the world of ideas it brings into being. By itself, an arrest in experience is an abstraction, something without significance and never as such known in experience; its meaning lies in its implications, in itself when joined to that which it is never without. And the character of this world of ideas, since it is created by abstraction, is to be determined only by considering its coherence, that is, by considering how far it succeeds and how far it fails to provide what is completely satisfactory in experience. Or again, a mode of experience is experience with reservation, it is experience shackled by partiality and presupposition; and its character lies, not merely in the particular reservations and postulates which distinguish it, but in the entire world of ideas which these postulates (and therefore this arrest in experience) imply, call forth and maintain. In short, since a mode of experience is a form of experience, it is a world of ideas, and the character of the mode is the character of the world.

The diversities in experience which I am to consider are, then, specific worlds of ideas; and it is these worlds of ideas, taken separately and by themselves, which are abstract. And when I speak of a mode of experience as abstract, I mean, not that it is a different kind of experience from any other, but that it is the whole of experience arrested at a certain point and at that point creating a homogeneous world of ideas. From one standpoint, such a world of ideas is free and self-contained; it has put itself outside the main current of experience and made a home for itself. But, from another standpoint, since every mode of experience is, in spite of its modification, still a form of experience, each abstract world of ideas seeks, not to escape from experience, but to be judged by the criterion of experience; each recognizes and appeals to the principle of coherence. No abstract world of ideas is independent of experience, for each is experience at a certain point. And no abstract world of ideas is independent of the totality of experience, for each derives its character from the whole from which it is an abstraction, and apart from that whole it has neither meaning nor significance. There is, of course, no theoretical limit to the number of such worlds, and the choice of which we are to consider in detail must, to some extent, be arbitrary. And further, no mode of experience can be represented as necessary to experience and unavoidable. Such a view belongs to the notion of modes of experience as stages through which experience must pass, or at least to some view which sees them as other than abstractions. It does not belong to the character of modes of experience, in the sense in which I am considering them, to be either necessary or limited in number.

(ii) I mean, then, by a mode of experience a homogeneous but abstract world of ideas. And when I speak of the relationship in which one mode of experience stands to another, I refer, not to experience itself as a single whole (which knows neither modes nor phases), but to the abstract worlds of ideas which arrests in experience create. And the general character of that relationship follows from the nature of the worlds concerned. It may be described in two propositions: that each abstract world of ideas is, as such and as a world, wholly and absolutely independent of any other; and that each, in so far as it is coherent, is true for itself.

The first of these propositions implies that there is no direct relationship between any two of these modes of experience, for each abstract world of ideas is a specific organization of the whole of experience, exclusive of every other organization. Consequently, it is impossible to pass in argument from any one of these worlds of ideas to any other without involving ourselves in a confusion. The fallacy inherent in any such attempt is in the nature of *ignoratio elenchi*. And the result of all such attempts is the most subtle and insidious of all forms of error—irrelevance. This, in an extreme example, seems clear enough. That what is arithmetically true is morally neither true nor false, but merely irrelevant, appears obvious. But, as we shall later have occasion to observe, though it appears not to be so clear in the case of some other abstract worlds of ideas, nevertheless this independence of one another lies in the character of the worlds themselves and cannot be avoided. No one of these modes of experience is, in any sense whatever, based upon or dependent upon any other; no one is derived from any other, and none directly related to any other. This does not, of course, mean that these modes of experience are merely separate and have place in no universe, for that is impossible. They are abstractions from the single whole of experience; they are separate, but misconceived, attempts to give coherence to the totality of experience, and consequently meet in the whole to which they belong. They arise from arrests in experience, and they derive their significance from their connexion with the totality of experience. My view is, merely, that these abstract worlds of ideas are not, as such and as worlds, in any way dependent upon or directly related to one another. And if the question were approached from the opposite direction, every case of irrelevance would be found to be an example of this attempt to pass in argument from one world of ideas to another, an attempt which, because it ignores the character of the worlds concerned, results only in error and confusion.

The second proposition, that each abstract world of ideas, in so far as it is coherent, is true for itself, means little more than that each of these worlds appears as, and is taken for, a world. And this character belongs to every world of ideas

whatever in virtue of its being an attempt to give coherence
to the totality of experience and its demand to be judged
in that capacity. Truth, in the end, is the character of the
coherent world of experience taken as a whole. But, in so far
as any world of ideas is taken to be coherent, it is taken to
be true. Each abstract world of ideas, in so far as it is coherent,
is, then, true so far as it goes, true if its postulates are accepted, true if its reservations are admitted. But, because
each is an abstract world of ideas, the product of an arrest
in experience, when whatever truth it may contain is asserted
absolutely and unconditionally, its truth turns to error. The
truth of a mode of experience is always relative, relative to
the degree of completeness which belongs to its world of
ideas, its organization of reality.

(iii) The relation of these abstract worlds of ideas to the
fully coherent world, the totality of experience, has been
variously conceived. We may, however, dismiss at once the
view that there is no world of experience beyond the various
modes of experience; the view that experience as a whole is
without unity or coherence.[1] Wherever there is modification
there must be a totality; wherever there is abstraction there
must be a concrete whole. And the view that this whole
can be resolved into or reduced to a totality of modifications
depends, I think, upon a misconception of the character of
modification or abstraction. Beyond this, there is the view
that the fully coherent world of ideas is the product of a
conflict between the various modes of experience. The notion
is that, in the struggle that ensues whenever abstract worlds
of ideas meet, that which is most complete survives and is

[1] 'But', it will be objected, 'you have said already that it is too
easy an escape from difficulty to find the concrete world of experience
*beyond* the modes of experience, in *another* world.' It is true, of
course, that a mode of experience is a world of experience and
consequently cannot be merely dismissed; but without some *other*,
which is neither the sum nor the product of the modes, there could
be no modes. A view for which there is nothing beyond the diversity
is one in which diversity is conceived in terms other than that of
modality.

what is satisfactory in experience. But, since the situation we have to explain is not one in which abstract worlds of ideas are seen to supersede each other, but one in which they are found existing side by side, and since there is no relevant contact—either for agreement or disagreement—between these worlds, as worlds, this view must also be dismissed. The conflict upon which it relies is made impossible by the character of the worlds concerned. A third and influential view is that the concrete whole of experience is a collection or combination of abstract modes of experience. Each mode of experience is conceived to contribute to the totality of experience. It is said, for example, that the world of experience as a whole cannot maintain itself as coherent unless it be 'in harmony with the results of the various special sciences'; and experience as a whole is thought of as a kind of 'synthesis of the sciences'. Now this, unlike the two former views, is a serious attempt to determine the relationship we are considering, but it cannot, I think, be called satisfactory. Setting aside many minor deficiencies, the chief defect of this view seems to be its assumption that each separate mode of experience, each arrest in experience, each abstract world of ideas, is necessary to the totality of experience. For each of these worlds of ideas is conceived as a body of results which must be thrown into the total world and without which that world would fall short of totality. It implies that the more half-truths we entertain, the more certain we are of achieving in the end a fully coherent experience; the more frequently we are mistaken, the more likely we are to reach the truth, so long as we have wit enough to hold on to our mistakes and (when we have made a fair collection) to 'combine' them. In short, this view loses sight of the fact that these modes of experience are abstract worlds of ideas; it misconceives the character of abstraction. An abstract world of ideas is an arrest in experience. It is not a part of reality, it is not an organization of a separate tract of experience; it is the organization of the whole of experience from a partial and defective point of view. And no collection or combination of such abstractions will ever constitute a concrete whole. The whole is not made of abstractions, it is implied in them; it is not dependent upon abstractions, because it is logically prior to them.

There are, of course, other ways than these in which the relationship between the concrete whole of experience and what falls short of that concrete whole has been conceived. Some I am unable to understand, and for that reason must leave on one side. Others, for which there is much to be said, appear to me to imply a conception of experience so different from that to which I have already committed myself, that it would be unprofitable to consider them here. These modifications of experience have, for example, been conceived as moments indispensable to the completeness of a dialectic (or logical development) which is the concrete whole. But here again this view appears to me either to involve a misconception of the character of modification; or to conceive the diversity of experience in some terms other than those of modification or abstraction, and for that reason to lie altogether to one side of the view I take to be implied in my conception of experience.

A satisfactory view of the relationship we are considering must, as I conceive it, avoid any notion of the concrete world of experience as a whole which implies that these abstract worlds are, as such, in any sense either alternative or contributory to it. From the narrow standpoint of process, the concrete world of experience is achieved by avoiding all modifications of experience. And, from a wider point of view, the concrete whole of experience is at once the completion and the supersession of its modes. It is the whole from which they are abstracted and to which they must, in the end, return. A mode of experience is an arrest in experience, it is an abstract world of ideas which, as a world, stands in permanent contrast with the concrete totality of experience. So long as the mode is insisted upon, experience must remain incoherent. In experience satisfaction depends, consequently, upon the avoidance of any modification: and avoidance may mean either the rejection of any form of experience which falls short of the full character of experience, or the mere failure to be diverted from the concrete purpose in experience. Every abstract world of ideas is, from the standpoint of experience as a whole, a limited and arbitrary point of view which must be avoided or overcome. But, on the other hand, each abstract world of ideas is experience, and there are neither separate kinds of experience, nor (in the end) permanently separable worlds of experience. Every experience whatever submits itself to the criterion of coherence, and in so far as it is abstract, an arrest in experience, it calls out for its supersession by what is complete. Thus, the concrete world of experience is not another, separate world, wholly different in character from any abstract world. It is the complete world which every abstract world implies and from which it derives its significance. But further, the difference between the concrete totality of experience and all abstract worlds of experience is that it possesses already what they require, what they attempt but cannot achieve without surrendering their character as abstract worlds, without self-extinction. And consequently, in completing them, it abolishes them. For, so long as these abstract worlds of ideas retain their character as modes, they deny their character as experience; and in claiming their character as experience (by appealing to the criterion of coherence), they implicitly surrender their character as independent modes. In short, as a world of ideas, as a mode of experience, every arrest in experience constitutes a self-contradiction which can be resolved only by the surrender of its modality, its character as a world of ideas. There is, then, the concrete whole of experience, a perfectly coherent world of ideas, governed by the principle that what is abstract is inadequate and what is inadequate must be superseded by the rejection of its inadequacy. And, at the same time, there remains the absolute exclusiveness of each abstract world of ideas, as such and as a homogeneous world. No experience save that which belongs exclusively to its mode can help to elucidate the contents of an abstract world of ideas; the experience which belongs to another mode is merely irrelevant, and that which belongs to the concrete whole is merely destructive of the abstract world as a world. The relationship between a mode of experience and the concrete whole of experience is the complex relationship which holds between what is abstract and what is concrete. There is, at once, the concrete unity of experience which gives meaning to and comprehends the diversity, and does not merely deny it; and there is diversity, in each case an arrest in experience, which is comprehensible only because it escapes the absolute nonentity of mere diversity and is recognized as modification or abstraction.

§ 5

There remain, of course, many important questions which this brief statement of my view of experience and its modes has left undiscussed, and to some of these I must return later. But, since this chapter is designed to be a preface to the main business I have undertaken, I propose to leave the view as it stands, perhaps imperfect, certainly imperfectly explained, and pass at once to other things.

Experience, I have suggested, is always thought. And further, in experience there is always the pursuit of a fully coherent world of ideas, and there is no point in the process short of absolute coherence at which an arrest can be justified. Experience, however, frequently suffers modification or abstraction, the process submits to arrest; and wherever this happens the full obligations of the character of experience have been evaded. Nevertheless, it is important to understand that there is, in the end, only one experience. In experience there are no doubt, different levels of achievement, different degrees of satisfaction, but there are never different ends pursued, never a different criterion admitted.

Now, wherever in experience the concrete purpose is pursued without hindrance or distraction I shall call it philosophical experience. And in doing so I shall not, I think, be attaching to the word philosophy any new connotation. Philosophy, for me and for others, means experience without reservation or presupposition, experience which is self-conscious and self-critical throughout, in which the determination to remain unsatisfied with anything short of a completely coherent world of ideas is absolute and unqualified. And consequently, whenever experience remains true to its concrete purpose and refuses to be diverted, to suffer modification or abstraction, philosophy occurs. Philosophy is, then, not a particular kind of experience, and certainly it has no peculiar and exclusive source of knowledge. It is merely experience become critical of itself, experience sought and followed entirely for its own sake.

But, as we have observed, the full obligations of the character of experience are frequently evaded, experience suffers modification, an end is sought in a direction different from that in which the end lies. And, from the standpoint of philosophy, from the standpoint of experience itself and for its own sake, this is, of course, deplorable. Nevertheless, it is difficult to see how it can be avoided, and it does not belong to the view I am presenting to show that it can or that it ought to be avoided. The concrete whole of experience is not a totality into which, historically, every mode of experience is caught up. It is the logical ground of every mode of experience, the totality of which each mode is a modification. The supersession of the abstract by what is concrete does not take place in the world of merely present fact, and cannot take place in any future world of present fact, but only in the world of logical fact. Philosophical experience is not the historical end in experience, but its logical end, its criterion. Nevertheless, if we determine to resign ourselves fully to the concrete purpose in experience, an abstract world of ideas, so soon as it is recognized, will cease to have fascination for us. It will be rejected because it fails to satisfy the criterion of experience. But experience does not merely pass through its abstract modes, for these will not, of themselves, if persisted in, lead us back to what in experience will be completely satisfactory; like the rivers of Persia, they perish of their own inanition. They must be avoided or overcome. And further, even when in experience we are successful in avoiding or overcoming certain abstract modes, we are not (for that reason) prevented from returning to move again in these worlds of abstract ideas. A mode of experience, a world of ideas seen to be abstract can, indeed, no longer satisfy the bare ambitions of experience itself, but we are not thereby for ever debarred from re-entering it. Philosophy, experience for its own sake, is a mood, and one which, if we are to live this incurably abstract life of ours, must frequently be put off. But wherever experience is persisted in for its own sake, we must avoid or overcome all abstractions. To avoid them is a council of perfection, and like all such, impossible to follow. And in order to overcome them, we require not merely a general criterion (like that of the principle of coherence), but a detailed criterion for determining what, in experience, is abstract; and we require the detailed and conscientious application of this criterion to the actual world of experience.

I conceive it, then, the main business of philosophy (the main business, that is, of unqualified experience) to determine its own character, and to extend its content by persisting in the concrete purpose implied in its character and by avoiding or overcoming every alluring modification which may offer itself as a distraction. But it is difficult to avoid what is imperfectly recognized and impossible to overcome what is only vaguely conceived. And consequently it must fall within the task of philosophy to consider the character of every world of experience which offers itself, but to consider it solely from the standpoint of its capacity to provide what is satisfactory in experience.

This task must, however, be distinguished from another which has frequently attracted the attention of philosophers. Sometimes what has impressed them is the fact that modifications of experience do not fall equally short, and they have attempted to determine in the case of each mode the exact degree of its defect and thus to determine a logical order or hierarchy of modes. Each mode is measured by the criterion of coherence, which all accept, and is assigned its place according to the degree of its shortcoming. Now, the difficulties which stand between this ambitious project and success are great enough to discourage any but the most confident thinker. But the reason why I have rejected it is not on account of its difficulty, but because it appears to me to involve a misconception of the business of philosophy. It is, of course, true that modes of experience do not fall equally short; in the end the distinction between them is, simply, that they represent different degrees of abstraction. But, from the standpoint of the totality of experience, from the standpoint of philosophy, the fact that one abstract world of ideas is more or less abstract than another is irrelevant; from that standpoint all that is visible is the fact of abstraction, of defect and shortcoming. In order to realize its purpose, in order to keep itself unencumbered by what is abstract and defective, it is not necessary for philosophy to determine the exact degree of defect belonging to any presented abstract world of ideas, it is necessary only to recognize abstraction and to overcome it.

Briefly, then, what I propose to consider is the character of certain highly developed modes of experience, and to consider them solely from the standpoint of the totality of experience. And the modes I have selected I have distinguished as Historical, Scientific and Practical experience. These seem to me to represent the main arrests or modifications in experience, the main abstract worlds of ideas. Moreover, they may be said to be established modes of experience; and each is a sufficiently well-organized and developed world of ideas to present material for analysis. My intention is not merely to discredit them, much less to attempt to abolish them, but to consider them from the standpoint of philosophy. I wish first, to show that each of these worlds of ideas is a modification of experience, an abstract world of ideas, and that consequently each must be avoided or overcome if experience is to realize its purpose; secondly, to consider in each case the exact form of the modification entailed, but to do so without involving myself in an attempt to determine in each case the exact degree of modification; and thirdly, to illustrate in each case the implications of the view I have already suggested of the relationship of abstract worlds of ideas with one another.

# III

## HISTORICAL EXPERIENCE

### § 1

I intend here to consider the character of historical experience from the standpoint of the totality of experience, that is, to consider the truth or validity of history as a form of experience. And this purpose, as I have already indicated, does not include the attempt to determine the exact degree of truth which belongs to history (as compared with other forms of experience); it does not include the attempt to place history in a hierarchy—either genetic or logical—of forms of experience. On the one side, it may be the case that, in the development of a civilization, an interest in history has been more primitive than (for example) an interest in science. But that belongs to the history of history, which is not what I wish to discuss. It is no part of my plan to indicate the place occupied by history in 'the development of human experience'. Nor, on the other side, am I able to discover the means by which the exact logical status of history as a form of experience might be determined. And consequently that also must lie outside my plan. My intention, precisely, is to consider the character of history in order to determine whether it be experience itself in its concrete totality or an arrest in experience, an abstract mode of experience; and further, to determine the general character of the relationship between history as a world of experience and other worlds of experience.

Now, it will be seen at once that what I am offering is a view of history from the outside. It is a view of history, not from the standpoint of the historian, but as it appears to one whose interest lies to one side of that of the historian. For, while my plan is to consider the truth of history, the validity of history as a world of experience, the historian is engaged in the attempt to establish truth or coherence in the world of history itself. And it will be said that, whatever else there is in favour of such a discussion, it cannot be contended that it will give us an adequate view of history. A view of the world of history from the outside may be an exercise which affords interest for the otherwise idle, but it can result in no extension of our knowledge of the character of history. And this suggestion must be noticed because it will be encountered wherever the character of any form of experience is discussed. Religion, it is said, can be understood only by the religious man; science by the scientist, art by the artist and history by the historian. It is, nevertheless, wholly misleading. The character of any world of experience is its place in the totality of experience and depends upon its capacity to provide what is ultimately satisfactory in experience. Consequently, if the world of historical experience be itself the world of concrete experience, the attempt to get outside it will be futile, but it will also be unnecessary; for there is no outside to the totality of experience, and experience as a whole is self-conscious and self-critical—is, in short, its own criterion. And if the world of historical experience discloses itself as a mode of experience, its character (because it is constituted by the place it holds in the totality of experience) can be determined only so long as we remain outside the postulates and presuppositions in terms of which it is constructed and maintained. A world of experience, except it be the coherent world of concrete experience itself, cannot be seen as a whole and as a world from within, and until it is judged as a whole its character must elude us. We may leave religious questions to religious men, the problems of science to the scientist, history itself to the historian; it is the business of each of these to organize and make coherent his own world of experience: but to suppose that the nature of history is an historical question, or that the character of religion is a question upon which a religious man, as such, is specially qualified to advise us, would involve (to say the least) unwarranted assumptions about the character of these worlds. Our business, then, is to discuss all that the historian merely assumes, to consider what he merely postulates. And if there is anything merely postulated in history, that, at least, is a symptom of unselfconsciousness, a symptom of modality.

It should be expected, then, that the view of history I have in mind may differ considerably from the historian's view of history, or (which is the same thing) history's view of its own character. The view which the historian, as such, must take of history is an historical view; and if (and in so far as) the history of a thing falls short of its definition, his view of the character of history must fail to be satisfactory in experience. If history be not the concrete totality of experience, of which all forms of experience are mere modifications, wherever the historian is found considering the character of history, the fact that he is an historian, so far from giving special authority to his speculations, will render them suspect. It should not be assumed, then, that all views of the character of history must be confined to the historian's view of its character. And it should not be supposed that any view of the character of history which differs from history's own view of its character, must therefore be false or inadequate. Indeed, unless history be itself the concrete totality of experience, it is the historian's view of its character which will be inadequate—as inadequate as history itself. The historian's view of history cannot, it is true, be replaced by any other view; within the realm of history itself his view is certainly the only relevant view. But it is a view which must be set on one side when we come to consider the validity of historical experience itself.

What I have to offer, then, is neither a description of how history has been written, nor advice as to how it ought to be written. I am not concerned with the historian's 'psychology', his methods of research or his speculations about history, but with history itself—to determine its character from the standpoint of the totality of experience. Consequently it must be my first business to establish history within the realm of experience, to establish it as a form of experience, for what is not itself experience can scarcely be expected either to meet or to fail to meet the demands of experience. And we are already well enough acquainted with the general character of experience to know that if history is to be established as a form of experience, it must be shown to be a form of thought, a world, a world of ideas; and be shown to recognize coherence as the sole criterion of achievement. But since, on more than one occasion, each of these characteristics has been denied to history, it will be necessary for me, in order to establish my view, to consider briefly the validity of these denials.

The view that history is experience but not thought, that it consists of experiences but not of ideas, may be dismissed at once. For not only has it never, so far as I am aware, been asserted, but also, were it asserted, we have already in our possession arguments enough to refute it. History does not consist of the sensations or intuitions of the historian; it is not a world of sensations, intuitions or immediate experiences: and if it were, it would, for that reason, be unable to maintain its independence of thought. History, if it be a form of experience, cannot avoid the character of thought.

But further, if history is to be established as a form of experience it must be shown to be a world. And on this point we are met, at once, with a denial. History, we shall be told, is not a world (of ideas or events—for the present it does not matter how we conceive it), but a series; it is not a world, but "a tissue of mere conjunctions";[1] it gives us "co-ordination" without "subordination or system".[2] History is not a whole or a world, but a sum; it enumerates, but cannot integrate. And, should it be possible to establish this view, the consequences for history would be important. If history be a mere series, a tissue of mere conjunctions, then it is something other than experience, it is something less than knowledge, and outside the world of thought. For

[1] Bosanquet, *The Principle of Individuality and Value*, p. 78.
[2] Schopenhauer, *Die Welt als Wille und Vorstellung*, B. ii, Kap. 38.

we have seen already that there can be no experience which is not a world. Here, then, is a precise view, an explicit denial of history as a form of experience. History is concerned, not with what is 'co-existent', with what belongs to a world, but with what is 'successive', with what belongs to a series. Nevertheless, it will, I think, be found impossible to establish this view. I take it, first, that history is concerned only with that which appears in or is constructed from record of some kind. 'Events' may have happened (if we choose this way of speaking) of which all record or suggestion has been lost, and these are certainly no part of the so-called 'historical series'. The 'historical series', that is, is not the same as what is spoken of as the 'time series'. Moreover, history does not consist in a bare, uncritical account of whatever has survived in record. Because an event is (in some sense) recorded, it does not imply that it is historical. 'History' has, indeed, been written in defiance or neglect of this principle, but it affords all the evidence we require to demonstrate the absurdities involved.[1] Much so-called 'religious' history, working with the non-historical concept of 'miracle', accepts without criticism and at its face value whatever is given, and for this reason falls short of the character of history. The mistake here is not mere credulity, but a failure to realize that the so-called 'authorities' (better called 'sources') of history are frequently not themselves the product of historical thought and require to be translated into the categories of history before they are used. What is a 'miracle' for the writer of any of the gospels cannot remain a miracle for the historian. History, like every other form of experience, must make its material as well as determine its method, for the two are inseparable. If, then, we conceive

---

[1] "Osiander (1498–1552), in his *Harmony of the Gospels*, maintained the principle that if an event is recorded more than once in the Gospels, in different connexions, it happened more than once and in different connexions. The daughter of Jairus was therefore raised from the dead several times,...there were two cleansings of the Temple, and so forth." Schweitzer, *Quest of the Historical Jesus*, p. 13.

history as a 'series', we are nevertheless obliged to admit that in this so-called historical series the terms are not merely successive, they offer criticism of one another. They do not stand isolated and self-evident, but are guaranteed by the series as a whole. What comes later in the series is part of the ground upon which the historian establishes what comes earlier, and *vice versa*. In short, it is impossible to exclude criticism from history, and where there is criticism there is judgment. Before a 'recorded' event becomes an 'historical' event, a judgment must have been interposed. But judgment involves more than a series, it involves a world. And the view that history is concerned with what is merely successive breaks down. What was taken for a mere series has turned, in our hands, into a world. For, wherever the terms of a 'series' so far lose their isolation and come to depend upon the criticism and guarantee of other, perhaps subsequent, terms, and of the 'series' as a whole, there is no longer a mere series of what is successive, but a world of what is co-existent. Nor is it possible to maintain that, although the world of history is constructed by means of this process of mutual criticism of what has been recorded (which implies a world), nevertheless, when it is completed, its character is that of a series and not of a world. This mutual criticism is not merely a stage in the construction of history, it is a permanent character of history—like the tensions and stresses always present in a building, maintaining its stability. History, then, must choose between remaining a mere series, an undiscriminating account of whatever appears in any record in the order in which it is recorded, or becoming a world of co-existent facts and by this means establishing itself as a form of experience. And there is no doubt which will be its choice. Whatever the historian may think, history is never a mere series, is never concerned with what is merely successive. It is a world because it is unable to maintain itself as anything else. And because, and in so far as it is a world, it is a form of experience. It is true that the notion of a series, the notion of successive events, is, as we shall see, one

of the notions which determine the character of the world
of history; but what I wish to establish here is that history
itself is not a series, but a world.

And it may be remarked, also, that the view that history
is not experience, is not knowledge, because it is concerned
with a series, with what is merely successive, and not with
what is co-existent, arises from an elementary misunderstanding. It is due to the assumption that the abstractions
of the historian must be accepted without criticism or modification by any view of the character of history which expects
a hearing. The world of history may appear to the unreflective
historian as a series of successive events, but that affords no
reason whatever for supposing that it is of this character.
For the historian (as we shall see) it is dangerous enough to
regard history in this manner; for anyone who desires a clear
view of the character of history it is disastrous. The 'historical
series' is a bogy, and we must rid ourselves of its influence
if we are to achieve a coherent view of the character of history.
There is, then, no ground for supposing that history is
nothing more than a tissue of mere conjunctions. And if no
more relevant objection than this can be raised, history will
have no difficulty in establishing itself within the realm of
experience.

Nevertheless history, if it is to be a form of experience,
must be, not only a world, but a world of ideas. And here
also we shall be met by doubt and denial. History, it will
be asserted, is an 'objective' world, a world of past events
to be discovered, unearthed, recaptured; it consists of what
actually happened, and that (at least) is independent of
what we think; it is a world, not of ideas, but of events.
History, in short, is the course of events. Or again,
the business of the historian, it is said, is to recall, not
to think; he is a receptive, not a constructive agent; he is
a memory, not a mind. This seems to have been Bacon's
view of the character of history; and Hegel appears to have
thought that there was at least one kind of history which was
not "reflective". Historians such as Herodotus and Thucy-

dides "merely transformed what was passing in the world around them into the realm of re-presentative thought (in das Reich der geistigen Vorstellung)". These historians "bind together the fleeting elements of story and treasure them up for immortality in the temple of Mnemosyne".[1] And other less judicious writers have believed this to be the universal character of written history. Written history, for them, is not a rebirth, not even a resurrection; it is a mere exhumation of the past course of events. But objections to this view are ready to hand. And the most comprehensive is that history cannot be 'the course of events' independent of our experience of it, because there is nothing independent of our experience—neither event nor fact, neither past nor future. What is independent of experience is certainly not fact; there are no facts which are not ideas. And equally certainly it is not event or happening. An event independent of experience, 'objective' in the sense of being untouched by thought or judgment, would be an unknowable; it would be neither fact nor true nor false, but a nonentity. And, in so far as history is a world of facts (which will scarcely be denied), it is a world of ideas, and a world which is true or false according to the degree of its coherence. The distinction between history as it happened (the course of events) and history as it is thought, the distinction between history itself and merely experienced history, must go; it is not merely false, it is meaningless. The historian's business is not to discover, to recapture, or even to interpret; it is to create and to construct. Interpretation and discovery imply something independent of experience, and there is nothing independent of experience. There is no history independent of experience; the course of events, as such, is not history because it is nothing at all. History is experience, the historian's world of experience; it is a world of ideas, the historian's world of ideas. And further, even if the task of the historian is conceived as recalling what has happened, nevertheless it is a gross fallacy to suppose

[1] Hegel, *Vorlesungen über die Philosophie der Weltgeschichte*, Lasson, I, 167.

that recalling is something less than a form of experience, to suppose that we can recall anything but ideas. To recall is not merely to lay side by side in present consciousness rigid particles of past event, it is to organize our present consciousness, it is to think, to judge, to construct. But even were it possible to find a world of merely recalled, exhumed events, it would not be a world satisfactory to the historian. For it is impossible to suppose that it would be free from internal contradictions, and if the historian were merely to recall, there would be no means by which he could overcome the disharmony of what he discovered. His world would be a chaos masquerading as a world, and its principle would be, 'Everything is true exactly as it is presented'. In short, discovery without judgment is impossible; and a course of events independent of experience, untouched by thought and judgment, is a contradiction.

And here, also, it may be remarked that this view of history as an 'objective' world is derived from the prejudices and assumptions of the historian as such, and comes to us backed merely by the fact that some historians seem to have believed it. The historian sometimes sets before himself the task of constructing an unbiassed account of the course of events; *er will blos zeigen wie es eigentlich gewesen.* But often he confuses this absence of bias with the achievement of a world of facts uninfluenced by experience. He supposes that what is independent of the particular ideas and prejudices of his own place and time must be what is altogether independent of experience. His criterion of objectivity is freedom from experience; and this, we have seen, is absurd. And moreover, this notion is, in the case of history, peculiarly vicious, because it involves us in a division of the world of history so radical as to amount to its total disintegration: I mean, of course, the separation of 'what has come to us' from 'our interpretation of it', the separation of 'the course of events' from the recollection of it in the mind, of history from historiography, of *Geschichte* from *Historie*. Written history appears to some historians as the attempt to build up in the present a world of ideas to correspond with a past and buried course of events. But since, in that case, the course of events must lie for ever outside experience, and consequently be unknowable, there is little to recommend the view. And further, written or experienced history itself is involved in the fall of the course of events, because it must always be impossible to ascertain the correspondence between the historian's world of ideas and the course of events which, *ex hypothesi*, is outside his experience. This 'course of events', this 'what has come to us' separated from 'our interpretation of it' is, in fact, a contradiction. It is what is experienced sundered from the experience of it and offered an independent existence which, nevertheless, it is powerless to sustain. When the course of events has been separated from the experience of it, it will be found impossible ever to bring them together again, and apart they are void of meaning. Or again, from a fresh standpoint, for the historian there appears to stand on one side the course of events, and on the other, the historical method, which he thinks of as specially adapted to the discovery of what actually happened. But the truth is that this course of events does not and cannot exist independently of the historical method. The method is correlative to the matter; when we consider the one we are considering the other also. There is, then, to be found among some writers on history a point of view, corresponding closely to the Naturalism of the last century, which attributes to the presuppositions of history a universal relevance and mistakes the abstractions of the historian for independent entities. It may be convenient for the historian to think of his work as the discovery and interpretation of a past course of events, to think of historical truth as the correspondence of his ideas with a past fact, but it is the first business of anyone who undertakes to consider the character of history as a form of experience to criticize these notions. They are not presuppositions which he is obliged to accept on the authority of the historian. And it is safe to say that he will find none of them satisfactory. History is a world and is a world of ideas.

And consequently it is not a world of mere ideas. We have seen already that mere ideas are abstractions and nowhere found in experience. And in asserting that history is the experience of the historian, I mean neither that it consists of his experience as such, merely as *his* experience, nor that it is a world of mere ideas.

In so far, then, as history is a world and a world of ideas it is a form of experience. But beyond these there are other characteristics to be looked for in experience. The datum in all experience is, we have seen, a world of ideas, and the process in all experience is to make a given world more of a world, to make it coherent. The given world in experience is given always to be transformed; nothing in experience is satisfactory merely because it is given. And if history is to be established as a form of experience, it must be shown to begin with a homogeneous world of ideas and to end with that world made coherent. But here again we are met with the prejudices of the historian. History, he says, knows very well where to begin and it is not with a homogeneous world of ideas. History begins with the collection of data, or, alternatively, it begins with the collection of material. "The search for and the collection of documents is a part, logically the first and most important part, of the historian's craft." After "isolated facts" have been collected, the historian proceeds to criticism and synthesis. "After the collection of facts comes the search for causes."[1] The data in history are fixed; they are given to be incorporated, not to be transformed. And they are isolated historical facts, and not a world of ideas. But there are many difficulties which stand in the way of our accepting this naïve theory of historical knowledge. First, there is the difficulty that, if it were taken seriously, this view would at once place history outside knowledge. No knowledge whatever, we have seen, can be supposed to begin with mere unrelated particles of data, isolated facts, for these are contradictions and lie in the region of the unknowable. The mind can entertain only that

[1] Langlois and Seignobos, *Introduction to the Study of History* pp. 18, 211, 214.

which has a meaning, that which belongs to a world. But further, if we consider what is in the mind of the historian as he collects his material, we shall find, in place of this supposed miscellaneous assortment of 'facts', first, a homogeneous system of ideas or postulates, in terms of which he is conscious of whatever comes before him. The collection of materials is certainly not the first step in history. And the data of the historian are certainly not facts. Indeed history, like every other form of thought, ends and does not begin with facts. What is given in history, what is original from the standpoint of logic, is a system of postulates. But secondly, the mind of the historian, even where it is free from mere prejudice and preconception about the course of events (even where it is free from the most crippling of all assumptions in history, that the past is like the present), contains not only a system of postulates, but also a general view of the course of events, an hypothesis, governed by these postulates. No historian ever began with a blank consciousness, an isolated idea or a genuinely universal doubt, for none of these is a possible state of mind. He begins always with a system of postulates (largely unexamined) which define the limits of his thought, and with a specific view of the course of events, a view consonant with his postulates. And whenever the historian imagines himself actually to *begin* with the collection of materials, he is suffering from an illusion which not only hinders him from achieving a true view of the character of history itself, but may also hinder him from the achievement of his own explicit end. The so-called 'scientific' historians of the last century placed their emphasis upon accuracy and the necessity of acquainting themselves with the 'original authorities', the necessity of 'research'; and the notion arose that the chief source from which the modification or correction of an historical writer should proceed was "the discoveries which have been made since he wrote".[1] And so far they were right. But their view of the

[1] Bury, Introduction to Gibbon's *Decline and Fall of the Roman Empire*.

character of history suffered from a radical defect. It neglected to urge the necessity of examining the hypotheses of the historian, the given world of ideas in terms of which the materials were understood, and into which new discoveries were incorporated. And it failed to recognize the necessity of transforming the hypotheses of the historian to meet new demands. But, not to have examined its initial system of hypotheses is as ruinous to history as to be without knowledge of the so-called 'authorities'. Historical research cannot take the place of historical experiment; historical experiment is barren without hypothesis; and hypothesis apart from a homogeneous world of ideas is impossible. My view is, then, that the theory of knowledge at the back of the notion that history begins with the collection of material and that the data in history are 'isolated facts', is erroneous, and that the notion itself is preposterous. We know nothing of a course of historical events apart from some system of postulates; and it is the first business of anyone who is considering the character of history to discover the nature of those postulates. And further, no line can be drawn between what is presupposed and what is known. What is known is always in terms of what is presupposed. The historian begins with a homogeneous world of ideas, and his task is to transform (though not wholly to transform) what is given into what is satisfactory.

History, then, begins not with the collection of isolated particles of data, nor with a universal doubt, nor with a blank and empty consciousness, but with a homogeneous world of ideas. No other starting place is to be found, none other is possible. And the work of the historian consists in the transformation of this world as a whole, in the pursuit of coherence. The problem of historical thinking is to detect what modification a new discovery, a new experience produces in the world of history as a whole. And the weakness of many historians is due to their inability to understand, first, that a new discovery cannot be appeased by being fitted into an old world, but only by being allowed to transform the whole of that world;

and secondly, that the character of a new discovery is not given and fixed, but is determined by its place in the world of history as a whole. The general scheme, the initial world of ideas, they imagine to have been given and to lie beyond the reach of criticism; and each new discovery is, for them, equally fixed, solid and independent. New knowledge may be used to illustrate or to extend the old world, but never to modify or transform it. But the fact is that this general scheme, with which the historian begins, is a world of ideas given only in order that it may be superseded. And to see the bearing of a new detail upon the world of history as a whole is at once the task and the difficulty of historical thought. For each new discovery, whatever it may appear to be, is, indeed, not the discovery of a fresh detail, but of a new world. Every experience is, by implication, a complete world of experience. And each new discovery must be seen in its place in that world, its effect must have been felt upon that world, before its meaning can be said to have been apprehended, before it is 'discovered'. The process in historical thinking is never a process of incorporation; it is always a process by which a given world of ideas is transformed into a world that is more of a world.

I take it, then, that history is experience, and not a course of events independent of experience. There is, indeed, no course of events independent of experience. History is not the correspondence of an idea with an event, for there is no event which is not an idea. History is the historian's experience. It is 'made' by nobody save the historian; to write history is the only way of making it. It is a world, and a world of ideas. It begins with a world of ideas; nothing can come to the historian which is isolated, meaningless or merely 'material'. And the explicit end in history is to make a given world more of a world, to make it coherent. The course of events is, then, the result, not the material of history; or rather, it is at once material and result. And the course of events is not a mere series of successive events, but a world of co-existent events—events which co-exist in the mind of the historian. And since, as we have seen, truth belongs only to a world of ideas as a world and as a whole, truth in history belongs only to the world of historical ideas as a whole. No detail is true in isolation: to be true is to belong to a coherent world. And further, since no world of ideas is merely true, but is always true of reality, history also, in so far as it is true is true of reality. History is nothing but experience, the course of events is nothing but thought, and it is objective not because it is free, or comparatively free from the 'interference' of thought, but because it is what the historian as such is obliged to think.

Nevertheless, there remains the prejudice that history, though it cannot throw off the character of experience, though it cannot avoid the necessity of judgment and is itself the product of inference, is not primarily reflective experience. History, it is felt, is likely to be falsified as often on account of too much thought, as on account of too little. To desert fact for inference, to interpose judgment too readily are temptations from which the historian must turn away. History, it has been said, is "the least artificial extension of common knowledge". And this appears to mean that it is knowledge least compromised by experience, that it is fact merely supplemented by thought, that in history there is a datum of raw material and that the historian contributes only a binding or co-ordinating element. And wherever the 'contribution of the mind' is in excess of some undefined quantity, the result is either false history or not history at all. But we must not give way to this compromise, this vestige of moderation which, in philosophy, is always the sign of makeshift. No distinction whatever can be allowed between the raw material of history and history itself, save a distinction of relative coherence. There is no fact in history which is not a judgment, no event which is not an inference. There is nothing whatever outside the historian's experience. And we must discard absolutely and altogether this notion of a course of events which the thought of the historian may represent but which too much thinking will distort. Either history is experience without compromise, a world of ideas without qualification, or it is not experience in any sense; and if it is not experience (I have contended) it is nothing at all. History may be a limited, deficient mode of experience (that we must consider in a moment), but it is certainly nothing but experience.

§ 2

My conclusions so far are meagre, nevertheless I take them to be not unimportant. History is experience and nothing but experience; and the attempt, implicit in the passing remarks of many historians and explicit in the theories of some philosophers, to place history outside experience must be considered to have failed. History, whatever else it is, is not "the doubtful story of successive events"; it is a world of ideas, a form of experience. And, because it is experience, it is the whole of reality; the whole, perhaps from a limited standpoint, but still, never a separable and independent part of reality. Here, then, is the *genus* of what we are considering; we are thus far towards determining its character. And our business now is to ascertain the *differentia* of history. Historical experience, we have seen, begins with a system of postulates; and, since it is in these postulates that the *differentia* of this form of experience lies, it is to this system that we must turn in order to fill out and make precise our view of the character of history. The character and status of history as a form of experience is determined by the character of its postulates. Nevertheless, to attempt an exhaustive account of the system of postulates implicit in historical experience would lead me too far afield, and I must be content to consider it briefly and under five heads—the ideas of the past, of fact, of truth, of reality and of explanation which belong to history and are explicit in history. These ideas are, of course, closely interconnected, and it will be both impossible and undesirable to keep them entirely separate. They belong to a world and must be seen together in and as that world.

(i) Now, whatever the historian may suppose, the historical past is not the only past. History is certainly a form of experience in which what is experienced is, in some sense, past. But the past in history is not the only past, and a clear view of the character of the past in history involves the distinction of this past from that in other forms of experience.

Certain pasts may be dismissed at once as alien to history. The past in history is not the remembered past. The remembered past may be historical, but it is not historical because it is remembered. For memory is always personal; we can remember only what has come within our personal experience. And if Thucydides wrote about what he remembered, it is not on that account that he wrote history. History is the historian's experience, but it is not the historian's autobiography, and it is not his experience merely as his. And further, the past in history is not a merely fancied past; the historical past is not a past which merely might have been. Nor is it a past which merely must have been. The historical past, whatever else it is, is categorical and not merely apodeictic. And again, the realisation that to claim for history the whole past would be to claim more than history is capable of mastering, has led some writers to make a vertical division, and others to make a horizontal division of the past, in order to stake out a moderate claim for history. Thus, the past in history is said to be the 'human' past or the 'political' past. But these, whatever their convenience, are distinctions without a principle; there is nothing in the human to distinguish it absolutely from the non-human past, nothing in politics to distinguish it finally from what is non-political, what is economic or religious. There is nothing more than a makeshift here. And, on the other side, the more recent past has been selected as the past in history, the less recent past being made over to pre-history. And it has been suggested that the historical past is confined to a certain geographical area: Hegel considered Africa to be no part of the world of history. But these also are distinctions without reason or justification, distinctions merely of convenience.

The historical past is not to be determined merely by leaving out this kind of event or that period or locality; some more rational distinction must be found to distinguish the historical past.

Setting aside these, the past which I take to be the most important for us to distinguish from that in history is what I will call the practical past. Wherever the past is merely that which preceded the present, that from which the present has grown, wherever the significance of the past lies in the fact that it has been influential in deciding the present and future fortunes of man, wherever the present is sought in the past, and wherever the past is regarded as merely a refuge from the present—the past involved is a practical, and not an historical past.

This practical past will be found, in general, to serve either of two masters—politics or religion. Patriotism, it is said, is a love of the past, a respect for the generations which have preceded us. This is sometimes a fancied past (though it is not thought of as such), and sometimes it is a remembered past. What is characteristic of it is that it is known as *our* past, and the love of it is inseparable from self-love. But this political past, our past as ours, is not, as such, the historical past. And so soon as we have relieved ourselves of the prejudice that every past is necessarily the same, and necessarily historical, we shall have no difficulty in setting aside this practical past as something alien to history. For the past is not 'there', the same for all who consider it and from whatever standpoint they choose to consider it. What it is depends entirely upon how we think of it; and the past which (in some sense) is what is experienced in history, is not the past in practical experience.

And when we turn from politics to religion this becomes even clearer. There belongs, for example, to the Christian religion a so-called 'historical' element, which has been the source of both pride and difficulty to its defenders. But when this element is considered more closely it will be found indeed to involve the past, but not the historical past. The view that the past is important to Christianity appears to have been

inherited originally from Judaism; but it would appear also
that the idea of a specifically historical past was unknown
to the Hebrew race. Like most primitive peoples, the past
had meaning for them only in so far as it was seen to be their
past; their concern was with its life, not with its deadness;
for them it was a saga, it was (in fact) a mythology, an effort
to make actual and impressive their beliefs about their
present world and about the character of God. The Greeks,
for the most part, did not call upon the past to give added
force and reality to the creations of their religious imagination; they called instead upon a present sensibility to nature
and life, to things which could be touched and seen and
heard. But the Hebrew language of imagination had in it
always some reference to the past; the world was seen not
as it appeared when they opened their eyes to the day but
as a process, and in this they were not unique. They did not,
of course, think of this past as a merely fancied past; its
power to capture the imagination was due entirely to the fact
that it was believed to be a past which had actually happened.
But this belief cannot of itself convert what is essentially a
practical past into an historical past; it is merely part of the
paraphernalia required to extract from the past the inspiration
and the life which practical experience seeks. This Hebrew
dependence upon the past was taken over by Christianity,
and has now become imbedded in our religion. Our mythology is built upon it, our imagination dominated by it.
When we wish to give to our beliefs the force and liveliness
which belong to them, we find in the *language* of history a
ready means for expressing our desires. And whatever
motive lies behind the composition of the Gospels, the past
which they are concerned with is a past of this character.
And it is not an historical past. The language may be mistaken for that of history, but the meaning does not lie in
the world of historical ideas.[1] Whether this dependence of

[1] It must be understood that my view is not that the writers of
the Gospels were unconcerned about the 'truth' of the past which
they presented, but that this past was not an historical past.

practical experience upon a past arises from some dark deficiency of the imagination or is due to some other circumstance, is not for me to say; certainly it has involved the civilization of Christendom in some momentous consequences, both practical and intellectual. What I have to suggest is that this past must be distinguished absolutely from that in history. In practical experience, the past is designed to justify, to make valid practical beliefs about the present and the future, about the world in general. It constitutes, of course, an argument the form of which disguises its real content and cogency; the language is that of history, while its thought is that of practice. But this, so far from detracting from its force, appears (in certain circumstances) to enhance its power.to persuade. It magnifies the intensity of sensitive affection. Strauss conceived a disbelief in the Christian religion based partly upon practical, partly upon theological grounds; but he expressed it in the language of history and persuaded many who would otherwise have remained untouched by his argument. In short, Christianity seems, almost from the beginning, to have provided a new incentive for studying the past, but it provided no incentive whatever for studying the historical past. It is only in recent times that new and specifically historical interest has arisen in connexion with Christianity. And how great a revolution this has involved is known to those who have followed it in detail.

The practical past, then, is a past alien to that in history. And whenever the past is regarded as a storehouse of political wisdom, as the authority for a body of religious beliefs, as a mode of expressing a philosophical system, or as the raw material of literature, wherever the past is seen in specific relation to the present, that past is not the past in history. To seek in legend and in myth, in saga and in religious biography, or in 'the birth of nationalism', the dawn of the historical consciousness, is to commit ourselves to a misconception which can only lead us farther astray the more faithfully it is followed.

So far, I have considered only those 'pasts' which separate

themselves from the historical past. And the question of the positive character of the historical past may perhaps be approached most conveniently by considering the character of the past *for* history, the past as the historian is accustomed to conceive it. And this past may be distinguished at once distinguished from the practical past and from all other pasts) as the past for its own sake. History is the past for the sake of the past. What the historian is interested in is a dead past; a past unlike the present. The *differentia* of the historical past lies in its very disparity from what is contemporary. The historian does not set out to discover a past where the same beliefs, the same actions, the same intentions obtain as those which occupy his own world. His business is to elucidate a past independent of the present, and he is never (as an historian) tempted to subsume past events under general rules. He is concerned with a particular past. It is true, of course, that the historian postulates a general similarity between the historical past and the present, because he assumes the possibility of understanding what belongs to the historical past. But his particular business lies, not with this bare and general similarity, but with the detailed dissimilarity of past and present. He is concerned with the past as past, and with each moment of the past in so far as it is unlike any other moment. But further, the historian is accustomed to think of the past as a complete and virgin world stretching out behind the present, fixed, finished and independent, awaiting only discovery. The past is something immune from change. And this view encourages the historian; he thinks that if he slips, the past does not fall. In short, the past *for* history is 'what really happened'; and until the historian has reached back to and elucidated that, he considers himself to have performed his task incompletely. There are occasions, he knows, when 'what really happened' remains obscure in spite of his attempts to discover it. And, at these points, history is thought of as falling short of its full character. Nevertheless, with care, with patience and with luck, the historian can often come at the past as it really was; and the occasional failures of history to fulfil its destiny, do not invalidate this view of its general purpose—the discovery and elucidation of a fixed and finished past, for its own sake and in all its dissimilarity from the present. Here, then, is a past different from the practical past—which is a past seen only in terms of the present and for the purposes of the present— and able to sustain itself on its own account. In history there is the elucidation of a past which really happened, in terms of that past and for its own sake. Nevertheless, this view of the historical past cannot, I think, be maintained unmodified. It is what the historian is accustomed to believe, and it is difficult to see how he could go on did he not believe his task to be the resurrection of what once had been alive. This is, and must remain, what the past is *for* history. But the view suffers from a fatal defect: it implies that history is not experience. And consequently it must be set on one side as a misconceived view of the character of the past *of* or *in* history.

That this view of the historical past contradicts the character of history as experience there can be no doubt. The notion here is of a fixed and finished past, a past independent of present experience, which is to be considered for its own sake. But with such a past we are back again with 'the course of events' sundered from 'our knowledge of it', we are back again with the view of history which makes it something other than experience. For what is sundered from present experience is sundered from experience altogether. A fixed and finished past, a past divorced from and uninfluenced by the present, is a past divorced from evidence (for evidence is always present) and is consequently nothing and unknowable. If the historical past be knowable, it must belong to the present world of experience; if it be unknowable, history is worse than futile, it is impossible. The fact is, then, that the past in history varies with the present, rests upon the present, is the present. 'What really happened' (a fixed and finished course of events, immune from change) as the end in history must, if history is to be rescued from nonentity, be replaced by 'what the evidence obliges us to believe'. All that history has is 'the evidence'; outside this lies nothing at all. And this is not a mere methodological scepticism; history is not merely obliged to *postulate* nothing beyond the evidence. What is beyond the evidence is actually unknowable, a nonentity. What is known in history is not 'what was', 'what really happened', of that we can know nothing; it is only and solely with 'what the evidence obliges us to believe'. There are not two worlds—the world of past happenings and the world of our present knowledge of those past events— there is only one world, and it is a world of present experience. The facts of history are present facts. And it is misleading to suggest that present facts are merely evidence for past events: historical events are facts, ideas in the world of the historian's experience, and there are no facts at all which are not present absolutely. The historical past does not lie behind present evidence, it is the world which present evidence creates in the present. And again, suppose 'what really happened' to have some independent existence and suppose the task of the historian be to construct a present world of ideas to correspond with it, how is he to determine the corre- spondence? Apart from his present world of ideas, he can know nothing of 'what really happened'; any correspondence he can establish, any comparison he can institute, must necessarily be confined within his present world. Immediately we think of history as the correspondence of the historian's ideas with 'what was', historical experience becomes im- possible, historical truth unattainable. Briefly then, to pursue 'what really happened', as distinct from simply 'what the evidence obliges us to believe', is to pursue a phantom. And the shortest way of disposing of history altogether is to sup- pose that what is known in history is a fixed, finished and independent past. A form of experience wedded to this purpose is infatuated with the impossible and joined with the contradictory.

The past in history is, then, always an inference; it is the product of judgment and consequently belongs to the his- torian's present world of experience. All he has is his present world of ideas, and the historical past is a constituent of that world or nothing at all. For, in historical inference we do not move from our present world to a past world; the movement in experience is always a movement within a present world of ideas. It is not possible in historical experience to separate any element which is merely past, for what is merely past is merely contradictory; there is nothing at all which is not present through and through. There is no 'what was' to contrast with 'what is', there are no 'facts of history' which are not present facts. The historical past is nothing other, nothing more and nothing less, than what the evidence obliges us to believe—a present world of ideas.

But with this we appear to be faced with a paradox: the historical past is not past at all. And it is a paradox which must be taken absolutely. It is not merely that the past must survive into the present in order to become the historical past; the past must *be* the present before it is historical. Nevertheless, the precise character of this paradox may easily be misunderstood. And it will certainly be misunderstood if the view that the past in history is present leads us to conclude that the historical past is indistinguishable from the practical past, which we have seen to be the past for the sake of the present, the past as merely present. There is a view, for example, which conceives the historical past to be a reflection of the present as merely present. History, it is said, can only be written backwards. Of course, some limiting conditions are recognized; nobody supposes that any reflection of any present, however random, deficient or distorted, will put us in possession of the historical past. Nothing, indeed, is more obviously ridiculous than some of these reflections of the present into the past. Nevertheless, the dependence of the past upon the present is taken to be the principal characteristic of history. The present dominates the past; all history is contemporary history. What I take to be the value of this theory is the emphasis it places upon the present, and its insistence that the facts of history are present facts. But, for all that, it cannot be counted a satisfactory view. Behind it lies this notion of a complete and virgin world of past events which history would discover if it could, but which it cannot discover on account of some radical defect in human knowledge. The past and the present still stand over against one another, and their relation is conceived as a compromise. The present is the present as merely present, and it dominates the past, not because it is seen to include the past, but because it is, in the historian's mind, prior to the past. In short, this view suffers from that fatal tendency to moderation, compromise and abstraction which cannot, in the end, be distinguished from logical inconsequence, and it is not the view of the historical past which I am recommending. The historical past, as I see it, is not present in the sense of being the present as such, in the sense of being merely contemporary. It is not the historian's world of ideas merely as present and as his. All this, we have seen often enough, is abstraction. The past in history is not whatever enters the historian's head, it is what he is obliged to believe. He can believe nothing which is not present, but it is not on account of its presentness that he is obliged to believe it. The historical past is a world of ideas, not a mere series of events, and consequently its criterion is coherence and not mere presentness. It is certainly present, because all experience whatever is present; but, equally certainly it is not merely present, because no experience whatever is merely present. The past in history is not a reflection of what is contemporary as such—that, we have seen, is the practical past and lies quite outside history. It is present, not in contrast with what is merely past, but in contrast with what cannot be in experience.

The historical past, then, because it cannot be mere past, is present; but it is not merely present. Nevertheless, the historical past, because it is past, is not present through and through. But experience, as such, is present through and through (although it is not merely present). Thus, the pastness of the world of historical experience involves a modification of its presentness, involves a modification of its character as experience. The pastness of the world of historical experience (although it is not mere pastness) is not merely a symptom of the abstractness of that world, it is one at least of the characteristics of that world which implies and constitutes its abstractness. History, since it is experience, implies an attempt to organize, to make and maintain coherent the whole world of experience. But the *differentia* of history is that in it an attempt is made to organize the whole world of experience in the form of the past and of the past for its own sake. The historical past does not stand over against the present world of experience, as a separate tract of experience; on the contrary, it is a special organization of that world, it is the organization of the totality of experience *sub specie praeteritorum*. The historical past is always present; and yet historical experience is always in the form of the past. And this contradiction must remain unresolved so long as we remain in the world of historical ideas. History, because it is experience, is present, its facts are present facts, its world a present world of ideas; but because it is history, the formulation of experience as a whole *sub specie praeteritorum*, it is the continuous assertion of a past which is not past and of a present which is not present.

(ii) Fact, I have observed, is what is achieved in experience, not what it is given. Or rather, fact is given (because there is nothing given which is not made), and more complete fact is achieved by the transformation of what is given. The significance of fact lies always ahead in the completed world, never behind in the given world. To be a fact means to have found a necessary place in a world of ideas. The world as a whole is the arbiter of fact; and fact is coercive, obligatory, absolute, only when it is complete and because it is complete, and never because it is mere 'fact' (that which has been made).

Historical fact, I take it, conforms to the general character of fact. It is a conclusion, a result, an inference, a judgment. And consequently it belongs to the world of present experience. Historical fact is present fact, because a merely past or future fact is a self-contradiction. And, because all historical fact is judgment, there are no historical facts about which mistake is impossible: where error is impossible, truth is inconceivable. Further, historical fact is not 'what really happened'; it is 'what the evidence obliges us to believe'. And the evidence is, comprehensively, the present world of experience. Moreover, in history there are no isolated facts, because there are none such in experience. An isolated fact, without world or relation, is a fact not yet made, a fact without significance, a contradiction. Whenever in history a fact is asserted, the world in which this fact is involved is asserted also: the fact and its world are not merely inseparable, they are (in the end) identical.

Nevertheless, among historians there will be found those who hold a different view of the character of historical fact. It is said, for example, of Gibbon that "while he put things in the light demanded by his thesis, he related his facts accurately".[1] This I take to mean that the relation (or recounting) of historical facts (which is, of course, indistinguishable from the relations between facts) is something external and inconsequent to the facts themselves. It means that the fact and its world are separate, that an isolated fact can be established while we remain ignorant of the world of facts to which it belongs, and that a fact can be true while its world is false. It means, in short, that historical facts may be adjacent but cannot be related, that they may belong to a series but cannot belong to a world. I need not, however, pause over this view; if it were taken seriously history would be impossible, and wherever it has been entertained none but defective history has been written. Each historical fact belongs to the whole world of history, and the whole world of history belongs to each fact. And, in the end, historical fact is nothing less than the world of historical ideas taken as a whole and seen to be coherent.

(iii) Fact is always judgment, and with the conception of fact is connected the conception of truth. And I must now

[1] Bury, Introduction to Gibbon's *Decline and Fall of the Roman Empire.*

consider what is meant when a fact is said to be 'historically true'. Truth, we have observed, is not outside experience, but is a condition of the world of experience. And, in general, whatever is satisfactory in historical experience must be taken to be historically true. The question for us, then, is, What condition of the world of historical ideas is satisfactory in historical experience?

Truth, in the view I have taken of it, is invariably coherence in a world of ideas. Wherever it is found, it is a coherent world of ideas; and where it is found in history, it is the coherence of the world of historical ideas. And this, I think, involves us in three important consequences. First, because truth belongs always to a world of ideas, it belongs only to a world of present experience. A past or a future truth is a mere contradiction. Truth, of course, is never merely present, and that is why it can be neither past nor future; nevertheless it is always present. Secondly, because truth is solely a matter of coherence, it can neither require nor recognize any external test or guarantee. That is, truth in history is never a matter of the correspondence of a present world of ideas with a past course of events, or the correspondence of present facts with 'what was'. And thirdly, it is impossible to establish the truth of historical facts piecemeal. The truth of each fact depends upon the truth of the world of facts to which it belongs, and the truth of the world of facts lies in the coherence of the facts which compose it. In historical experience, as in all other experience, there are no absolute data, nothing given which is immune from change; each element rests upon and supports every other element. Each separate 'fact' remains an hypothesis until the whole world of facts is established in which it is involved. And no single fact may be taken as historically true, and beyond the possibility of transformation, until the whole world of facts has achieved a condition of stable coherence. It is impossible, for example, to 'fix' a text before we begin to interpret it. To 'fix' a text involves an interpretation; the text is the interpretation and the interpretation is the text.

What comes to the historian is, then, a world of ideas. It comes to him as a world of facts, but in order to transform it from a merely given world into a coherent world, the given 'facts' must be considered as hypotheses to be verified. And the process of verification involves not merely the acceptance or rejection of this or that constituent of the given world, but the transformation of the given world as a whole. Nothing which comes to the historian is wholly false; and nothing, until he has established the coherence of his world, is wholly true. But, since his world is a world of facts (and therefore present), and since history is a form of experience (and therefore involves an attempt to establish coherence in the world of experience as a whole), the question for the historian is not (as he commonly supposes), Does this set of past events hang together when taken in this way? but, Does my whole world of experience gain or lose in coherence when I take these facts in this way? Truth in history, I repeat, is a matter of the coherence of a world of facts, and there is no world of facts apart from the world of present experience taken as a single whole. An anachronism is not (as is often supposed) a contradiction in a world of past events, it is a contradiction in a world of present experience: it is something which comes to us as a fact, but which fails to establish its factual character on account of the incoherence it introduces into our world of present experience.

But, it may be objected, the truth of an historical fact depends upon 'the original authorities'. If we abandon the notion that the original authorities are the touch-stone of historical truth, we shall find ourselves committed to a conception of history in which truth is independent of evidence, the product of 'pure reason' or (in the debased sense of the phrase) *a priori* thought.

Let us consider, then, the character of what actually guarantees our beliefs, for this, I take it, is what we must suppose to be fully authoritative. First, it is not external to our experience. We are deceiving ourselves if we attribute any of our beliefs whatever to a ground less than our world of experience as a whole. The so-called 'authority' of an eye-witness, of a tradition, of a report, of a document or of an expert, if it be supposed to stand on its own feet and take the place of first-hand experience, is no authority at all. Whatever comes to us from these and similar sources must enter our world of present experience before it can influence our belief, and to enter this world means, in every case, to be absorbed, transformed, interpreted, made part of that experience, means (in brief) to be known at first-hand. Secondly, what actually guarantees our beliefs for us is always present. A past 'authority', as such, is no part of our world of ideas; it is beyond the region of possible experience. "A past judgment holds not because it was once made, nor merely because it is not in actual conflict with our present. It holds because, and so far as, we assume identity between our present and our past, and because, and so far as, our past judgment was made from the basis and on the principle which stands at present. An assumption of the same kind, I may add, is all that justifies our belief in testimony, and, so far as you cannot infer in the witness a mental state essentially one with your own, his evidence for you has no logical worth."[1] Thirdly, the real ground of our beliefs is always single and indivisible. A belief is never guaranteed by a 'series of reasons' or a 'number of witnesses', for these (and the testimony they offer) must themselves be believed before they can influence our belief, must submit to our world of experience as a whole. And lastly, the real authority of a belief is not reached until something absolute and in-escapable has been found. To speak of the sanction of an authority is to commit a pleonasm: an authority is always its own sanction. It is authoritative because it is absolute; it is absolute because it is complete, because it is impossible to look beyond or outside it. With a real authority there can be no question whether or not we shall accept it; we have no choice in the matter, for an authority we can escape is an impostor. In short, then, what alone governs our beliefs (and

[1] Bradley, *Essays on Truth and Reality*, p. 406.

what is, consequently, their only final authority) is our present world of experience as a whole.

And when we turn to the so-called 'original authorities' of history we shall find no difficulty in recognizing them, when taken alone, as abstractions. Taken by themselves they fall outside the world of experience and consequently are unable to stand alone as the ground of belief. It is not, of course, because they are the source or origin (as distinct from the ground) of our historical beliefs that these 'authorities', taken by themselves, are not authoritative. For the distinction between the origin of a belief and its ground is not one which can be maintained in the end. There is no 'cause' of belief which may not be 'reason' for belief. These 'authorities' are not authoritative only because they are never the *whole* ground of belief, because they are abstractions. Nor should they be thought of as part of the ground of our historical beliefs, for a ground can have no parts. These 'authorities' come to us from the past, written records, traditions, eye-witness's accounts and the like; and in so far as they retain their character as past, they remain strictly outside experience. They may be in some sense original, they are certainly necessary for history, but they are not, as they stand and by themselves, authoritative. They are abstractions which, taken by themselves, have no independent existence, and taken in their place in the world of experience must submit to criticism and suffer transformation. The ground, the authority of a belief in an historical event, is neither that it is recorded by an historian, nor that it is asserted by a contemporary, nor that it is attested by an eyewitness, but is an independent judgment we make, based upon and guaranteed by our entire world of experience, about the capacity of the event to enhance or decrease the coherence of our world of experience as a whole. The grounds of our historical belief are not two—conformity with our own experience and the testimony of others' experience—they are our single world of experience taken as a whole. Historical truth is certainly not independent of evidence; but evidence is not something, coming to us from the past, which has merely to be accepted. Evidence, the testimony of others' experience, can never take us outside our own world of experience; and the evidence of an historical fact is this present world as a whole and nothing else. If history is to maintain itself as a form of experience, we must abandon at once and altogether this notion that the so-called 'original authorities' of history are, taken by themselves, the touchstone of historical truth.

But, it will be objected, if the 'authorities' are no longer to be considered the criterion of historical truth, we shall find ourselves left with history as the construction of 'pure reason', with history as *a priori* thought, with history (in short) which is not history at all. History, it is said, is an unpredictable course of events, the connexions in which are not necessary or logical, but merely temporal and accidental. Consequently, nothing can be known of this course of events except by considering it in detail. And historical truth can be nothing save the correspondence of the historian's ideas with this essentially 'empirical' course of events.

Now, this view raises many and important questions, some of which I must consider later, but in order to refute it, it is not necessary for me to embark upon a consideration of the meaning of *a priori* truth. The view I have suggested is that in all experience whatever we begin and end with a world of ideas, and that any view which introduces or implies a linear conception of knowledge is misleading and false. It is impossible to think in advance of experience, and no experience is merely empirical. *A priori* and *a posteriori* are alike vicious abstractions. And further, history is not a 'course of events', it is not a series of happenings, not a temporal development; it is a world of facts in which the truth of each fact is based, not upon specific attestation, but upon that world as a whole. The truth of each historical fact is a function of its place in the world of historical facts. And nothing, in the end, is true, and nothing false save that world as a whole. 'Pure reason' is, indeed, powerless to determine the relations and the truth of historical facts, but it is powerless also to determine any truth whatever: 'pure reason' is something unknown in experience. And historical truth is not *a priori* (in the sense of being derived from merely general considerations or in the sense of being independent of experience), because no truth whatever is of this character.

Historical fact and historical truth suffer, then, from this limitation; they are necessarily present, because all fact and all truth is necessarily present, and at the same time they are conceived of in the form of the past. Historical truth is not present truth about what happened in the past—that is a view I have dismissed as self-contradictory. It is the entire world of experience seen as a single and coherent world of ideas *sub specie praeteritorum*. And it is the business of the historian to introduce into the world of experience whatever coherence this category of the past is capable of introducing.

(iv) History is experience, a world of ideas; and because it is this, it is not a world of mere ideas. The ultimate reference of historical judgment (like that of all other judgment) is to reality. And the criterion of reality recognized alike in all forms of experience is the criterion of self-completeness or individuality. The absoluteness of this criterion is not, however, recognized equally in all forms of experience, and the *differentia* of a form of experience may be taken to lie in the degree of thoroughness with which the criterion is applied. And our present business is to consider the world of historical ideas in relation to its conception of reality or individuality.

It will be observed at once that historical reality involves the same contradiction as we have seen to be involved in historical fact and historical truth. Reality, because it is experience, must be present; and yet, in history, it must also be past. And there is no need for me to repeat here what I have said already in connexion with historical truth. The historical past is not a *part* of the real world, it is the whole of reality *sub specie praeteritorum*, it is the whole of reality subsumed under the category of the past.

But beyond its character as 'past', I take reality in historical experience to be comprised of events, things (or institutions) and persons. The distinction between them is not, of course, an absolute or ultimate distinction; no such distinction could be maintained between the elements of what is real. It is a distinction of convenience. The fall of the Bastille and the Reformation are examples of what I mean by historical events; the Roman Empire and Christianity are historical institutions; and what the person or self is in history will appear in a moment. The generic reality to which these abstractions belong, I will call the historical individual. And the question for us to consider is, What is the character of the individual in historical experience?

It seems that there is a widespread belief that time and place, taken together, offer a principle of individuation appropriate to historical experience, and I will consider this view first. History, it is said, is concerned with what is absolutely particular, what exists 'here' and not 'there', what exists once and no more than once. Every historical event is fettered by time and place. And again, history deals only with that which cannot be repeated; it recognizes only that aspect of reality which is merely successive or which never recurs in the same way. The absolute uniqueness of each moment of space-time is the fundamental postulate in historical experience. Now, I am not disposed to deny that there is some truth in this view, and what truth there is we shall see later on; but taken as a whole it appears to me to suffer from two defects. First, history of this kind has never been written. This, of course, is not a conclusive objection; the history that has been written cannot be taken as a kind of absolute datum for a view of the character of historical experience, but it is suggestive. Secondly, such history never could be written. What is absolutely singular is absolutely unknowable, it is neither idea nor fact. Merely successive unique events, as such, belong not to a world but to a series and consequently lie outside the world of possible experience. This view reduces the degree of individuality in historical events, things and persons to zero. It is a view which cannot be taken absolutely; and a view which cannot be taken absolutely is no view at all. Once modification is attempted, the principle (such as it is) which is offered here disappears. For if these unique units of space-time are not absolute, how are we to determine them? Merely, I suppose, by drawing arbitrary lines across the continuous flow of experience. But since no reason is offered why we should draw them 'here' rather than 'there', we are left without guidance in determining what, in history, shall be considered a real thing.

I do not, however, intend to dismiss this view—that what is real in history is that which is absolutely singular—unconditionally. Behind it there lies the truth that the individual in history is presupposed, that it is designated and not defined. History itself does not and cannot provide us with the historical individual, for wherever history exists it has been constructed upon a postulated conception of individuality. The history of Natural Science, of Christianity, of Napoleon, of Cambridge, involve and depend upon a presupposed conception of their subject; and it is never a fully criticized, but always a merely designated conception. What is required of it is that it should be stable and should be consistently adhered to, not that it should be absolutely clear and coherent. "I have described", says Gibbon, "the triumph of barbarism and of religion." But his conception of barbarism and of religion does not amount to a definition; he has made no enquiry into the ultimate character of these things. Barbarism and religion are, for him, easily distinguished from their environment, and his business is merely to make sure that the distinction he works with is consistent. And those historians who see in the Reformation the triumph of secularism over a religious view of the world, have not asked themselves for more than a superficial, almost a conventional, conception of these things. Historical individuals are, then, designated; the determination of their character involves settling no ultimate questions. But the designation is not merely arbitrary, it is not without a principle.

Mere place and time I have rejected already as the principle of historical individuality; taken by themselves they offer no principle at all. But if this notion of place and time be enlarged and transformed by means of the double conception of continuity and discontinuity, we reach a principle which offers us an individual, neither absolutely singular, nor absolutely complete, nor merely arbitrary, but an individual in some degree separable from its environment and consequently suited to the purpose of history. The explanation of this principle belongs to a later stage in my argument, and I will offer here only an example.

First, in respect of what I have called an historical thing, it appears to me that its individuality can be established by means of this conception of continuity and discontinuity, and can be established in no other way. It is, I believe, the tacit assumption of all sound historical thinking. The Roman Empire, for example, stands out from what, for history, is taken to be its environment, not because it can show no change at all, no variation in shape, size or content, nor because the historian has chosen the line of least resistance and has restricted the name either to the thing as it first appeared before change had made its individuality ambiguous or to some core which he supposes to have remained untouched by outward circumstances, but because its beginning is marked by an apparent break in the continuity of what went before, and because, having once been established, it could maintain a continuous existence. Into this individuality, place enters very little; Rome itself is scarcely significant at all; now West, now East preserves the continuity. What establishes it for history is the fact that there appears to be some discontinuity at its beginning, and subsequently no absolute break in the Empire's existence, various as were the circumstances of its life. And when such a break is seen to occur, then and not till then, is the individuality shattered. Secondly, the principle of continuity and discontinuity is that by which historical events are determined. An historical event is never a mere point-instant; it is something with a meaning, and something which can maintain itself relatively intact and self-complete. Its capacity for establishing its individuality lies in the discontinuity, the relative break which seems to precede it; and its capacity for maintaining its individuality lies in the continuity, or relative absence of break, which it can show. Anyone who has considered the matter knows well enough how arbitrary the individuality of an historical event is. One historical event is distinguished from another by the flimsiest partition; there is nothing solid or absolute in their character. The historian is constantly to be found joining and separating them: the Reformation, the invasion of the Crimea, the Charge of the Light Brigade, the fall of the Bastille and the fall of Jerusalem, are alike historical events. But their determination as events is not arbitrary; it is always a question of relative continuity and discontinuity and a question of scale. And thirdly, in respect of historical persons, the same principle seems to be required, and to be all that is required, to establish their individuality. The persons of history are constructed upon the analogy of the persons of practical experience. Birth is the discontinuity which establishes their individuality, death the discontinuity which shatters it. The self in history is centred in the body; where the body is, there is the man. And the principle of mere time and place, the principle of the bare particular, is quite foreign to the conception of the individual person postulated in historical experience.

But, although this principle of continuity and discontinuity is absolute in determining the individual in historical experience, it can be and is applied in history in varying degrees of thoroughness. History begins with a world of presupposed individuals, but in the attempt to make it coherent, to make it more of a world, there is a constant temptation to abandon the terms of the presupposition. The historical individual is relatively stable, but it is also abstract and to some extent arbitrary, and it is difficult for the historian to remain unaware of this. Historical experience, like all abstract experience, is always on the verge of passing beyond itself. Its movement tends to supersede the conception of individuality upon which it is based, while at the same time it insists, as it must insist, upon retaining it. The historical individual, determined upon the principle of relative continuity, is conceived in terms rather of separateness than of self-completeness and passes almost unnoticed into its environment. Where does an historical event begin, and where end? Political and religious beliefs are sometimes sufficiently separable to appear as distinct historical individuals; but who shall separate them in ancient Greece, or in sixteenth-century England? And even the historical self shows this same tendency to coalesce with its environment. Principal and agent are often indistinguishable. Selves which are inseparable tend to be acknowledged as a single individuality. And there appears no limit to this process. But carry it too far, allow the designated individual of history to disappear altogether into its environment, and history is destroyed. And what rises from the wreckage is not (as some writers seem to suppose) reinvigorated historical experience, but a hybrid and barren world of pseudo-historical ideas. The possibility of history depends upon the maintenance of this balance.

The individuality of the historical individual is, then, established by means of the principle of discontinuity; it is maintained by means of the principle of continuity. And this involves us at once in the difficult problem of change and identity. For nothing can be continuous which is not a changing identity. Happily, however, it is not necessary for my purpose to consider this problem in full; all that is required here is for us to understand the solution satisfactory in historical experience itself.

The historical individual is a changing identity. And this is true not less of events in history than of institutions and persons. A bare particular, a mere point-instant; the complete and concrete individual, the universe as a self-explanatory whole; an abstract individual designed to exclude change, like the individual of scientific thought, a quantitative abstraction statistically determined—to these, it is true, neither change nor identity may be attributed; but it is true also that they are not historical individuals. The individual in history changes and is identical; it persists through a period of time, and a mere change of place is not held to destroy it. An historical event is never a mere point-instant; an historical thing or institution never exists merely 'there' and 'then'; and an historical person is taken to maintain his identity from day to day and from place to place, so long as death does not intervene. And the principle upon which the identity of the historical individual is maintained is what has been called the principle of the Identity of Indiscernibles. This means, briefly, that "what *seems* the same *is* so far the same, and cannot be made different by any diversity, and that so long as an ideal content is identical no change of context can destroy its unity".[1] "It implies that sameness can exist together with difference, or that what is the same is still the same, however much in other ways it differs."[2] But historical experience itself does not attempt to establish or examine this principle: for history it is a sheer, uncriticized postulate. The historical individual is established on this presupposition, on this presupposition it is maintained and, since somewhere there must be a limit, this presupposition supplies also its limit. The problem of identity is not solved in historical experience, it is merely perfunctorily settled. The historical individual is not constructed upon an examined foundation, but upon an uncriticized, a merely postulated foundation.

The world of historical experience is, then, a past (though not a merely past) world of historical individuals, a world governed by the ideas of change, of continuity and discontinuity. The world of history is the real world as a whole comprehended under the category of the past. And the individual, the real thing in history, is not a defined individual, but a merely designated individual, and consequently an abstract, unstable and incomplete individual. Whatever distortion the real world may suffer when seen *sub specie*

[1] Bradley, *Logic*, I, 288.
[2] Bradley, *Appearance and Reality*, p. 347.

*praeteritorum* is increased by the distortion which mere designation in place of definition never fails to introduce.

(v) The last of the structural concepts of the world of history which I have undertaken to consider is that of historical explanation. In experience, we have seen, there is always meaning; experience is explanation. And history, because it is experience, is explanation: in history what is attempted is to give a rational account of the world. But, since the explanation offered in history will necessarily be in terms of the categories of historical experience, in considering the character of historical explanation we shall be considering again, and as a whole, the categories which determine the world of history.

The world of history, besides being past, is a world of changing identities. Change and identity are of the essence of the historical individual. And history, from one standpoint, may be taken to be the attempt to account rationally for historical change. For it is only by explaining the changing character of its world that historical experience can hope to introduce coherence into it. Historical explanation is, then, an explanation of the world in terms of change, and an explanation of change in its world. But it must be observed once more that the categories of historical explanation are, for history, presuppositions. And this means that they are to be thought out (or assumed) *first*, and that they are not to be learnt from the study of history itself. The view is frequently to be met with that the categories of historical explanation are the product of some kind of inductive study of the course of events, that they are the result, not the ground of history. It is suggested that the 'historical method' is determined by the character of the world. But that this is a preposterous view can scarcely be doubted. Without historical experience there is no historical world, no course of events from which to gather the principles of historical knowledge. The course of events is the result, not the material of history, and more cannot be got out of it than the historian has put into it.

Now, of all the methods of accounting rationally for change, that which has most frequently been attributed to history is an explanation in terms of cause and effect. The categories of cause and effect have been used by historians since history began to be written. "The description of the course of events is interesting", says Polybius, "but the indication of cause makes history fruitful." Indeed, cause and effect have become ingrained in our view of historical knowledge. History, we scarcely question, is concerned with past events and causal connexions. And for this reason it will be proper for me to consider first this conception of the character of historical explanation. And I must consider it with a view to discovering whether it affords an explanation of change relevant to the character of the historical world.

The notion of cause as a category of explanation covers, however, a variety of conceptions; and my first business must be to distinguish and set on one side those causes which, although they are not altogether absent from the writings of historians, are nevertheless not consonant with the character of historical events and are consequently unable to provide an explanation satisfactory in historical experience. And among these must be placed those causes which offer so liberal and extensive an explanation that they end by explaining nothing at all. For, it is well known that what can be used indifferently to explain everything, will in the end explain nothing.

"Of all causes the remotest are stars", says Burton, writing of the causes of love. But since the stars are the cause of everything (or nothing, according to our view), they explain so much (or nothing at all) that the historian is obliged to leave them out of account. It may be possible to explain every event in this way, but history, unless it is to disappear altogether, must find some other way. This is an explanation which contradicts the character of the historical past, and consequently it is unable to offer anything acceptable in history. And again, the idea of God suffers, from the standpoint of history, from the same defect. He explains everything and consequently affords no rational explanation of any one thing. Whatever there is to be said for the view that God works directly in the world, he cannot be supposed to work directly in the world for history—the world of historical experience—without destroying that world altogether. 'God in history' is, then, a contradiction, a meaningless phrase. Wherever else God is, he is not in history, for if he were there would no longer be any history. Where in history he is taken to be a cause, nothing has been said and nothing remains to be said. And this, among other reasons, is why we must deny to the ancient Hebrews any proper historical consciousness. 'God in history' indicates an incursion of the practical past into the historical past, an incursion which brings only chaos. Nor is it possible to bring God into history by a back door. Polybius, for example, thinks it permissible for an historian to impute an historical event directly to the gods whenever he can discover for it no other cause. But an event without a cause (other than God) is not in any sense an historical event. It may belong to 'what really happened' (whatever that may mean), but it certainly does not belong to history. In short, what may be called purely general causes are not a category of explanation consonant with the presuppositions of historical experience.

But further, there is another kind of cause which must be rejected in historical explanation because to recognize it involves the destruction of history. A cause in scientific experience is, briefly, the minimum conditions required to account for any example of an observed result. But this, clearly, is a form of explanation foreign to historical experience; and it is possible in science only because the world of scientific experience is a world, not of events but of instances. Were he to adopt it, the historian would be obliged to eliminate all causes save one, of existing effects; and this would resolve history into an infinite regress of abstractions in search of an absolute beginning, or limit its reference to whatever lay immediately behind the given event. And moreover, the historian would find himself obliged to consider (by a kind of ideal experiment) what *might* have happened as well as what the evidence obliges him to believe did happen; that is, he would find himself becalmed outside the current of historical thought. History must reject not only those causes which are too comprehensive, but also those which are too limited. For example, history has no use for abstractions such as climate, geographical conditions or national character as the sole causes of events. When Lessing ascribes the eminence of Greek art to the climate and the government of Greece, he has quitted altogether the region of historical thought. Or again, to say of an event that it is due solely to 'economic causes', is not bad history; it is not history at all. This is not a question of evidence, not a question to be decided by the historian as such, it is a way of thinking excluded by the presuppositions of his thought. A cause in history must belong to and be consonant with the character of the world of history.

But there is a third conception of cause which must be rejected from history if history is not to suffer extinction. There is the notion that some events are causal in the sense of being decisive. The 'great events', the 'turning-points' of history are regarded as causes, and the world of history is explained in those terms. For example, it is possible that had St Paul been captured and killed when his friends lowered him from the wall of Damascus, the Christian religion might never have become the centre of our civilization. And on that account the spread of Christianity might be attributed to St Paul's escape. Or again, the upbringing of the Emperor Frederick II in Sicily has been made a turning-point of this kind, a decisive, causal event which accounts for and explains the subsequent, or parts of the subsequent history of the Empire. Had he not been in Sicily when he succeeded to the Empire, all would have been different. And once more, the Reformation, or Protestantism, has been isolated as the sole cause of modern capitalistic industry, democracy, republicanism, or religious toleration. Now, that causes of this kind are foreign to the character of history is clear enough when it is realized that the process by which an event is made a cause is a process which deprives it of its historical character. Explanation of change in terms of these causes implies that a single historical event may be abstracted from the world of history, made free of all its relations and connexions, and then spoken of as the cause of all that followed it or of certain selected events which followed it. And when events are treated in this manner they cease at once to be historical events. The result is not merely bad or doubtful history, but the complete rejection of history. Indeed, the distinction, which this view implies, between essential and incidental events does not belong to historical thought at all; it is a monstrous incursion of science into the world of history. The so-called 'great events' of history are either those which are seen to have great practical importance (in which case they belong to a non-historical past), or events possessing a high degree of individual completeness because they concentrate and include within a single whole a number of smaller events. The birth of Jesus of Nazareth and the battle of Salamis are examples of the first; the fall of the Roman Empire in the West and the Reformation are examples of the second. But 'great' historical events cannot be supposed to be those which are in some special sense causes and not effects, those which fall outside the process as a whole.

The principle in all this is that we desert historical experience whenever we look outside history itself for the cause of historical events or whenever we abstract a moment in the historical world and think of it as the cause of the whole or any part of what remains. Thus, every historical event is necessary, and it is impossible to distinguish between the importance of necessities. No event is merely negative, none is non-contributory.[1] It is, then, a contradiction of the

---

[1] This principle will be found, somewhat differently stated, in the writings of some historians. "There are conditions", says Lord Acton, "in which it is scarcely an hyperbole to say that slavery is a stage on the road to freedom." "The first lesson of history", says

character of history whenever we attempt to explain this world of changing identities by means of a cause which is either altogether outside the world of history itself (such as the stars, or God), or an arbitrarily selected moment in the world of history. Whatever else historical explanation must be, it must be consonant with the conception of fact and event which determine the structure of the world of history; and these causes contradict that conception.

However, it will perhaps be suggested that there is one important exception to this principle. What is true of historical events is not equally true of historical persons. In the individual human will is to be found the cause of all events; all other causes are subsidiary to this; history cannot look behind it and does not require to look beyond it for a principle of explanation. "The aggressive action of Prussia which astonished Europe in 1740 determined the subsequent history of Germany; but that action was anything but inevitable; it depended entirely upon the personality of Frederick the Great."[1] The grounds of this view are not, however, as clear as I should wish. The individual human will is, indeed, something which may be distinguished within the world of history, but why it should be relieved of all its connexions, placed outside that world and then made the sole cause in it, is difficult to understand. If it be placed outside, it can no longer have anything to do with history, it is become an abstraction foreign to historical thought; and if it remain inside, it must lose all appearance of being the sole cause of everything else. 'The personality of Frederick the Great' is

Creighton, "is the good of evil." But the principle that nothing in the world of history is non-contributory (or, if we choose to speak the language of morality, evil) is not a "lesson of history", it is a presupposition of historical thought. And this affords one more example of the confusion which exists with regard to the presuppositions of historical thinking. It is impossible to get more out of history than has been put into it; and if you learn from it the good of evil, it means that you have built your world of events on that principle.

[1] Bury, *Selected Essays*, p. 38.

not something absolute, self-explanatory, self-contained, and
it is not this even for historical experience. It is true that
certain historians have written on the assumption that it is.
With Thucydides personal character and motive is a first
cause behind which, as a general rule, he does not press.
But in this he is not only a peculiar, but also a defective
historian. 'Personality' cannot be placed in this manner outside history without becoming irrelevant to history. And
further, to speak of a single, ill-distinguished event (for no
historical event is securely distinguished from its environment) as determining, in the sense of causing and explaining,
the whole subsequent course of events is, again, not bad or
doubtful history, but not history at all. In scientific experience, on account of its assumptions, it is possible to
circumscribe and analyse both the antecedent and the consequent situations and to determine which elements of the
latter were caused by which elements of the former, but in
history this is impossible—not, of course, because the evidence is insufficient, but because the presuppositions of
historical thought forbid it. And, unless we are to return
to the distinction between essential and incidental events,
there is no more reason to attribute a whole course of events
to one antecedent event rather than another. The beginning
of a course of events might, I suppose, be spoken of as in
some sense essential; but a mere beginning explains nothing,
is logically neutral and cannot take the place of a cause.
And besides, history knows nothing of beginnings; it is not
in any sense a study of origins.

These, then, are some of the causes which, because they
contradict the presupposed character of the historical past,
cannot offer an explanation acceptable in history of the
changes in that past. These causes either explain too much,
or turn out to be no causes at all. And when we pass from
these causes and pseudo-causes to the more general conception of cause, we shall I think be obliged to conclude that
it also has nothing to offer of which history can make use.
What, I take it, is fundamental to this conception is that we

should be able to separate the cause and its effect, and endow each with a certain degree of individuality; but it is just this which is impossible while we retain the postulates of historical experience. It cannot be achieved by selecting some single event and attributing to that any subsequent event or the whole course of subsequent events. No single event in history is isolable in this manner, and if it were there would be no more reason to isolate *this* event rather than *that*. And abstractions like geographical or economic conditions cannot for one moment be considered to have the character of historical causes because these do not as such belong to history. It might, however, appear that the conception of cause could be saved for history by taking it to be the complete course of events antecedent to any single event or subsequent course of events. But here again the separation of cause and effect is arbitrary, random and meaningless; it affords no explanation; there is no more reason why it should be made at one point rather than another. Unless the emphasis is placed upon the *complete* antecedent course of events, this conception of cause shows no advance upon those we have already found to be unsatisfactory; and if it is placed there, *post hoc* and *propter hoc* are indistinguishable, and all semblance of a cause and of an explanation is lost. And finally, the suggestion that all these are manufactured difficulties, that single historical events are legitimately created by a rupture in the single whole postulated in historical experience, and that there is no reason why historical causes should not be made in the same manner, puts us on no firmer ground. It is one thing to break up the single whole of history, but quite another to force one of the pieces outside the whole itself and then call it a cause. The strict conception of cause and effect appears, then, to be without relevance in historical explanation.

These remarks will not, of course, have been mistaken for a general criticism of the idea of cause. That lies beyond what is necessary for me to consider here. All I have suggested is that the strict conception of cause, and all that it involves, when introduced into historical experience, instead of bringing light, brings darkness; instead of order, added chaos. And there appears to me no reason whatever for supposing that, because no place can be found for it in the world of history, historical experience is (on that account) defective. That all explanation must be in terms of cause and effect is a view we need not stop to consider. But if the strict conception of cause breaks down as the explanatory principle in historical experience, because it contradicts the postulated character of the historical past, it is necessary for us to find some other category of explanation with which to replace it.

This question is not one frequently discussed by historical writers, nor is there any reason why they should discuss it, but a distinguished modern historian has advanced a view of the character of historical explanation which deserves consideration because it is proposed as an attempt to get beyond the category of mere cause and effect.[1] In the course of his study of history, Bury appears to have conceived a dissatisfaction with explanation in terms of general causes, especially when used to account for what he calls the 'great events' of history. And the grounds of this dissatisfaction seem to lie in the fact that, if we observe events as they actually happen, many of them are not to be accounted for by means of this category of general cause. Indeed, wherever we are able to observe events closely and in detail this category of explanation breaks down. Consequently, Bury proposes a conception of 'contingency' to replace that of cause. The historian is to explain the course of events not by referring it to general causes, but by seeing it as the product of accident. Change in history is the result of accident, not specific cause.

Now, the first point to be remarked here is that, if accident is to afford an explanation of historical change in some terms other than those of general cause, it must be distinguished from mere chance. For if accident meant mere chance, then it would be merely one of the most general of all causes—like God and the stars—and consequently useless to the historian.

[1] See Bury, *Selected Essays.*

Whatever else it is, the course of events in history cannot be a mere series of miracles. "Fortune has caused the whole world and its history to tend towards one purpose—the Empire of Rome", says Polybius; but he can scarcely be held to have explained the history of the world. Chance belongs to one of the types of causes which we have already dismissed as inappropriate in history. And Bury is certainly not guilty of a mere appeal to τύχη Σώτειρα. An accident for Bury is, then, not a mere chance, but a 'contingent event', a 'coincidence'.

The character of Bury's view of historical explanation may be seen best in application. "The truth is that the success of the barbarians in penetrating and founding states in the western provinces cannot be explained by any general considerations. It is accounted for by the actual events and would be clearer if the story were known more fully. The gradual collapse of the Roman power in this section of the Empire was the consequence of a series of contingent events. No general cause can be assigned that made it inevitable."[1] And Bury's general explanation of the fall of the Roman Empire in the West has been summed up as follows: "It was the conflux of coincidences which proved decisive. The first contingent cause was the invasion of the Huns from Asia, a 'historical surprise' and resulting from 'events in Central Asia strictly independent of events in Europe.' It was an 'Asian mystery' how these Huns arose and poured into Europe. And to this first contingency was added a second, for the valiant Goths fled before them and poured into the Roman Empire. In their flight they met and defeated a Roman army and slew a Roman Emperor. This great defeat was mainly due to the contingent accident that the Roman Emperor was incompetent and rash. Theodosius, who succeeded Valens, set 'the unfortunate precedent' of settling the Visigoths—a new barbarian people—as a unit inside his borders. The fact that he died at the age of fifty was 'a third contingency', for had he lived longer his great ability might

[1] Bury, *Later Roman Empire* (1923), I, 311.

have averted the evils of his blunder. But a fourth event, dependent on causes which had nothing to do with the condition of the Empire, was the mediocrity of his two sons who divided his Empire. The Eastern Arcadius was incompetent, and the Western Honorius was 'feeble-minded'. The final or fifth event was the fact that in the West poor Honorius was controlled by a German, Stilicho. His character is 'a puzzle', and he admitted barbarians wholesale into the Roman Empire till he brought disaster on himself and it".[1] Bury was prepared to apply this principle of explanation to all historical events, and one more example of it may be given. "The American War of Independence may furnish another illustration. It may be said that the separation of the colonies from Great Britain must inevitably have occurred. This is a proposition on which it would be rash to dogmatize. But granting it for the sake of argument, there can yet be no doubt that if George II had been still reigning when the difficulties arose, or if George III had been a man of different character, the differences between the colonies and the mother country would have been amicably composed. If the independence of the colonies was inevitable, it would have come about at a later time and in another way. The American War, one of the most far-reaching events of modern history, was determined by the contingency of the personal character and political ideas of George III, which were the result of a chain of causes, unconnected with the relation between the interests of the colonies and those of England."[2] "The course of events", says Bury, "seems, then, to be marked at every stage by contingencies, some of greater, some of smaller import."

This view, it will be seen, involves two presuppositions. First, it presupposes the whole world of history to consist of a complex of separate series of events, each of which (taken by itself) is a causal sequence—a sequence of events which the category of cause and effect is adequate to explain. There

---

[1] Bury, *Selected Essays*, Introduction, by H. Temperley, pp. xxvi–xxvii.

[2] *Ibid.* pp. 63–4.

is no event in history which does not fall within one of the causal sequences. And each of these causal series of events is governed (in the absence of interference by another similar series of events) by its own principle of "natural development". "The irruption of the Huns into Europe", for example, is seen as "the result of a series of political events in Central Asia which was strictly independent of the events in Europe." "The disarrangement of the Germanic world by the descent of the nomads altered at many points the natural development of events in Europe, with which it had no causal connexion." And secondly, this view implies that all historical events may be divided into those which must have happened, inevitable events, and those which need not have happened, accidents. Inevitable events are those which have place within any one of these causal sequences which is permitted to follow its own course of development unhindered; accidents or contingent events are the product of any conflux of these independent causal sequences.

The explanation of change in history which Bury offers in this theory is, then, in terms of two different but co-operative categories: cause and effect, and accident or contingency. Cause is required to explain, and is all that is required to explain events falling within the separate series of events of which the totality of history is composed. And these events, because to each of them a specific cause can be assigned, are inevitable events. Contingency is required to explain and account for events which lie at the meeting place of any two or more of these causal sequences. And such events are accidental or coincidental.

Now, as a rational explanation of historical change this theory suffers from many and obvious defects: it is in fact both self-contradictory and contradictory of the presuppositions of historical experience, and must, I think, be rejected. I will not stay to consider all its defects, but only those which lie upon the surface. In the first place, in the form in which Bury presents it, it purports to be not a postulate of historical thought, but a principle derived from a study of history itself. It is a lesson of history. And since we have seen that history has no lessons of this kind to teach, it stands convicted of misconception at the outset. History, indeed, for Bury, is not a world of experience; it is 'what actually happened'. And he thinks that a rational principle of historical explanation can be deduced from the study of what actually took place. We speak of coincidences and accidents in practical life, and for that reason (he thinks) these things belong to history. "It is obvious that daily life, and therefore history, is full of such chances." Modern history he thought particularly instructive because there, owing to the fullness of our information, we can observe the extent to which history depends upon accident. But, of course, all this is beside the mark. Such a principle is not to be found in history unless we have first put it there. No course of historical events exists until it has been constructed by historical thought, and it cannot be constructed without some presupposition about the character of the relation between events. And it does not follow that because, in practice, we speak of accidents, they remain accidents in history. Indeed, as we shall see, accident is itself a conception altogether foreign to historical experience.

Secondly, this theory of historical explanation, although it modifies the use of cause as the principle of explanation, yet retains it. And in so far as cause is retained, this theory suffers from the defects which we have seen belong to all attempts to use the category of cause and effect in historical explanation. But, thirdly, where this theory attempts to limit or modify the use of cause as the principle of explanation in history, it introduces a distinction between the characters of certain events which is, in fact, meaningless. On the one hand, there are causal sequences; on the other hand, conflux of coincidences. But in what sense, if we are willing to accept coincidences in history at all, can we retain these causal sequences? How, in short, does the advance of the Huns, taken by itself, or the spread of Christianity before it was adopted by Constantine, or the rashness of Valens, or the feeblemindedness of Honorius or anything else which Bury takes to be the effect of a rigid causal sequence, to be an inevitable event, differ in principle from the fall of the Empire in the West? What, in fact, we are given here is a distinction without a difference. Every one of these so-called rigidly causal sequences is, in fact, merely an unrecognized conflux of coincidences. There is not one of them which may not be broken up into subsidiary events and series of events, the independence of which is no more and no less indisputable than that of the original series. And we are left with the position that, if we admit coincidence (in Bury's sense) into history, its first action is to swallow up cause; every historical event becomes an accident. How satisfactory an explanation of historical change this affords, we need not wait to enquire.

But the defects of this theory do not stop here. For if, on the one side, taking the conception of accident seriously leaves us with nothing but accidents, on the other side, any attempt to maintain the genuine causality of the independent sequences of events of which history is represented as being composed, leaves no place at all for accident. An accident or coincidence is, for Bury, the meeting point of two or more causal sequences, it is a collision of two or more "strictly independent" series of events. Now, if we suppose such a collision between two independent causal sequences of events to have taken place, the point at which it occurred certainly belongs to both sequences concerned. Both have been led to this point by a rigid sequence of cause and effect. How, then, can it be maintained either that the two series are strictly independent, or that the point at which they collide is an accident? That point falls within both series concerned, they have it in common; and it is absurd to maintain that two rigidly causal sequences of events which have one or more events in common are "strictly independent". And since the point of collision is the 'effect' not of one but of two causal sequences, its 'accidental' character appears to be to seek. Where, then, causal sequences such as Bury postulates exist, there is no room for accidents.

Two other objections to this theory may be noticed. It presupposes a complex of separate causal sequences of events each with a "natural" or "logical" development of its own, from which only a collision with another such course of events can cause it to diverge. But history knows nothing, and cares less about a natural or logical development apart from the actual development which the evidence obliges the historian to accept. The question in history is never what must, or what might have taken place, but solely what the evidence obliges us to conclude did take place. Had George II been King of England when the trouble arose with the American colonies, it is possible that the differences might never have led to war; but to conclude from this that George III was an odd chance, which at this critical point altered the "natural" sequence of events, is to have abandoned history for something less profitable if more entertaining. When Dicey says that "in the ordinary course of events" the law of England with regard to property would have been emended before the end of the eighteenth century, or soon after the beginning of the nineteenth, had not the French Revolution and the Napoleonic wars delayed the changes, he speaks as a lawyer and a man of affairs, not as an historian. This 'ordinary course of events' is, so far as history is concerned, a pure myth, an extravagance of the imagination.[1]

And lastly, Bury's theory of contingent events implies that in history there are accidents, surprises, abnormalities. But the notion of the accidental is contradictory of the whole

[1] "As for it having been unlikely that Shakespeare should have the literary power at 21 to write the Sonnets—Shakespeare proved to have such transcendent literary power that there is no arguing as to what he might or might not be able to do when he was 21. The only question should be one of fact, as to whether the evidence leads us to suppose or no that he wrote the Sonnets at that age. We cannot argue in Shakespeare's case from what other young men are commonly able to do. If this kind of argument is permitted, may we not have someone presently maintaining that Pitt cannot have been born so late as 1759 because that would make him only 24 in 1783 when he became Prime Minister?" Samuel Butler, *Correspondence*.

character of the historical world. It is a notion which the historian, when he sits down to write history, must dismiss from his mind. History knows nothing of the fortuitous or the unexpected; in history there is nothing extraordinary, because there is nothing ordinary. The hard winter of 1812 which ruined Napoleon's expedition to Russia, the storm which dispersed the Armada—these, from the standpoint of the participants, were distressing mischances; all (from that point of view) might so easily have been different. But the attitude of the historian is not that of the eyewitness or the participant. Where they see mischance and accident, he sees fact and event. And he is never called upon to consider what might have happened had circumstances been different. For himself and his friends the death of William I was an accident; for the historian it is no more accidental than if he had died in his bed. To think, as Bury does, of the death of Pericles as in some sense accidental because he died of the plague is to have abandoned history altogether. If we consider Napoleon abstractly, merely as a human being, it was an accident that he was born in Corsica. But when he is considered as the historical Napoleon who (evidence obliges us to believe) was born in Corsica, his birthplace is no more accidental than any other event in the whole range of history. In short, chance or accident is a mask which it is the precise duty of the historian to tear away, it is a way of thinking which he cannot understand. In the historical past there are no accidental events because, in the scientific sense, there are no necessary or inevitable events. Nevertheless, if history has no place for the accidental, it does not replace it with 'providence' or a 'plan'; it replaces accident with the actual course of events which the evidence establishes.

For these reasons, then, I take it that the attempt to establish historical explanation as explanation in terms of cause and effect and of the conflux of coincidences must be held to have failed. It is both self-contradictory and contradictory of the postulated character of the historical past. Nevertheless, it cannot be considered a wholly worthless attempt. Any view which has the effect of relieving history from the incubus of bare cause and effect must have some merit. For no attempt to explain change in history can come within sight of success unless somehow it avoids any arbitrary arrest or disjunction in the flow of events and any arbitrary distinction in the character of events. The conception of cause is unsatisfactory because it requires false and misleading interruptions in history: the conception of coincidence is unsatisfactory because it entails the separation of historical events into those which are inevitable and those which are accidental. And the chief defects of Bury's view are, first, that it retains the category of cause, and secondly that it modifies cause only by means of the contradictory concept of accident.

However, in looking elsewhere for a more satisfactory view of the character of historical explanation, we shall do well, I think, to consider a sentence which I have already quoted from Bury. The fall of the Roman Empire in the West is, he says, "accounted for by the actual events and would be clearer if the story were known more fully". For this suggestion contains, I believe, at once a view of historical explanation quite different from that which Bury worked out in detail, and a view less objectionable than any other. Change in history carries with it its own explanation; the course of events is one, so far integrated, so far filled in and complete, that no external cause or reason is looked for or required in order to account for any particular event. The historian, in short, is like the novelist whose characters (for example) are presented in such detail and with such coherence that additional explanation of their actions is superfluous. This principle I will call the unity or continuity of history; and it is, I think, the only principle of explanation consonant with the other postulates of historical experience.

The unity or continuity of history is, of course, a conception not unknown to historians. But most writers of history, because they conceive it to be a lesson of history, must be taken to have misconceived it. History teaches no lessons of this sort. Freeman, for example, believed the unity of history to be a principle derived from the study of history: "as man is the same in all ages, the history of man is one in all ages". Bury thought it had been established by the Darwinian theory of evolution. And, on the other hand, Stubbs denied that it is possible to discover unity in the course of events: there are breaks and "new points of departure in human history". But for our present purpose, the unity of history must be regarded as a presupposition of historical thought. We shall not find unity in history unless we have first constructed history on a principle of unity. And what I have to suggest is that this principle is capable of offering an explanation of historical change alternative to that supplied by the presupposition of cause, and free from the defects inseparable from the conception of cause.

The first implication of this principle I have noticed already: it is that nothing in the world of history is negative or non-contributory. All relationship between historical events is positive. And to show an event to be non-contributory is the historian's method of denying it the character of an historical event. Moreover (to extend this implication a little) history has no place for mere error or mistake. The belief that the Donation of Constantine recorded a genuine 'donation' was erroneous; the document was a forgery. But, for the historian, the belief is a positive fact, an event which makes a positive contribution to our knowledge of the Middle Ages, and not a mere mistake. A forgery is not, of course, the same thing to the historian as a genuine work, but it is no less and no more important. History is never a balance of debit and credit; it is a positive unity. In short, the unity of history implies a world of positive events in which such negative concepts as 'evil', 'immoral', 'unsuccessful', 'illogical', etc., have, as such, no place at all. Historical explanation, consequently, involves neither condemnation nor excuse. Secondly, it is implied in this principle that in the course of events for history "everything goes by degrees and nothing by leaps". Whatever may happen in 'daily life', nothing appears in history *de novo*. Events which, in the world of practice, appear sudden catastrophes, strange, unexpected occurrences, in history are seen as elements in a completely integrated world. It is a presupposition of history that every event is related and that every change is but a moment in a world which contains no absolute *hiatus*. And the only explanation of change relevant or possible in history is simply a complete account of change. History accounts *for* change by means of a full account *of* change. The relation *between* events is always other events, and it is established in history by a full relation *of* the events. The conception of cause is thus replaced by the exhibition of a world of events intrinsically related to one another in which no *lacuna* is tolerated. To see all the degrees of change is to be in possession of a world of facts which calls for no further explanation. History, then, neither leaves change unexplained, nor attempts to explain it by an appeal to some external reason or universal cause: it is the narration of a course of events which, in so far as it is without serious interruption, explains itself. In history, "pour savoir les choses, il faut savoir le détail". And the method of the historian is never to explain by means of generalization but always by means of greater and more complete detail.[1]

There are, of course, other implications of this principle of the unity of history which it is not necessary for me to consider in full. It requires, for example, that we should reject any notion of a 'plot' or 'plan' in history, in the sense

---

[1] To Lord Acton's advice—"Study problems in preference to periods"—we must reply first, that there is no difference; a period in the hands of the historian is as much a problem as anything else. The historian's business with a 'period' is to make it coherent, not merely to narrate the course of events; to understand it historically, not merely to recount it. And secondly, while many of the 'problems' which historians have undertaken to study are not historical problems at all and have succeeded only in leading them astray, 'periods' are beyond question historical individuals and the writer who undertakes seriously to discuss a period, may write bad history, but he certainly cannot be convicted of not writing history at all. Nevertheless, ideally, I suppose, the subject of a history is not so much a 'period' as a society or social whole.

of an outline skeleton of important events, the abstract story without the details. History and the plot of history are the same thing, to know one is to know the other. There is no 'main stream', no essential core in terms of which explanation can be offered. "Au fond, le détail c'est tout l'histoire:" history has neither husk nor kernel.[1] But it is, perhaps, important to notice that 'the unity of history' does not (as Freeman supposed) require us to "cast away all distinctions of 'ancient' and 'modern', of 'dead' and 'living'".[2] Without distinctions of some kind there can be no historical individuals, and without separate individuals there can be no change. This principle does, however, require us to recognize only historical distinctions, only the individuals of history. It excludes the recognition both of individuals which lie outside the world of history, and of individuals created by the arbitrary grouping of historical events in order to give the appearance of a cause and an effect. And finally, it is by means of this principle that accidents are dismissed from history and the contrast between freedom and necessity, freewill and determinism, is made meaningless. These conceptions are relevant in the world of practical experience, but in historical experience they have no meaning. Events, things and persons in history are neither free (in the sense of being ungoverned by relations), nor determined (in the sense of being governed by 'logical' or cosmic causes). They are both free from the influence of external determination, and determined by their place and relations in their own world. The 'human will' is no more uncertain or unaccountable than any other individual of historical experience.[3] In short, what the principle of mechanism is in scientific experience, this principle of unity or continuity is in historical experience. It is a structural presupposition (assumed and left uncriticized in history) which enables the historian to build a specific and homogeneous world of ideas. In history

[1] Cp. R. G. Collingwood, *Proceedings of the Aristotelian Society*, 1924–5, pp. 151 sq. [2] Freeman, *Comparative Politics*, p. 197.
[3] Cp. Freeman, *Methods of Historical Study*, p. 148.

there is the attempt to explain the historical past by means of the historical past and for the sake of the historical past.

## § 3

My purpose, I have said, is to consider historical experience from the standpoint of the totality of experience, to consider (that is) the truth of history. History is the whole of reality from a certain standpoint, and not a separable part of reality. Historical thought belongs to the attempt to find a world of experience satisfactory in itself, and history cannot be dismissed as a "tissue of mere conjunctions". The undertaking of Schopenhauer and others to thrust history outside experience must be considered to have failed. The world of historical fact is certainly true and history is certainly reality, so far as it goes. But, beyond this general character, historical experience is a specific, homogeneous world of experience, an organized whole, and the problem of the character of this world of historical ideas, taken by itself and as a self-contained whole, remains. Is the world of historical ideas, taken as a whole and by itself, satisfactory, or must a means be discovered of superseding it in order to achieve what the character of experience implies? Is the world of history the world of concrete reality, or is it an arrest in experience? For we have seen, whatever be the character of the world of historical experience, it must be accepted or rejected as a whole. Either it is, when taken as a world and by itself, abstract, defective, unable to satisfy the ultimate demand in experience; or it is itself the concrete world of reality. Our question, then, remains: What is the status of this world of historical experience, taken as a world and by itself, in the totality of experience?

In considering the actual structure of the world of history I have not concealed my view that it is, when regarded from the standpoint of the totality of experience, abstract and defective. And in order to answer the question now before us, I have only to point out the implications of the view of historical experience to which I am already committed. What determines the world of historical experience as historical, determines it also as an arrest in experience.

The first characteristic of the world of historical experience I have had occasion to notice is that its form contradicts the nature of its content. And this alone obliges us to consider it no better than an abstract world, a defective mode of experience. The world of historical fact, truth and reality appears to lie in the past; historical reality is a past reality, and the notion of the past cannot be dismissed from history without dismissing history itself. But to suppose this world of history *actually* to lie in the past, to accept it (that is) in the form in which it is satisfactory in historical experience, involves us in a radical contradiction. It obliges us to suppose a world which is not a world of ideas, to suppose facts which are not in experience, truths which are not true, reality which is not real. For no fact, truth or reality is, or can be, past. And, at this point, what is satisfactory in historical experience fails to satisfy in experience itself. The world of history is the world *sub specie praeteritorum*; but only by becoming present through and through can this world become an adequate organization of experience, and to become this would involve the renunciation of its own specific and distinguishing character. In historical experience the attempt is made to establish and maintain the real world, but the world which is actually established and maintained, the world which corresponds with its actual character and represents its explicit purpose, is a world vitiated by this abstraction, the past. Historical experience, because it is experience, implies the assertion of reality; but what is explicit in historical judgment is not what it asserts of reality, for what is explicit is abstract and unable to qualify reality directly. And again, the world of history appears to be an extension of our present world, a newly discovered tract in experience; and unless it actually is this, it stands convicted of defect and ambiguity. But to suppose that this is its character involves us at once in the contradictory notions of events which are not facts, facts which are not ideas, ideas which are not experiences. In short, what is past is, as such, an abstraction, and any attempt to make a system of experience upon the basis of this abstraction can result only in an abstract world of experience. The world seen under the category of the past is the world seen imperfectly.

This world of historical events, then, taken as a whole and by itself, must be thought of as a certain abstracted aspect of the real world. Or, alternatively, it must be considered a defective organization of the world of experience taken as a whole. It adds nothing to that world, and by introducing this contradictory notion of the past, it succeeds only in rendering a satisfactory organization of the world of experience impossible. Taken by itself, the world of history is abstract and defective from end to end: and only by abandoning it altogether shall we find ourselves once more on the way to a world of experience satisfactory in itself. Pretending to organize and elucidate the real world of experience *sub specie aeternitatis*, history succeeds only in organizing it *sub specie praeteritorum*. And consequently the world of historical experience constitutes an arrest in experience and a renunciation of the full, unmitigated character of experience.

But there is a second characteristic of the world of history which establishes its abstract character on an even firmer foundation. If, after what I have said, the notion is still entertained that history can be freed from its attachment to the past without at the same moment being freed from itself, we need only consider the character of the historical individual (what is real in history) to be convinced of the abstractness of the world of history. The historical individual, besides being past (and for that reason abstract and beyond redemption), is, I have said, the creature of designation. And designation is not a separate kind of thought, but a defective mode of thought. The end in all experience is definition; and wherever in experience satisfaction is achieved in a world of merely designated individuals, in place of a world of defined individuals, experience has fallen short of its own character.

The individual of designation is always more or less arbitrary; its limits are arbitrary, its identity insecure. Everything, we have seen, is real so long as it is not taken for less than it is. But mere designation is a mode of thought which consistently takes everything for less than it is; it is abstraction as a special process. And this is the condition of history. What in history is taken to be real falls short of the character of reality. The subject in history is not, of course, a mere name, or it is not always so. There are degrees of designation, degrees of falling short of definition; and history certainly passes beyond any form of experience satisfied with singular judgments, the subjects of which are proper names. Nevertheless, it always falls short of definition. And any world of designated individuals falls short of what is satisfactory in experience. History postulates something more than a mere name, and something less than a definitive individual.

Moreover, the historical individual is a changing identity. And identity and change, we have seen, belong only to abstract individuals: they postulate incompleteness. Wherever identity can be asserted or denied, what we are dealing with is an abstraction, an individual which falls short of being a world and complete in itself, an individual which has failed to achieve and cannot maintain individuality. The historical individual is, then, the result of an arrest in the conception of individuality at a point short of absolute coherence. And consequently there is nothing in history which can be supposed to provide what is ultimately satisfactory in experience.

Historical experience, I conclude, is a modification of experience; it is an arrest in experience. History is a world of abstractions. It is a backwater, and, from the standpoint of experience, a mistake. It leads nowhere; and in experience, if we have been unable to avoid it, we can regain the path to what will afford satisfaction only by superseding and destroying it. In short, everything I have taken to be true of a mode of experience is true of historical experience; and everything I have taken to be true of a world of abstract ideas, is true of history. This, of course, does not mean that in historical experience there is nothing which affords any degree of satisfaction whatever, that historical experience is abstract absolutely—such a position is, in my opinion, untenable and I have already dismissed it. Historical experience means, in the end, nothing else than experience which in a certain specific degree is satisfactory in itself. That historical experience is in some degree satisfactory is not untrue, but (from my point of view) irrelevant. My standpoint is that of the totality of experience, and from that standpoint historical experience is a failure and consequently an absolute failure. And the limited satisfaction to be found in historical experience is unable even to contribute to the ultimate satisfaction looked for in the totality of experience. The world of history, as a formulation of experience, stands in the way of a finally coherent world of ideas.

It will, perhaps, be thought that I have reached this conclusion somewhat rapidly and without having given sufficient attention to the views with which it conflicts. And in order to remedy this defect, I propose now to consider what I take to be the two most important forms of the view that historical experience is concrete experience and that the world of historical ideas is the world of concrete reality. Briefly, this view asserts that in order to understand things we must understand their history, and that when we have understood their history we have understood the things themselves. Experience, it is said, "is historical altogether and the fact is happily one there is no gainsaying".[1] "History", remarks Lord Acton, "rescues us from the transient": and for that reason must be supposed to provide what is satisfactory in experience. Experience itself is historical, and all abstract modes of experience are modifications of historical experience.

Before considering this view in detail, there are two general observations to be made. First, it will be seen that any view

[1] Ward, *Naturalism and Agnosticism*, II, 281.

which asserts that in order to understand 'things' we must understand their history, rests, from my point of view, upon a *petitio principii*, and is entirely worthless. It assumes the existence of 'things' independent of experience, it takes these 'things' to be the absolute and unchangeable data in experience, and then enquires what interpretation or view of them reveals their essential and intrinsic character. The world of 'things' and the world of experience are sundered, and all attempts to reunite them must remain futile. And secondly, so far from history rescuing us from the transient, it is the organization of experience under the category of transience. It rests upon the assumption that transience is real and gives us a view of experience from this standpoint. History could rescue us from the transient only if the past were separate from and independent of the present, a storehouse of past events and past experiences, and history a kind of universal memory—and this view involves us in so many difficulties that I have already been obliged to reject it.

The claim to concreteness or absolute self-completeness, in the first of the forms in which I shall consider it, is made on behalf of history itself. By this I mean that history itself (and not any refinement upon history) is represented as concrete experience, and the world of historical events (and not something derived from that world) is represented as the world of concrete reality. And it is difficult to conjecture how this notion can ever have gained currency. On the surface it presents difficulties enough: but these are negligible when compared with the mass of contradictions which does duty as a foundation. I do not, however, propose to unearth these systematically; many of them I have discussed already, and it will be sufficient for my purpose to consider only the main arguments which are used to recommend this claim.

Historical experience, it is said, is concrete experience because the object in historical experience is what is individual and not (like scientific experience) what is merely general. In history we have knowledge of what is absolutely individual, what is real without qualification. Now, anyone who has followed the remarks I have already made on the subject of individuality will understand the objection I must take to this view. For me individuality is a question of degree; but for this view it is either present in or entirely absent from any world of experience. For me the end in all experience is to distinguish individuality; but for this view there are modes of experience which are wholly without a notion of individuality; the generalities of scientific thought are not a modified form of individuality, they are the mere denial of individuality. For me the only absolute individual is the universe as a whole, for this alone is self-complete, without either environment or relations; but for this view the universe is as full of absolute, self-existent individuals as it is full of historical events, things and persons. In short, this view of history is based upon a notion of experience and of reality which I have already examined in detail and rejected. And further, that the historical individual is a self-complete whole, ultimate, irreducible and absolute, is, when we compare it with the shaky and uncertain individuality which actually belongs to history, a notion so absurd that it is difficult to take it seriously. The individual in history is both past and merely designated, and on account of either of these characteristics it stands convicted of abstraction. And if what this view of history intends to claim is, not that history is concerned with and reveals what is absolutely individual, but what is singular, it is merely another attempt to thrust history outside experience in the hope that it may, on that account, demonstrate its intimacy with reality. And, as we have seen already, the effect of this procedure is the reverse of what is intended.

Another argument (if it may be called so) used to support the world of historical events in its character of the world of absolute reality takes this form: all knowledge is historical knowledge, because all knowledge is the product of experience, and experience is necessarily historical, necessarily derived from 'what has happened'. But this argument relies upon a conception of experience which identifies it with something standing over against reflection providing the material or data of reflection—a common conception, but one for which there is nothing at all to be said. And further, even if we were able to maintain the possibility of such experience, it would still be something different from historical experience. For history, we have seen, is not concerned with 'what has been' as such, with every and any past, but only with the historical past. Historical knowledge is not knowledge of 'what has happened', but of the past in so far as it conforms to the categories of historical experience. What, no doubt, lies behind this notion of historical knowledge as complete knowledge is the idea that in history we enjoy a kind of extension of present knowledge which must be supposed to enrich it and make it more profound, and without which it must remain partial and restricted. But history, we have seen, is anything but an extension of present experience; it is, on the contrary, a mutilation of present experience, it is present experience deformed and restricted by being thrown into the mould of the historical past, by being conceived under the category of the past. The view, then, that the world of history is the world of concrete reality, that historical truth is absolute truth, can find no adequate support for itself in the notion that history is somehow an extension of present experience, that history "rescues us from the transient".

But further, this view appears sometimes connected with the notion that history is not a mode of experience at all, but the direct presentation of the objective life of the universe, uncompromised by experience and unmodified by interpretation. In the 'pageant of history' we perceive naked reality, unencumbered with the generalities of philosophy and the abstractions of science, passing before our eyes. We see the whole, of which the present is but a part; the detailed whole, from which science abstracts a mere aspect and of which philosophy grasps a mere outline. But in so far as a connexion with this extraordinary notion is insisted upon it cannot fail to discredit rather than advance the claim we are considering. Unless history is experience it is nothing at all; and if it be experience it must conform to the character of experience, which knows nothing of a whole separated into parts; there are no separate tracts of experience and no separate kinds of knowledge.

So far, then, from it being impossible to gainsay the view that experience is "historical altogether", it must remain conjectural how such a notion could ever have been entertained. That experience itself is historical experience; that the only valid criticism which can be offered of any modification of experience is an historical criticism; and that when history itself is made the subject of thought, all that can be said of it, relevantly, must be comprised in a mere history of history—all this, and much else, seems to be involved in this claim. And there can be no doubt that, to appear in this exaggerated guise, history must be living beyond its means, and the last state of such extravagance can be only bankruptcy.

But the assertion that historical experience is absolute experience is to be found in a second form. The claim is not only made on behalf of history itself, but also on behalf of what is called the 'philosophy of history'. The world of historical events, as it leaves the hand of the historian, is admitted to be incomplete and defective, but it is asserted that 'philosophy' working upon this world can somehow transform it into the world of absolute reality. And I must now consider this view. It should, however, be remarked that the claim cannot be said to be on behalf of history, or the world of historical events, unless the 'philosophy of history' itself stands for some form of historical experience. The transformation which 'philosophy' is to produce in the world of history must not be so radical as to involve the destruction of that world and the substitution of another in its place. Yet it must be a real transformation, for otherwise the result would be indistinguishable from history itself and would suffer from the defects which we have seen belong to history. And it appears to me that the 'philosophy of history', in its attempt to serve two masters, will succeed in satisfying neither, and must reveal itself as a hybrid and homeless form of thought.

Now, the phrase 'the philosophy of history' cannot be said to have a single and unambiguous meaning for all who make use of it. It will, I think, be found to cover at least three entirely distinct conceptions. And in what I have to say I will confine myself to these. In the first place, the 'philosophy of history' has been taken to mean the attempt to discover and establish some general laws which govern the whole course of history. The materials are supplied by the mere historian; the philosopher generalizes them. Historical facts are regarded as ephemeral instances of the unchanging truths which the philosophy of history propounds. I do not, however, propose to consider this type of philosophy of history in detail now, because it represents a form of thought which I should prefer to call the 'science of history', and I must discuss it later when I come to consider the relation of historical to scientific thought. All that need be remarked at this point is that this so-called philosophy of history involves the complete destruction of history. The moment historical facts are regarded as instances of general laws, history is dismissed. Historical individuals are, of course, themselves generalizations, but any form of generalization which reduces them to instances of a rule must involve the complete destruction of history. An historical individual, it is true, tends always to pass beyond the conception of individuality upon which it is based, but there is a limit beyond which it ceases to be an historical individual. And I may say also that I can find no reason whatever for speaking of this attempt to generalize history as 'philosophy'. The first form of the philosophy of history appears, then, to be neither philosophy nor history; it is of too nondescript a character to be able to maintain itself either as concrete experience itself, the world of absolute reality, or as the world of history.

But secondly, 'the philosophy of history' means for some

writers a kind of general review of the course of human life, a view of finite existence from some standpoint outside the actual course of finite life. A notion of this sort is, I think, to be found in Lotze.[1] But its excessive vagueness makes it difficult to describe. Its difficulties, however, are obvious. Such a form of thought might be philosophy, but it could have nothing whatever to do with history. The transformation it effects in the world of historical events is so radical that nothing recognizable as history remains. A view of finite existence from the standpoint of the Absolute is, indeed, an intelligible conception, but it is grossly misleading to speak of it as a 'philosophy of history'.

A third conception of the 'philosophy of history' is to be found in the notion of the discovery and elucidation of the plan or plot of history. And this may be taken in two quite distinct senses. It may mean either the skeleton of history, the general plan from which the details have been omitted; or, history seen as one, all-inclusive whole in which each detail has its place. It may mean either a selective simplification of history based upon some assumed notion of general significance[2]; or what is called 'universal history'. If, however, the discovery of the plot or plan of history be taken in the first sense, the result may possibly be philosophy, but has certainly nothing to do with history; it is, in fact, the denial of all that we have seen history to be. To omit the details involves the destruction of history. And if it be taken in the second sense, it is quite indistinguishable from history itself: for, merely to extend the region of history cannot be supposed to convert an abstract mode of experience into the concrete whole of experience. And consequently it suffers from the defects which we have seen belong to the world of history itself.

I conclude, then, that the attempt to find the world of unqualified reality in the world of historical events or in the

[1] Lotze, *Mikrokosmus*, VII, Kap. ii.
[2] The writings of Hegel and Schlegel on the philosophy of history appear to fall into this class.

'philosophy of history', has failed. And no argument the cogency of which can be recognized has yet been proposed to persuade me to alter this opinion. Any attempt of historical experience, or any form of experience derived from history, to pass itself off as the concrete totality of experience can result only in the grossest error. And similarly, any attempt on the part of experience itself, philosophical experience, to enter the world of historical experience, except in the form of historical experience, must constitute an *ignoratio elenchi*, and be productive only of confusion. The world of history is a world of abstractions, historical experience is abstract experience; it is a homogeneous, self-contained mode of experience which falls short of self-completeness. And those who have made it their business to press experience to its conclusion can choose only between avoiding or superseding it.

§ 4

From this review of the categories of historical thought and the character of the world of historical experience, I will pass now to consider briefly the relation of this world, as a world, to other worlds of experience. In so far as these other worlds are what I have called abstract, they are (of course) in no sense whatever related to the world of history, and there can be no passage from one to the other in argument without *ignoratio elenchi*; that is a principle I have already discussed. Whenever they attempt an incursion into the world of history, the result can be only the destruction of history; and whenever history invades any other world of experience, the result is always the general disintegration of experience. Nevertheless, it is important to see *what* worlds of experience are thus excluded from history and why in detail they are excluded. And in what I have to say on this topic I shall confine my attention to two worlds of experience which have, on occasion, been confused with that of history, but which, since they are different modifications of experience from that of history, must be taken to fall outside the world of historical experience—I mean the worlds of practice and of science.

(*a*) I have already considered in some detail the result of an incursion of history into the world of practical experience and of practical experience into the world of history; and I have contended that from neither can anything but error arise. The notion, however, is common that the aim in historical thought is the elucidation of the world of practical experience. "The understanding of the present is always the final goal of history. History is just the whole life experience of our race, in so far as we are able to remember it well and apply it closely to our present existence."[1] The goal in history is, in short, the elucidation of our world of practical ideas, the organization of our present practical life. Two connected notions appear to be involved in this view of the character of history, and both of them I take to be false. First, it is implied that "our present existence" can be isolated in such a way as to leave part of our experience outside it. It is a world of experience which can be elucidated by 'applying' to it some other experience which lies behind it. And secondly, it is implied that history is an extension of our world of present knowledge. The appeal to history as a guide to conduct, as a school of statecraft, as a basis for present practical life is conceived to be an appeal to a wider world of experience than what belongs to the present.[2] This, for example, is how the matter seems to have appeared to Burke. But history, we have seen, can in no sense be considered to open to us a world of 'past experience' lying outside our world of present experience. And whenever history is joined to practical experience an appeal is made, not to an extension of our present, practical experience, but to experience as a whole disguised and misrepresented *sub specie praeteritorum*, to a mode of experience wholly without relevance to practical life. And whenever history finds itself joined with

[1] Troeltsch, *Die Bedeutung des Protestantismus*, p. 6.
[2] "Die Geschichte ist das γνῶθι σεαυτόν der Menschheit, ihr Gewissen", Droysen.

practical experience, the result can be only the destruction of both. No guidance for practical life can be expected to follow from the organization of the totality of experience *sub specie praeteritorum*. The world of history has no data to offer of which practical experience can make use; and to conceive it as offering such data is to misconceive its character.

This does not mean that in matters of practice any form of appeal to any past is always irrelevant. We have seen already that such an appeal is both possible and intelligible as an incentive to belief or action; though it never amounts to more than a *façon de parler*. What it means is that this practical appeal to a practical past is not even an abuse (much less a 'use') of history, it is merely not history at all. Unless history is released from this proposed alliance with the world of practical experience it must remain a hybrid and sterile mode of experience. History is not a bar of judgment; it passes no verdict; *die Weltgeschichte* is not *das Weltgericht*. Neither the truth nor the character of history depend, in any way, upon its having some lesson to teach us. And if ever we persuade ourselves that the past has taught us something, we may be certain that it is not the historical past which has been our teacher. The worlds of history and of practice are different arrests in experience, different modifications of experience, and, taken as worlds and by themselves, there can be no relation or commerce between them.

(*b*) The relation between the world of history and that of science calls for a more detailed consideration; and in what I have to say now I shall be compelled to anticipate some of the conclusions of the next chapter, for the view which I wish to present of the relationship depends, naturally, as much upon the character of scientific experience as upon the character of historical experience.

There have been historians who believed that this so-called relation between history and science is the very condition of historical truth. History, they thought, is itself a science. Sometimes it is not clear what exactly they intended to convey by this assertion; at other times it is only too clear that they did not intend to convey the meaning to which, I think, we must hold the words. But briefly, the view I wish to suggest is that history and science are different modifications of experience and that whenever they are brought together, associated or combined only irrelevance, a hybrid and non-sensical world of ideas is produced. I do not say that the phrase 'the science of history' has no intelligible meaning; I say that "a science of history *in the true sense of the term* is an absurd notion".[1] The assimilation of history to science is, on account of the different characters of these worlds of ideas, impossible.

The relation between history and science has appeared to some writers to be a matter merely of words. Freeman, for example, takes this view. History is certainly knowledge; 'science' is merely Latin for the Teutonic 'knowledge'; therefore history is a science.[2] But since on this view all knowledge whatever is also science, it cannot be considered to have greatly extended our ideas on the subject. Few will deny that history is knowledge; but the question for us is, Does history belong to that subspecies of knowledge called 'science'? Again, 'scientific history' sometimes means little more than 'accurate history', history unclouded by prejudice, or history based upon a critical examination of the original sources. But this also is in the nature of a metaphor and does not help us to determine the relations of history and science. No attempt is made to advance from mere designation to a definition of the terms in question. And the whole of that grotesque (and now happily obsolete) con-troversy as to whether history is an art or a science must be considered, from our point of view, quite beside the mark. What, however, appears to lie at the root of any serious assertion that history and science belong together is the notion that, for some reason, history must be assimilated to science before it can be considered to be a valid form of knowledge: history must be science in order to be valid. And

---

[1] Jevons, *Principles of Science*, p. 761.
[2] Freeman, *Methods of Historical Study*, pp. 117, 152.

further, what I take to be the ground of this notion is the view that history, if it is to be a form of knowledge, cannot avoid generalization, and that the only valid form of generalization is that which belongs to science. The first of these ideas would seem to contain some hint of truth. Without some kind of generalization history would be a "tissue of mere conjunctions", would fall altogether outside experience. The second, however, is certainly false. And since I cannot here anticipate the whole argument of my next chapter, I will content myself (so far as scientific generalization is concerned) with the assertion that if the character of science and scientific generalization be what I there suggest it is, then it is different from anything which can be found in history. But with regard to the character of historical generalization a few observations may be made.

First, it will be observed that historical individuals are themselves the product of generalization, though not (of course) of scientific generalization: a scientific generalization can result only in a scientific individual. The fall of the Bastille, the Roman Empire and Napoleon are all generalizations, and they are constructed (we have seen) by means of the principle of continuity. And since the principle of continuity implies that there is in history nothing apart from 'details', this historical generality cannot be secured by suppressing what, from another and non-historical point of view, might be regarded as mere details, accidents. But, it will also be observed that these historical generalizations are limited. Press them too far, and we shall find that we have pressed them outside the world of history; abandon (in the interests of universal generalization) the limits of historical individuality, and we shall have abandoned history itself. Historical facts, then, are limited generalizations constructed by means of the more or less arbitrary principle of historical continuity. But the important point is yet to come. Historical individuals, themselves the product of generalization, do not admit of further generalization. There is no process of generalization by means of which the events, things and persons of history can be reduced to anything other than historical events, things and persons without at the same time being removed from the world of historical ideas. For, once an historical individual is established it is, for history, absolute. It is not, of course, absolute in the sense of being ultimately complete and self-sufficient; but, with all its limitations, it remains the irreducible unit of history. And what appear to be universal generalizations in history are, in fact, merely collective or enumerative judgments. *All the Reformation Parliaments were packed*, is an historical judgment, but it is in no sense a generalization.[1]  In history there are no 'general laws' by means of which historical individuals can be reduced to instances of a principle, and least of all are there general laws of the character we find in the world of science.

But the real difficulties involved in the notion of a science of history appear when a world of ideas is considered which, in the opinion of some, unites historical and scientific thought; I mean the world of ideas pursued and maintained in Anthropology.

There are not many points upon which anthropologists are unanimous, but there seems to be tolerable agreement upon the propositions that anthropology is an historical study, that it is a science, and that "it is a science in whatever way history is a science". And we may be excused for supposing that some explanation beyond these assertions is required before an intelligible world of ideas is even in sight.

Anthropology is an historical study—this is certainly intelligible. The men it is concerned with are historical persons, the societies it studies are historical facts, the events it records are historical events; in short, the abstractions it works with are the abstractions of history. The subject of anthropology is the evolution of historically determined individuals. "Anthropology is the whole history of man as fired and pervaded by the idea of evolution. Man in evolution—that is the subject at its full reach. Anthropology studies man as

[1] Bradley, *Logic*, I, 46, 82.

he occurs at all known times. It studies him as he occurs in all known parts of the world. It studies him body and soul together—as a bodily organism, subject to the conditions operating in time and space, which bodily organism is in intimate relation with a soul-life, also subject to those same conditions. Having an eye to such conditions from first to last, it seeks to plot out the general series of changes, bodily and mental together, undergone by man in the course of history."[1] Anthropology, in short, is the application of an historical idea of evolution to the history of man.[2] And, whatever difficulties we may find in this view, even if it must be admitted that this prepossession with the idea of evolution or development and with a merely "general" series of changes may lead to bad history, it is impossible to suppose that the mode of experience involved is other than historical, and that the world of ideas is other than the world of historical ideas.

The second proposition asserts that anthropology is a science. And this, if it means anything, means that anthropology is not concerned with historical events, that its data are not perceptual objects, and that its conceptions and abstractions are not those of history. It appears, then, that whatever else the character of anthropology is, it cannot be both history and science; and to advertise it as such is to advertise an absurdity. And it appears, further, that although it has frequently claimed the character of a science, no serious attempt has been made to create a genuine science of anthropology. No anthropologist, in fact, is to be found willing to surrender the abstract world of history for the abstract

[1] Marett, *Anthropology*, pp. 7–8.
[2] The scientific or biological conception of evolution must, of course, be distinguished from the historical (or pseudo-historical) conception. To speak of the Darwinian theory as an invasion of science by the historical method, the introduction of an 'historical biology', is certainly to misconceive its character. Evolution for biology is not an historical change. And the tendency of some biologists to express their views in pseudo-historical language is, to say the least, misleading and belongs to an ill-thought out conception of scientific experience.

world of science, to adopt (that is) a purely quantitative conception of man and of society, of civilization, moral development and religion, and to be content with measurements in place of historical events, statistical inference in place of historical fact, statistical generalization in place of historical enumeration.[1] And the reason for this is, perhaps, that the conclusions of such a science would be relatively unimportant. If anthropology is to be a science, it must begin with a world conceived *sub specie quantitatis*. And it is difficult to imagine the process of abstraction which would produce a scientific conception of 'society', or of 'man', sufficiently different from that of biology, psychology or economics, to distinguish this science of anthropology. Beyond this lack of distinctive scientific conceptions, the relative unimportance of the conclusions of a science of anthropology would be due to a lack of data. A science which aimed at establishing general laws with regard to 'races', 'nations' or communities distinguished upon the basis of creed or culture would have comparatively few measurements and observations at its command. This, of course, would not make such a science impossible. What makes a science impossible is never merely the quantitative limitation of its data. All scientific generalization is statistical generalization and refers directly only to a series of observations as such; and wherever there is a series of observations of the right character there is material for scientific generalization. But a scantiness of data will certainly render scientific generalizations insignificant. And such is the inevitable condition of a science of anthropology.

The assertion that anthropology is a science may, however, be made in a modified form. It may mean merely that what is sought in anthropology is, not strictly scientific laws, but

[1] The attempt to correlate 'societies' with their standard of civilization on a purely numerical basis, whatever its validity, might appear to be an exception to this. But, while societies are taken to be pure measurements, the standard of civilization is not similarly conceived, and the argument consequently fails to be genuinely scientific. Cp. Sutherland, *Origin and Growth of the Moral Instinct*, ch. xi.

general laws of some kind. "The aim of this science," says Frazer, "as of every other science, is to discover general laws to which the particular facts may be supposed to conform."[1] This, in so far as it refers to "every other science" is, of course, if not untrue, at least misleading. It is never supposed that the "particular facts" of science "conform" to general laws; it is always and only the series of observations as a series which in science is taken to conform to law. And further, whatever we may suppose the character of "the general laws which have regulated human history"[2] to be, we cannot suppose them to be scientific laws; for scientific laws can refer only to scientific observations which are of a wholly different character from those in history. They are neither past, nor percepts, nor observed under the category of historical continuity.

And even when they attempt generalization, many writers on anthropology do not, in fact, venture beyond a merely historical treatment of this subject. Such 'generalizations' as: "Among certain races and at certain times superstition has strengthened the respect for government, especially monarchical government, and has thereby contributed to the establishment and maintenance of civil order",[3] or, "No society has ever passed into full civilization without passing through patriarchy. No matriarchy has ever given rise directly to a full civilization",[4] are merely enumerative judgments; they are certainly not scientific (because they are not statistical), and they are certainly not generalizations because they rely upon the supposition that the observations on which they are based are exhaustive. They are, however, valid, and for what they are worth, historical.

But when a more extended form of generalization is attempted, it becomes (to say the least) doubtful, without becoming scientific. When, for example, a "pre-exogamic stage of human society" is spoken of, or when it is said that primitive societies recognize no purely self-regarding acts

---

[1] Frazer, *The Scope of Social Anthropology*.
[2] *Ibid.*          [3] Frazer, *Psyche's Task*, p. 4.
[4] G. Heard, *The Social Substance of Religion*, p. 39.

because they recognize no independent individuals, an attempt has been made to pass beyond judgment about the mere history of particular societies, to pass beyond enumerative judgment about all observed societies, to judgment about human society in general. Again, a similar attempt is made in such a statement as this: In England scrofula was believed to be curable by the king's touch, "and on the analogy of the Polynesian superstitions which I have cited, we may perhaps conjecture that the skin disease of scrofula was originally supposed to be caused as well as cured by the king's touch".[1] And it becomes necessary to enquire into the character of these generalizations. We should notice first that, though these judgments purport to be real generalizations, to go beyond what has actually been observed, they take, nevertheless, the form of historical judgments; they are in terms of historical concepts and they refer directly to historically determined events or occurrences, and not to a series of quantitatively conceived observations as such. And for this reason, if for no other, they are not scientific. But, we are told, the generality of anthropological judgments (whether or not it is scientific) is based upon the Comparative Method, which is described as "borrowing the links in one chain of evidence to supply the gaps in another".[2] And the method, in turn, "rests upon the well-ascertained similarity of working of the human mind in all races of men",[3] rests upon "correspondence among mankind",[4] the fact that "one set of savages is like another". And this view of the character of anthropological generalization is important because it is the only coherent suggestion yet made for a method of generalizing historical observations. We should not, however, allow ourselves to assume the validity of this form of generalization before we have considered the ground upon which it rests and the presuppositions which it involves.

First, it is clear enough that the Comparative Method is

[1] Frazer, *Psyche's Task*, p. 17.
[2] Frazer, *The Scope of Social Anthropology.*     [3] *Ibid.*
[4] Tylor, *Primitive Culture*, I, 7.

sterile unless it is dealing with instances which are demonstrably separate. If one event or custom has influenced another, either directly or indirectly through the mere knowledge of the fact that it has happened, they are no longer separate instances, and to compare them can result in no valid generalization whatever. Unless, for example, it is demonstrated that the change from mother-right to father-right in one community was uninfluenced by a corresponding change in another community, or by the knowledge of a corresponding change, we cannot begin to collect data to verify the hypothesis that changes in lineage are always from mother-right to father-right and never *vice versa*. And not only is this condition difficult to satisfy, but also, were it satisfied, anthropology would at once become something other than history (for where comparison begins, as a method of generalization, history ends), without becoming scientific.

But secondly, assuming this condition to be satisfied, the position of the Comparative Method is still precarious; it rests, indeed, upon a *petitio principii*. If the world of anthropology does not possess the characteristics of atomism and limited variety which this method assumes it to possess, then the method ceases to be of value. And the assumption that it does possess these characteristics involves the assumption that the world of anthropology is a world of scientific concepts—which it is not, because it is not a world of quantitatively determined observations. Science secures for itself a world of limited variety, a world of repetitions and recurrences, by assuming a world of pure measurements. But this assumption, we have seen, is impossible for anthropology, and with it goes the validity of the Comparative Method.

Anthropology, then, has in the main none but historical observations at its command, and these observations depend upon the rejection of the one condition upon which the Comparative Method depends, the rejection of a world of limited variety, a world of distinguishable cause and effect. If generalization in anthropology depends upon the Comparative Method, then anthropology is a scientific study and not an historical study; but it cannot be scientific for the reasons I have already given. It must, then, be concluded that the generality of the 'laws' of anthropology, in so far as they pass beyond genuine historical generalizations and in so far as they are based upon the Comparative Method, is mere conjecture and without logical validity. Anthropology certainly provides no scientific generalizations, and its attempt to produce non-scientific laws has been without legitimate issue. And we must not allow ourselves to be misled by the suggestion that, because this historico-scientific form of thought has produced results, it is therefore absurd to question its validity. Any mode of thought, however hybrid or diseased, can produce results, but they are not necessarily legitimate. The Comparative Method is not a method which unites science and history; it dismisses history and never achieves the full condition of science. And since the scientific character of anthropology is an illusion, its conceptions and presuppositions being those of history, we must conclude that it is history or it is nothing. Any attempt to find in it, or to make of it, an historico-scientific world of ideas must always fail.

What reforms a full realization of the historical character of anthropology (and the consequent rejection of the view that it is a science) would produce in this study need not now be considered. But it may be remarked that one effect would be a shifting of emphasis from similarities to differences. The anthropologist, intent upon developing the pseudo-scientific character of his subject, has in the past concentrated upon the observation of similarities; but history is regulated by the pursuit of differences. Whenever the historian is presented with an apparent identity, not merely are his suspicions aroused, but he knows that he is passing beyond his own presuppositions; for it is posited from the beginning that the world of history is a world from which identity has been excluded. The question whether or not history repeats itself is not one to be decided by examining the 'course of events' itself, it is answered in the negative by the postulates which determine the only course of events known in history. History never repeats itself because to do so would involve a contradiction of its own character. And the institution of comparisons and the elaboration of analogies are activities which the historian must avoid if he is to remain an historian.

I have embarked upon this discussion of the character of anthropology because it appeared the most comprehensive way of dealing with the question of the relation of historical and scientific experience. And I conclude from it that in fact science and scientific conceptions have never contributed to the elucidation of the world of historical ideas. Wherever science and history have been associated, nothing but recognizable error and confusion has followed, and in logic such a contribution is impossible. The conjunction of science and history can produce nothing but a monster, for these are abstract and separate worlds of ideas, different and exclusive modifications of experience, which can be joined only at the cost of an *ignoratio elenchi*.

# IV

## SCIENTIFIC EXPERIENCE

### § 1

The purpose of this chapter is to consider the nature of scientific experience from the standpoint of the totality of experience. The world of science, I take it, is a world of experience, and is consequently the world of reality. In all experience, we have seen, there is an assertion of reality. And we have seen also that no experience is a mere part or department of the real world; reality has no parts in this sense, and everything asserted of reality is asserted of it as a whole. Further, science, because it is experience, is a world of ideas, and contains a specific and homogeneous assertion of reality. And my business is to discover the explicit character of this world of ideas, the explicit content of the assertion of reality contained in scientific experience, for the character of science from the standpoint of the totality of experience lies in the character of this world of ideas as a whole and in the adequacy of its assertion of reality.

'Natural history', a kind of semi-detached observation of uniformities in the world of perception, may be taken to be the point at which scientific thought springs from the main stem of experience; and the desire which prompts it is for an escape from the private, incommunicable world of personal experience as such, into a world of common and communicable experience, a world of experience upon which universal agreement is possible. The entire history of science may be seen as a pathetic attempt to find, in the face of incredible difficulties, a world of definite and demonstrable experience, one free from merely personal associations and independent of the idiosyncrasies of particular observers, an absolutely impersonal and stable world. The sole *explicit* criterion of scientific ideas is their absolute communicability.

Now, that natural history itself will not itself provide us with a world of experience of this kind is clear enough.[1] The mere attribution of a common name to what is given in perception, even when perception is freed so far as possible from merely personal associations, will give only a small degree of communicability, of stability to our experience. Every science has started upon its career as a kind of natural history, but every science has discovered the necessity of passing beyond the world of experience which a natural history gives if it is to satisfy its explicit purpose. For the end in scientific experience is not merely a world of experience of a high degree of communicability, but a world of absolutely stable, impersonal, communicable experience. Science, it may be said, is the assertion of reality as a world of absolutely communicable experience. And only when natural history has been superseded can this assertion be achieved fully. For the definitions and observations of a natural history, though they may achieve a high degree of impersonality, are always in terms of common names. It gives us a world of only roughly determined entities. Its language remains, for the most part, the language of the senses, and its world is confined to the world of perception.

In scientific experience, however, in pursuit of this world of absolutely communicable experience, it is found necessary to leave behind the world of perception; for so long as we are bound to this world what we are seeking must elude us. Science may be said to begin only when the world of perceptible things has been left on one side, only when observation in terms of personal perception and sensation has been superseded. For, although the attempt to discover a world of absolutely stable experience must be considered to have begun long before this decision is taken to abandon the world of perception, it is only in virtue of this decision that scientific

[1] 'Natural history' implies a modification of history which ends in its destruction.

experience is able to achieve its end. This, so to say, is the Pisgah of scientific thought. Henceforward science is disconnected from the various extraneous interests which hindered the achievement of its specific purpose, and becomes a world of absolutely stable and communicable experience, the assertion of reality as communicable. And what, more than anything else, hinders the full development of scientific thought is the practical interest, for this interest serves only to discourage science from passing into the world of abstractions in which alone it can fully satisfy itself. Practice is not concerned with absolute communicability, but with only a certain degree of communicability. But when it disengages itself from the world of perception, science disengages itself also from this extraneous practical interest.

The world of scientific experience is, then, created by a transformation of our familiar world; in science there is no attempt to elucidate the character of this world of perception in which we live, what is attempted is the elucidation of a world of absolutely stable experience. And it is one of the signs of the present growth of the scientific mind that it has become reconciled to the fact that, though it may be said (in a sense) to begin from our world of ordinary, practical experience, science can borrow and use no component of that world which it has not learnt how to transform. Scientific knowledge is not 'organized common sense'; it is a world of knowledge which begins to exist only when common sense and all its postulates have been forgotten or rejected. Experience becomes scientific experience when it is a world of absolutely communicable experience. Scientific experience is based upon a rejection of merely human testimony; its masterconception is *stability*.

And there is no doubt about the general character of this world which science, in pursuit of its goal, enters when it has left the nursery of natural history. It is a world conceived under the category of quantity. For to abandon a world conceived in terms of common names, and a world of observations executed in terms of the senses, for a world conceived in terms of quantity, and a world of observations executed in terms of precise measurement, is to renounce a world which could never satisfy the explicit purpose in science for one which is capable of satisfying that purpose. Scientific experience, because it is a world of absolutely communicable experience, because it involves the assertion of reality as absolutely communicable, is a world of purely quantitative experience, involves the assertion of reality under the category of quantity.

Now, there are, of course, other views of the character of scientific experience than this, and some of them I shall be obliged to consider in detail later on. There are the views, for example, that scientific thought is the attempt to discover and elucidate an 'objective' world, a 'material' world, an 'external' world, or the world of experience which is 'common to all normal people'. But these views, and others like them, I regard as misleading and ambiguous. From one standpoint they may be seen as fumbling attempts to establish scientific experience as a world of absolutely communicable experience, and from this standpoint they are true so far as they go. But, from another standpoint, each of them is a failure to grasp the fact that it is stability alone which will satisfy scientific thought. Each of them introduces some notion extraneous to that of stability. And from this standpoint they are false. Stability or communicability is not merely the most important characteristic of scientific beliefs, it is the sole characteristic in virtue of which they are scientific. And until these ambiguous and extraneous notions of a 'material', and of an 'external' world are swept aside, our view of the character of scientific experience will be merely superficial.

§ 2

In order to achieve my purpose—a view of scientific experience from the standpoint of the totality of experience—there are two main topics which I must consider. First, the general character of scientific experience, and secondly the logical structure of the world of scientific ideas: first, scientific thought from the standpoint of what it achieves, and secondly, scientific thought from the standpoint of the validity of its achievement. And I ought to remark at once that neither of these studies is itself a part of science. The discussion I wish to engage in is not a scientific discussion; and such conclusions as I may reach should, in no sense or degree whatever, be considered to rest upon the conclusions of scientific thought, or to be doubtful because they are without this foundation. This fact alone, upon which I will not enlarge at present, that scientific experience is not, so to say, self-conscious experience (experience which can take account of its own character), is enough to indicate that what we have to consider here is a limited and consequently defective mode of experience. But I do not press the point; it is a symptom of, rather than a reason for the failure in scientific knowledge. And the particular defects in scientific experience will reveal themselves more conclusively from a detailed examination of the character of the world of science than by means of any such general consideration.

But, in this connexion, there is a danger of which, perhaps, warning should be given: I mean the danger of accepting too readily what scientific writers tell us about the character of scientific experience. In our careless way, we are apt to give special attention to what scientists say in this matter, because they appear to speak with something like authority. And when what they say seems to us difficult or absurd, we put it down to our own lack of scientific knowledge. But this claim of the scientist (which, to say the truth, is more often admitted than preferred) to speak with some special authority about the character of scientific experience is, in fact, baseless. The question of the character of scientific experience is not itself a scientific question.

It seems that there was a time when the scientist supposed that he put nothing (mentally) into the world. The real world was there, awaiting discovery; and the only valid means of apprehending it was the scientific method, because this alone could lead to 'objective' knowledge, knowledge independent

of personal predilections and subjective fancies. But fortunately we are no longer required to take seriously the
absurdities of nineteenth-century speculation about scientific
knowledge. But a new, and even more strange, apology for
scientific experience has now appeared to take their place.
What is called (oddly enough) the 'subjective element' in
scientific knowledge is admitted, and the world is again
partitioned between the 'objective things' that are real, and
the 'subjective ideas' that correspond more or less with them.
A part of scientific knowledge is spoken of as "the contribution of the mind", and the rest is just the universe as God
made it and as it really is. In short, scientists have come to
regard science as a form of thought, as the construction of
a world of ideas, and they conclude that it is consequently
debarred from a true knowledge of the world of reality.
Naturalism has given place to a mild and unintelligent
scepticism. I have, however, indicated already the line of
argument which forces me to place this explanation of
scientific experience among the regrettable curiosities of philosophy; and we shall see later that what debars science from
full knowledge of the real world is its character of a defective
and abstract mode of thought, and not the mere fact that it
is a form of thought. This distinction between the 'subjective
element' and the 'objective element' in scientific experience
can be compared only with the worn-out fantasy of the
primary and secondary qualities of matter. Indeed, it is
almost the prerogative of the scientist to attach himself to
worn-out philosophical ideas; and he does this because his
preoccupation with other things leads him to adopt those
philosophical ideas which appear plausible without making
any attempt to think them out for himself. He takes over (for
example) what he can understand of Kant, not because his
thought has followed Kant's mind to Kant's conclusions, but
because the general point of view to be found in Kant's
philosophy is congenial to his preconceptions. His philosophy
is essentially uncritical; that is, it is not a philosophy but a
jargon. Naturalism was the result of an abortive attempt of

scientific experience to achieve self-consciousness, to conquer both itself and its world, based upon the ignorant prejudice that "there is no way to gain a knowledge of the universe except through the gateway of the scientific method". And the dualism which this new, psychological apology for science involves is merely the importation of another of the postulates of scientific experience into a consideration of the character of science itself. And, if we are on our guard against what is misleading in the opinions of the scientist about the character of science, we shall be better placed to take advantage of what he has to tell us of his methods and interests.

In considering the character of scientific experience I will begin by accepting a distinction which I shall not, in the end, be able to maintain. It is a distinction between the method and the matter of science. The view I find commonly expressed is that the method of science is dictated by its matter, and that these are so far distinguishable as to make it possible to consider them separately. The view I shall ultimately suggest is that they are two aspects of a single whole, that the method is no more dictated by the matter than the matter by the method, and that whenever we are considering the one we are considering the other also. However, if by assuming this distinction I can show how far and for what reason it is not absolute but merely relative and (as I believe) misleading, I shall have gone far towards elucidating what I take to be the true character of scientific experience. In science, as in every other form of experience, what is experienced and the manner in which it is experienced are inseparable aspects of a single whole. I will consider first the method of science.

The world of scientific experience, from this point of view, is a world of knowledge reached by a certain method, and the unity of scientific knowledge is the product of a strict adherence to this method. A study is scientific if it is conducted in a certain way and if its results are stated in a certain manner. Now, the method of science is designed (or, from another point of view, has developed) in order to achieve the end in scientific experience—a world of common and communicable ideas. And, in pursuit of this end, what I take to be the prime character of the scientific method, which is at once a method of observation and of explanation, is its quantitative character. Science is the attempt to conceive of the world under the category of quantity. From the standpoint of observation, science is never satisfied with mere observation. Scientific observation is designed expressly to replace observations in terms of personal feelings by observations of an absolute stability, by quantitative measurements. All scientific observation whatever is measurement of one kind or another. The scientific method is a method of measurement; and in scientific observation measurement is anterior even to enumeration. When we say that scientific observation is 'exact', we mean no more than that it is conceived in terms of quantitative measurement. Similarly, from the standpoint of explanation, the scientific method is dominated by quantitative categories. Scientific explanation is always in terms of quantitative concepts. The scientific method offers us an escape from the world of merely personal explanations and descriptions in terms of the unstable categories of personal experience as such, by substituting for these an explanation in terms of categories which are absolutely stable, common and communicable, in terms of purely quantitative concepts. Sensations, feelings, perceptions are set on one side as categories of explanation by this method which recognizes only what is impersonal and quantitative. And the history of science, from one point of view, may be said to be the development of the possibilities inherent in quantitative conception and measurement. Each new departure has been a fresh attempt to rid the world of scientific knowledge of whatever is incapable of quantitative statement and to discover methods of measurement less and less at the mercy of a particular observer and his situation. The development, for example, of atomic and molecular conceptions into the modern theory of structural formulae is an advance of this kind.

The scientific method is, then, a quantitative method, and it is this because science is the pursuit of a world of stable, communicable and impersonal experiences. And this view may be expressed by saying, first, that what has come to be called 'physics' is in the van of scientific development, it is scientific experience least contaminated by what is extraneous to science; and secondly, that the explanation of the world offered by the scientific method is a mechanical explanation.[1]

On the first of these propositions it is not necessary to say much. That physics is the prototype of science and that it shows the scientific method in its purest form have been common-places among scientists ever since they began to be conscious of the meaning of science. At one time this was spoken of as the tendency of all scientific knowledge towards the form of mechanics—die Zurückführung aller Natur-erscheinungen auf die Mechanik. But it is now seen to involve a more intimate resemblance than this, to involve, indeed, a relationship that goes beyond merely formal resemblance. Physics has acquired a character very different from that of the old mechanics; and not only is it taken to represent the furthest achievements of the scientific method, but the actual conceptions of physics have (often under other names and in modified forms) besieged and invaded the less developed sciences, deposing the conceptions which formerly ruled them. All sciences not merely resemble physics in so far as they are genuinely scientific, but tend actually to become transformed into, or reduced to physics, because this alone provides the opportunity of purely quantitative explanation of which every science seeks to avail itself. The process has not, of course, been simple and direct. Biology, for example, has been reformed and made more scientific under the influence of chemistry. But physics remains the prototype and the inspiration of all scientific knowledge. Nor are

[1] I have not distinguished between 'explanation' and 'description' because I believe them to be, in the end, indistinguishable. And when we come to consider the matter of science, these words will appear equally misleading.

the reasons at all obscure why there remain sciences which fall short of the condition of physics. Not only is it clearly a task requiring the utmost patience and skill to achieve this reduction of what is (in some degree) arbitrarily designated to what is designated quantitatively; but also, in the case of many sciences, an irrelevant, non-scientific interest has frequently entered in to hinder the process. The development of biology and scientific psychology has been inhibited by a moral interest, and a radical confusion between the scientific and the historical mode of thinking still stands in the path of sociology. It would, of course, be a mistake to suppose that the golden age of science can be hurried in by dismissing at once all the non-quantitative conceptions and relations which many sciences still harbour. But it is equally mistaken to suppose that the growth of biology, psychology and sociology in this direction would encounter any difficulties peculiar to themselves. What is peculiar in these sciences is nothing inherent in their character, but merely the prejudices by which they have suffered themselves to be hindered. Physics, then, by which I mean not the results and conceptions of physics at the present time, but the principle of the method by which these have been obtained and the world of results finally implied in this method, is the logical end of scientific experience. What is important for us, however, is not to determine the relations of physics and biology, but to see that, in so far as they are sciences, they have a common character, and to see what that character is. Science and physics are identical, in the sense I have suggested, merely because a science which fell short of physics, in this respect, would fall short of the end in science—the construction of an essentially stable and communicable world of ideas.

The phrase 'mechanical explanation' has, of course, more senses than one, and I must make clear what I take to be the limit of its meaning in this connexion. It must be said at once that scientific explanation can be conceived in terms of mechanism only in so far as it is possible for a world of quantitative concepts to be a mechanical world. The world of scientific experience is primarily a world of quantitative concepts, and it is a mechanism only in so far as the relations of quantitative concepts can be spoken of as mechanical relations. A mechanical explanation in this connexion means, then, in the first place, the simplest or most economical explanation. Concepts which are unnecessarily complete or unnecessarily complex are rejected for those which are simple and sufficient. "Science in its most ultimate formulation seeks objects with the most permanent definite simplicity of character and expresses its laws in terms of them."[1] Secondly, a mechanical explanation is a general explanation; it is an explanation which refers not merely to this or that observation, but to a whole class of observations. The aim of scientific thought is to explain not *this* observation, but any instance of this observation; and an explanation which takes account of the mere thisness of an observation is useless in science. Further, a mechanical explanation is a quantitative explanation, an explanation in terms of quantitative concepts. All change and modification in the world of science is explained by being represented as a quantitative difference or variation within that world. Consequently, also, such an explanation makes no appeal to what is outside that world; change and variation, or the situation itself are explained by reference to what is closest and most immediate, not to what is distant and universal. And finally, such an explanation will be, in the end, always in terms of motion and concepts related to, or derived from that of motion.

I do not conceive it my business to prove that no science has ever offered an explanation of its world other than this kind of explanation; or to prove that any science has ever actually achieved a perfect explanation of this sort. Frequently this kind of explanation has been disowned by professors of one or other of the sciences. Descartes was willing to 'mechanize' all sciences save psychology, and modern scientists are not lacking who wish to make an exception in favour of

---

[1] Whitehead, *Concept of Nature*, p. 172.

biology and physiology.[1]  Such demands as vitalism in biology and philosophism in psychology, however, appear to me anachronistic, if not absurd, and (if persisted in) will succeed only in reducing the sciences on behalf of which they are made to the sterile condition of all such hybrid forms of

[1] I know of no argument in favour of this demand which does not involve a wholly erroneous view of the character of nature and the method of science. The argument, to which all others may be reduced, seems to be that in science we must adapt our method of study to the character of the objects we are considering. And this, as I hope to show, is a vicious fallacy. All these difficulties arise from the ruinous supposition that the end of scientific thinking is to discover something which is called "the truth about the external world".

I may remark also, in this connexion, that the introduction of the notions of 'indeterminism' and 'determinism' into a discussion of the character of nature has never failed to mislead. It appears that some scientists have believed that nature was 'determined' in the sense that its future was predestined. But since the mere notion of 'nature' having a future (or a past) belongs, not to science, but to pseudo-science, we may dismiss this view without further argument. Others have asserted that nature is 'indetermined', in the sense that it contained some principle of freedom; but what this can mean it is difficult to conjecture.

Another objection to the view of the world of science as a mechanism which must, in these days, be met is this. "The old mechanical view of the universe", we are told, "is giving place to the conception of it as a poem in the course of creation." But when we enquire for the reasons of this break-down of mechanical explanation we are met with two suggestions. First, it is said that mechanism must go because science has 'discovered' something better. But what? And if mechanism means, as I have taken it to mean, a world constructed so as to reach the maximum of stability and communicability, how can science 'discover' or attend to what is incapable of a mechanical explanation? The end of science is an absolutely communicable world, and so long as it pursues this end, only a mechanical view of the universe can succeed in satisfying it. And secondly, it is said that mechanism must go because some ingenious scientists have conceived a doubt concerning the completeness of the scientific explanation of the universe. But this, so far from implying a condemnation of mechanical explanation in science, assumes and asserts such an explanation. A complete explanation of the universe would be (as I hope to show), by reason of its completeness, non-scientific.

knowledge. Instead of making these sciences less abstract, compliance with these demands will succeed only in making them less scientific.

Thus, a mechanical explanation is the logical satisfaction of scientific knowledge, and consequently the purpose of the scientific method. Science, intent upon the discovery of a world which shall be, before all else, a common, communicable, impersonal world, fixes its attention upon a world of quantitative concepts. And such a world is, on account of the character of its components, susceptible only of a mechanical explanation.

But we must come closer to the character of the scientific method. In general, we have seen, it is a quantitative method; but the implications of this view must remain obscure until it is seen in conjunction with the generalizations in terms of which science explains or describes the world, and with the actual procedure of scientific thought. I am not, however, concerned with the details of the psychological process by which a scientist may reach his conclusions, I am not concerned with the procedure of scientific research, but only with the process of argument which lies behind the establishment of scientific conclusions, in virtue of which such conclusions are said to be proved or valid.[1] And I take it that the final explanation or description which science offers of its world is in terms of generalizations.[2]

Now, anyone in search of an account of the process by which scientific conclusions are reached will be offered a great variety from which to choose. But, without staying to criticise these, I will present at once my view of the matter. And it will be seen that it differs from some other views only in the order in which it conceives the various steps or stages of the process to follow. Scientific experience, as I see it, begins neither with the 'collection of data', nor with measure-

---

[1] Of course, the separation of discovery from proof cannot, in the end, be justified. What is not proved is not discovered.

[2] These generalizations are often spoken of as the 'laws of nature'; but this, I think, introduces more difficulties than it avoids.

ment, neither with experiment nor with observation, but with a world of scientific ideas. That it must begin with a world of ideas is involved in the character of science as a mode of experience. And scientific experience is distinguished from all other experience merely on account of the character of the ideas with which it begins. From the beginning the world of scientific experience lies before the scientist in outline; the limits of his pursuit are laid down. The world within which he is to move is to be a world of common and communicable experience, a world of quantitative concepts. When I say 'from the beginning' I do not, of course, refer to an historical beginning, nor do I mean that the individual scientist is conscious of this world in outline lying before him as he makes his own personal beginning. What I refer to is the *logical* beginning of scientific knowledge. Historically science, no doubt, began with crude, imperfectly apprehended attempts to find a stable world from which all that could be called superstition was banished: it was certainly some time before it became clear that such a world must be a world of quantitative ideas. And as for the individual scientist, so far as his consciousness is concerned he begins with a highly complicated inheritance of scientific knowledge. But this knowledge itself implies the delineated world of science; he inherits his millions, but these imply the monetary system. Scientific experience begins, then, with a world of ideas which, though it may require endless amplification and even transformation, itself lays down the main lines upon which that amplification and transformation must run. The process in scientific experience is the continuous modification of a world of ideas in terms of the main structure of that world.

All the generalizations of science, the whole body of generalized scientific knowledge, is in terms of these structural concepts; these are the categories of scientific thought. But the primary generalizations of science are not only in terms of these concepts, they are actually implied and involved in the concepts themselves. The primary generalizations of science are analytic generalizations, derived from the analysis of the structural concepts of the world of scientific knowledge, and they express the relations between these concepts which are inherent in the concepts themselves. The integration of the world of science is, first, in terms of the relations which can be deduced directly from the structural concepts of that world. The generalization, for example, that gravity is proportional to inertia, the generalizations about the conservation of energy and momentum, the generalization that the extension of a body is proportional to the force acting upon it, belong to this class. Indeed, it may be said that the main concepts of mechanics constitute the structure of the world of scientific thought; and the generalizations deduced directly from them are statements of definite, invariable and quantitative relationships between quantitative concepts. That these generalizations are definite requires no demonstration; what is indefinite is of no value to science in this connexion. And again, since the concepts which these generalizations join are quantitative, not in the sense that they are themselves measurements, but in the sense that they are subject to judgments of 'more' and 'less', of 'intensity' and of 'duration', it follows that the relationships directly deducible from them will be of the same character. But the invariability of these generalizations depends upon the invariability of the concepts they join: they are invariable only so long as the concepts they bring together retain the meaning attributed to them. For these concepts are not, as they stand, separable from the generalizations which relate them; and out of relation to these generalizations they must have either no meaning, or a different meaning. But, since these concepts do not, in any sense, refer to the world of practice, to the world given in sensation, the invariability of the generalizations which express their necessary relations cannot be taken to imply that any event or occurrence will invariably take place. The concepts do not refer to events; and the generalizations are not in respect of events.

These main structural concepts of scientific thought, together with the generalized statements about their necessary relations to one another give us, then, a world, but a world in outline, the sketch of a world; they give us a homogeneous and partially integrated world of ideas, but not a fully coherent world. Consequently, science cannot remain satisfied with this and nothing more. Science is not merely mechanics; and mechanics is not, in the full sense, scientific knowledge. And the advance from this outline of a world to a more fully integrated world is achieved by means of, in the first place, hypothesis. Scientific thought, in possession of its world in outline, sets about the integration of that world, not with experiment or observation, but with hypothesis. And this, it will be seen, is involved in the view that in experience what is attempted is to make a given world more of a world. Hypothesis is the assertion in supposal that the character of a given and known world of ideas would appear, were it more fully known, to be of a certain sort. It involves and is based upon what is known, and it is an attempt to extend this known world in order to make it appear more of a world. Scientific hypothesis is, then, in terms of the structural concepts of the world of scientific experience. It may lead to the modification of these concepts, it may even end in the transformation of this world, but it begins with the assertion of it as fact in order to discover it more fully.

From hypothesis, scientific thought proceeds to observation and experiment. Scientific hypothesis is framed always in terms of the general structure of the world of science with a view to the further determination of that structure; scientific observation and experiment is conducted in terms of scientific hypothesis. The observations and experiments of science are, then, limited and controlled by hypothesis. Science knows nothing of a collection of miscellaneous data, it knows nothing of a haphazard accumulation of materials. But further, scientific observation is not only controlled by a specific hypothesis, a direct supposal about the character of the world of science; it is limited and controlled also by the postulated character and end of scientific knowledge—the achievement of a common and communicable world of experience. Scientific observation and experiment is quantitative; what are observed are measurements. And again, still in pursuit of a stable and communicable world, observation and experiment in science are conducted always with a view to the achievement of statistical generalizations. Of course, a great distance divides the first correlation of observations, the solution of a particular scientific problem, from the establishment of an important generalization in the world of scientific experience, but they belong to a single and continuous process. And though it is given to few to formulate a new major generalization in science, or even to reform an old generalization to meet the conclusions of fresh and more extensive observation, no single observation can be said to have found its place in the world of scientific knowledge so long as it is not seen to be part of the evidence (though never an independently essential part) upon which a significant generalization may be or has been established.

The exact status and significance of single observations in scientific knowledge is a question which must engage us in a moment, but for the present what should be noticed is that scientific observation is observation for the purpose of statistical generalization; what is characteristic of the scientific method is not that it is inductive, but that it is statistical. By this I do not mean that none but a statistical procedure is open to science. I mean first, that science will adopt another procedure only when circumstances—the present state of our knowledge, or special difficulties of observation—make a statistical study difficult; and secondly, that the generality of scientific knowledge is due to the statistical character of scientific thought and not to its so-called inductive character. This statistical method I take to be implied in the end in the character of scientific experience; a stable world of quantitative conceptions is to be obtained in no other way save this. The method of Difference, the method of Residues and the method of Concomitant Variations are none of them relevant or useful in scientific experience unless they are applied to more than a single set of observations and unless their conclusions are stated in the form of a calculated mean, mode or median. In science even so elementary a procedure as the reference of an observation to a class of similar observations is based upon a statistical study wherever such is possible. Writers are, indeed, to be found who conceive the statistical method as supplementing or replacing the experimental method in those sciences where experiment is difficult or impossible. Nevertheless, not only can no such absolute distinction be maintained between observation and experiment, but also it is characteristic of every scientific experiment that it is designed and seen to be a contribution to a statistical conclusion. The whole tendency of science is towards this form of observation because by this means alone is it able to construct and establish a stable world of quantitative ideas. It is for this reason alone that all generalizations in science which are not merely analytic are statistical.

In so far, then, as it signifies anything to speak of a stage in scientific thought as the 'collection of data', this stage is a collection of measurements. The 'collection of data' and measurement are not, in science, two stages, but a single act: measurement is the scientific method of recognizing and designating the materials of scientific study. The eye of the scientific observer is a measure; scientific perception is itself measurement. The data of scientific knowledge are never mere 'observations'. And an interest in mere observation, in 'things' seen is not, as such, a scientific interest; it belongs rather to the world of natural history—science before it has realized its own character. Science begins only when the world of 'things' opened to us by our senses and perceptions has been forgotten or set on one side. There are, of course, sciences which appear to have very little notion of measurement as the sole means of observation; but then there are sciences which are imperfectly scientific.

Scientific observation is measurement; the materials of science are measurements. And the only way of generalizing measurements is statistical. Scientific thought is the attempt to elucidate a given world of ideas, first in terms of the necessary relations of those ideas, and beyond that in terms of the statistical generalization of its observations. The character and significance of statistical generalization must engage our attention when we come to consider the nature of scientific experience from the standpoint of its validity. But it may be observed now that a statistical generalization is a *résumé* of scientific observations, but a *résumé* independent of the character of any single observation. It is a generalization which refers to a series or body of observations as a series or body; it is an attempt to assign a precise character to a series of observations as such. Thus, a statistical generalization sustains the character of generalization; it is not a mere collective or enumerative judgment, but a judgment about the character of a specific, complex whole. Moreover, such generalizations are definite and precise; they are susceptible of mathematical statement. And further, they are invariable in respect of the series of observations to which they refer. The uniformity which they express is the uniformity of averages, and (up to a point) the larger the number of separate observations upon which the conclusion is calculated, the more nearly it will present a stable character. But a statistical generalization refers directly to the series of observations upon which it is based, and to that alone; and it is invariable in respect of this series, however inadequate a sample of the whole body of possible observations this series may be. The more successful scientific generalizations are the result of, at once, so large a number and so large a variety of observations that their stability can scarcely be doubted or overthrown, and deviation from the uniformity asserted is sufficiently small and sufficiently remote to be disregarded. But it is never supposed either that the hypothesis to be verified is the only possible hypothesis, or that further observations may not modify or even overthrow the generalization. Modification of this kind, however, cannot touch the invariability of the generalization so long as it is taken (as it must be taken) to refer directly and only to the world of observations which it was created to explain. Such a generalization when super-seded may cease to be important, may lose some of its stability, but does not cease to be invariable and true for its own world of observations. Thus, so long as statistical general-izations are based upon a sufficiently large number, and a sufficient variety of observations, and are not taken to refer directly to any one of these observations or to any other observations outside the series in question but to the series as such, they may properly be spoken of as invariable in respect of the series of observations from which they were derived, and stable in respect of all possible observations.

But this conclusion clearly falls short of what scientific thought requires: it discovers to us no comprehensive world independent of the peculiarities of particular observers and the particular circumstances of individual observations. Scien-tific thought seeks generalizations which will remain relevant beyond what has actually been observed, and it must find some valid method of extending and enlarging the scope of these statistical conclusions. This extension cannot, of course, take the form of a direct application of these statistical general-izations to a wider field than that from which they have been drawn, for these can refer directly and only to this series of measurements. Consequently, in place of a direct application of these generalizations beyond their field of reference, science achieves its end by an extension in terms of probability. What is true categorically of the observed series of measurements as a series can be shown to be relatively true of any member of the series and of what may lie altogether outside the observed series itself. And the closeness of the relation is calculable in terms of probability. Thus, science can achieve, on the basis of its statistical observations and inferences, generalizations no less invariable and no less definite than the statistical observations themselves; for, whatever its short-comings, any specific probability is both definite and in-variable. What all this involves, and the grounds upon which this whole process of thought and the conclusions in which it issues can be held to be valid, we must consider later.

## § 3

I pass now from the method of science to the matter of scientific knowledge. Science is distinguished, in this aspect, by what it studies. And this I will call Nature. The word 'nature' has, of course, a variety of meanings and many associations, but if I am to adhere to the view I have already recommended of the general character of scientific experience, I must set on one side all meanings and implications of this word which take us beyond the notion of a world which is in the highest degree common and impersonal. And the question for us now is, What is the matter of scientific knowledge more than merely common and communicable? What, in short, is the character of nature when it is taken to be the matter of science? The matter of scientific knowledge has called forth various descriptions, but before attending to what I take to be the more important of these, I wish to present, as briefly as I can, the view of it which I believe to be involved in my view of the scientific method.

Nature, then, is primarily a world of ideas independent of particular persons and particular types of sensation, a world of ideas which admits of universal agreement. For this reason it has sometimes been supposed that nature is a world of mere ideas, that the matter of scientific experience is "l'œuvre artificielle du savant". *Natura non fecit saltus* means no more than, *Mens non fecit saltus in naturae cogitatione*. This view, however, we have seen to be misconceived. Because a world is a world of ideas it does not follow that it is a world of mere ideas; indeed, we have seen already that no world whatever can be *that*. Ideality is never more than an abstract aspect of any world of ideas. Experience is always reality; and of this we cannot too often remind ourselves. It is true that

> We receive but what we give,
> And in our life alone does nature live;

but to take this as casting doubt upon the reality in what we experience, is (once again) to divide the universe between 'what we experience' and 'what is real', and to condemn ourselves to the whole miscellany of absurdities involved in this division.

Nature, then, is a world of ideas; it is a world of 'impersonal' ideas; and consequently it is a world of quantitative ideas. For such a world as this can alone be supposed free from the encumbrances from which scientific knowledge endeavours to rescue us. Whatever is not quantitatively conceivable cannot belong to nature. Nature, in short, is the world conceived coherently under the category of quantity. This is the nature which is 'inexorable', which acts only through immutable laws; but, of course, it is not the 'nature' we observe. This nature is the correlative of the scientific method; it is the product, not the datum, of scientific thought.

It is sometimes suggested that the end in scientific knowledge is the classification, correlation or elucidation of its 'objects' in terms of the character of these 'objects' themselves: what is sought is a 'natural classification'. The aim in science, it is said, is to express the relations between the facts of nature in terms of the character of those facts. And usually this view implies the belief, not only that the facts of nature dictate the categories under which they are explained, but also that these facts are more than merely quantitative ideas. But in so far as this second belief is involved, the suggestion appears to me to be founded upon the most vicious and crippling fallacy the theory of scientific knowledge has ever entertained. Nature, 'matter' or what is experienced in science are nothing other than the world conceived under the category of quantity, because the method of science is incapable of elucidating any other world; and the method of science is restricted in this way because the world sought is a world satisfactory to the purpose in scientific experience, a world of ideas before all else common and communicable. There is no contract here between method and matter, no mutual agreement, no accommodation, because where there are no parties a contract is impossible. The method and the matter of scientific knowledge are not two partics, each with claims which the other must recognize, they are inseparable aspects of a single whole. Between them there can be neither agreement nor disagreement, for they cannot be separated. And the notion of the categories of scientific knowledge or the instruments of scientific measurement interposing themselves between the scientist and his object is a notion utterly foreign to the character of scientific experience. Without the categories and the method, there is no matter; without the instruments of measurement, nothing to measure.

Furthermore, nature is a mechanism or a mechanical world within the limited meaning of this expression which we have seen applies to the explanation offered by scientific knowledge. That is, nature is a quantitatively conceived whole of interconnected parts such that every variation within that whole is seen to be a quantitative change, a rearrangement of the distribution of forces. And it is a self-contained, self-determined whole in which every change is conceived to be the product, not of the whole as such, nor of the whole of what is antecedent to the change, nor of some occurrence outside that whole, but of as little of the antecedent situation as is necessary to explain it. In a mechanism there is nothing undetermined, and nothing inexplicable. Thus, nature is a uniform, mathematically integrated, self-contained world of quantities. It is a closed system, determined solely from within. The 'uniformity of nature' is not established by observation, it is not even an hypothesis to be verified, it is, for scientific experience, a postulate, a *conditio sine qua non* of scientific thought. Uniformity is secured to nature by definition. And, for the same reason, nature is self-contained. No scientific 'discovery' can either shake, or help to establish this general character of the world of scientific experience.

And finally, it is a mistake to suppose that nature itself changes, or that scientific explanation is (for that reason) asymptotic, for ever nearing a complete explanation of its world but never achieving it. Nature, this integrated world of quantitative ideas, is static, complete in itself, present and beyond change or decay. It is static, not in the sense of being 'there', awaiting 'discovery' (for 'discovery' is a misleading word in scientific or in any experience), but in the sense of being wholly implicit in the imperfect, incoherent world of quantitative concepts with which scientific experience begins and which it is the purpose of science to elucidate and complete. There are, of course, modes of experience in which change has significance, but science is not one of these. The world of science is fixed and delineated from the moment when its elucidation was begun. Thus, it is not meaningless to speak of science approaching the stage when it will be complete—as it *is* meaningless to think this of the world of practical experience. And even if science should never reach this stage, its shortcoming will be due not to the fact that what is experienced in science is itself changing, is "a poem in the course of creation", a universe in the course of evolution (because this is not the case), but to the intricacy of the world of quantitative ideas it has presumed to elucidate, or to a failure of the interest which first started it on its career.[1]

[1] There is, no doubt, much in scientific experience in its present state which appears to contradict this view of its character. But that, in the main, arises from the fact that the present world of science is imperfectly scientific. For example, if we were to believe what some scientists *say*, the theory of evolution implies an actual change in the world of perception and is, in fact, a theory of history. But this, of course, is not what they think. What evolves, what changes is not, for biology, an historical entity, and the biological theory of evolution is not designed to account for changes in the historical world—if it were, it could never be a theory relevant to scientific experience. It is a theory designed to relate and explain certain scientific observations, observations (that is) not of what *has* happened in the past, but present, recurrent, statistically determined observations. Time for scientific thought is not what it is for history; the only time of which science is cognizant is an entirely intrascientific time. Biological evolution refers to the phylogeny of the race, and the 'race' is not an historical fact, or something that can be seen, it is a scientific abstraction. The theory of evolution is, of course, insecure and unscientific in so far as it falls short of a statistical generalization expressed mathematically; and it is a theory

It appears, then, that nature, the matter of science, is not what we ordinarily mean by 'nature'; it is an abstraction created by a division in our ordinary experience, and is neither what the poet means by nature, nor what the philosopher means, nor is it "what we observe in perception through the senses". It is, in short, the creation of the scientific mind for the sole purpose of satisfying that mind. Scientific experience begins by abandoning the world of ordinary, practical experience in favour of a world of its own, a world of quantitative concepts. None of the objects in our ordinary experience is, we may suppose, without this particular quantitative or measurable aspect, but none of them is merely a quantity, and the world of science is a world of mere, abstract quantities, quantities as such. Such a world, of course, can be neither perceived nor imagined. And those scientists who spend their time making pictures of the world of scientific experience may entertain, but certainly mislead both themselves and those who listen to them. We ought not, then, to speak of 'the scientific view of nature', for science and nature are inseparable correlatives (if by 'nature' we

which has been applied and misapplied to many different ends, both in science and out of it. But since the so-called evolutionary theories of philosophy and history have nothing in common with the biological theory of evolution but a name, and since to argue from the establishment of some kind of scientific 'law' of evolution that the same or a similar law is relevant in historical or philosophical thought involves the grossest confusion of mind, it would perhaps be best to confine the word to its scientific meaning. And when it is limited in this way, the theory of evolution does not imply, and is not designed to account for, any change in the perceptual or historical worlds: it is designed to explain the relationship of scientifically determined abstractions. Science is concerned with instances as such, with generalizations and wherever possible with statistical generalizations, and the theory of evolution relates to these and never to individual observations; although it is perhaps not too much to say that the quantitative study of the theory of evolution has as yet scarcely begun. And geology and zoology have the appearance of being historical studies only because they are imperfectly thought-out sciences; and the appearance is a mere appearance.

mean the matter in scientific experience), or they are without any direct or recognizable relation (if by 'nature' we mean what we ordinarily mean). 'Whatever can be measured is real', says the scientist; but what he means is that whatever can be conceived quantitatively belongs to nature, and nature is the world from the standpoint of scientific experience. The assumption in scientific thought is not that everything is measurable, but that in a world of quantitative concepts we have a world of absolute communicability. And again, the scientist does not dream (as we dream) that nature is a riddle without an answer; he knows that an answer is often difficult to find, but he knows also that what he means by nature is, *ex hypothesi*, a completely explicable world. The planets, apples and stones are not parts of the nature of which science is cognizant: the law of gravitation does not refer to the movement of these or any similar objects, but to the movement of mass. The world of scientific experience is, then, a world of abstractions, so far as our ordinary, practical experience is concerned. The nature which we perceive and which we fear or enjoy is not the nature in scientific experience.

The natural world which is the matter in scientific experience is, then, from the standpoint of our ordinary experience, a world of abstractions. Scientific thought is, from this standpoint, abstraction as a special process and for a particular purpose—the discovery and elucidation of an impersonal world. And it remains for us to consider the character of this experience from the standpoint of the totality of experience. But before turning to this, I wish first to notice some of the views of the character of scientific experience and of nature which I take to be excluded by the view I have suggested.

It is a notion still fashionable enough to require remark that nature in scientific experience is a 'purely objective' world: a world, as one writer says, of "naked facts". And this seems to mean not only that nature is independent of the inner life of particular experients, the same for every mind with which it comes into relation, but also that it is independent of any experience whatever. Science is "the photography of the bare fact"; generalizations in scientific experience are discovered and formulated, but not made. But the defect of this view is not so much that it fails to explain adequately the character of scientific experience, but that it is conceived in direct denial of what we have seen to be the character of experience in general. A world of facts which is yet beyond the so-called tyranny of experience and the influence of thought is a wholly nonsensical conception. A world which is 'purely objective' could not be a world of facts; it stands, *ex hypothesi*, outside experience and it is therefore a world to which it is absurd to attribute either truth or reality. And further, not only is a misconception of the character of experience involved in this view, but science itself has no use for this conception of a purely objective world; it is not necessary for science even to assume the existence of such a world. The elementary assumption of an 'external' or 'objective' world is something which belongs not to science but to common-sense.

And with the conception of nature as a 'purely objective' world must go the conceptions of it as "those things which are outside us" (Claude Bernard) and as 'the physical world'. In scientific experience the phenomena of nature are assumed to be external to us only in the sense of being independent of particular observers, and in no other or more extended sense. Science does not explain the character of those things which are outside us; it explains the world in so far as it can be explained when conceived under the category of quantity. And again, the world of nature is not 'the physical world'; it is the world of physics, a world of pure, quantitative abstractions which can be neither seen, touched nor imagined.

Akin to these views of the character of nature is that which conceives it as a 'book'; nature is 'there', awaiting interpretation. But this conception of scientific knowledge, by separating 'what is there' from 'our interpretation of it', divides what is indivisible and gives us two vicious abstractions in place of recognizable experience. We have seen already that the notion of 'interpretation', because it requires the assumption of a prior and fixed 'something' upon which the interpreter works, is a notion which will never fail to mislead us when we are considering the character of experience. Science does not construe a 'book of nature'; the notion of such a book is merely one more example of the misleading presupposition necessary to all forms of the view that reality is somehow separate from experience. Scientific truth does not lie in the correspondence of our ideas with 'nature', because apart from our ideas there is no nature.

Over against this view of the character of nature as a 'purely objective' world stands another, its direct opposite. Nature, in this view, is not a world of 'naked facts', it is a world of mere ideas, a subjective world. This view, no doubt, affords to some a welcome release from the absurdities of the 'book of nature' theory, but it ought not, for that reason, to be counted more satisfactory. Indeed, this view of the character of nature seems to be based upon no firmer foundation than the belief that because nature is a world of ideas, it must consequently be a world of mere ideas, that because it is experience, it can be neither true nor real. This belief, however, is one which we have met before. All experience, we have seen, is subjective, but no experience is merely subjective. All experience is somebody's experience, but no experience is merely the experience of a particular mind as such.

A more plausible and more important view of the character of nature is one which lies between the 'purely objective' and the 'purely subjective' notions. It is plausible because it has the charm of a compromise and appeals to that love of moderation which has as frequently been fatal to English philosophy as it has been favourable to English politics: and it is important merely because it is plausible. "Nature", it is said, "is not natural rock, but a concrete in which the

cement is mainly human assimilativeness." Nature is 'fact'
supplemented by what is called "the contribution of the
mind". Since "nature's own intrinsic system of government" is to a large extent unascertainable, the scientist, in
order to make nature intelligible, contributes subjective
principles of his own. "Die ganzen Zahlen hat Gott gemacht:
alles anderes ist Menschenwerk." But it will be found, I
think, that this view of nature and of scientific knowledge
suffers from the same defects as those which belong to the
two previous views. It asserts and depends upon a separation
of inseparables, and it postulates a world of reality beyond,
outside and independent of the world of experience. The
"contribution of the mind", this so-called 'subjective element' is not a separable element in knowledge, it is the
whole of knowledge, the whole of nature from one abstract
point of view. It is impossible to separate nature from our
knowledge of it. And the notion of experience working upon
raw material which is not itself experience is one which we
have been offered before and have seen reason to reject.
Compromise here (as elsewhere) increases, instead of miti-
gating, the errors of the extremes.

A fourth view which perhaps deserves notice is that which
asserts a pre-established harmony between nature and the
human mind. Science can discover the laws of nature because
nature happens to be of so complaisant a character that her
laws are discernible. Some writers even confess themselves
amazed at the correspondence between the intrinsic order
of nature and man's capacity for deciphering it. But, in spite
of this capacity, the subtlety of nature (it is believed) sets
a limit to scientific knowledge. Nevertheless, in this view
also, with its implicit reference to a game of hide-and-seek
between nature and the scientist, we are faced with a separation of the matter from the method of science; and whenever
these are separated it is impossible to bring them together
again without some such makeshift notion as that of a pre-
established harmony. My plan, however, has been to avoid
analogies and not to manufacture difficulties where there are

none. The method and the matter of scientific experience, science and nature, do not agree and are not adapted to one another; they are inseparable correlatives, aspects of a single whole. Nature is not a composite world, half the work of God and half of man; it is the world conceived under the category of quantity, it is the world *sub specie quantitatis*.

The last topic in this connexion I wish to touch upon before turning to other matters is the character of scientific experiment. An experiment in science is, of course, an observation, it is a controlled and regulated observation, and this may be taken to be the most elementary aspect of its character. Experiment is a method of discovery. Of the character of scientific observation I have said something already, and I will add here only the remark that we should be mistaken were we to suppose that every step in a scientific argument represents an actual observation, or that the scientist regards each observation as a fixed and unalterable datum. For scientific thought observation or 'the way of the senses' (which itself is not, of course, exclusive of judgment), if it is not exactly the way of error, is certainly the means neither of establishing nor of verifying its conclusions. Experiment as a method of discovery is certainly necessary in science, but it is never the whole process in any scientific research. Scientific generalizations are the result, not of the acceptance of what is given in observation, but of a critical analysis of observations.[1]

But there is another and more important aspect of the

[1] "L'expérience ne nous donne qu'un certain nombre de points isolés, il faut les réunir par un trait continu; c'est là une véritable généralisation. Mais on fait plus, la courbe que l'on tracera passera entre les points observés et près de ces points; elle ne passera pas par ces points eux-mêmes. Ainsi on ne se borne pas à généraliser l'expérience, on la corrige; et le physicien qui voudrait s'abstenir de ces corrections et se contenter vraiment de l'expérience toute nue serait forcé d'énoncer des lois bien extraordinaires. Les faits tout nus ne sauraient donc nous suffire; c'est pourquoi il nous faut la science ordonnée ou plutôt organisée." Poincaré, *La Science et l'Hypothèse*, p. 169.

character of scientific experiment. In scientific experience, we have seen, observation and experiment are undertaken always under the control of some hypothesis, and with a view to testing the validity of that hypothesis; and an experiment may be seen not only as a means of discovery but also as a method of verification. Verification is necessary before an hypothesis can be converted into a valid generalization, and this process of verification is thought of as a process of observation. Actual observation, it is believed, is the criterion of validity. Now this is a plausible and popular view, but it is not without its difficulties. It suggests, in the first place, that a valid scientific generalization is a concept or hypothesis which, when referred to an 'external world', proves itself satisfactory. It suggests that the end in scientific experience is to find an objective correlate to a subjective idea. It suggests that nature and scientific experience are separable entities. And all these suggestions we have seen to be false and misleading. But further, if actual observation were regarded by the scientist as a process of verification, we should expect to find him pay equal attention to each observation and to regard his hypothesis as invalid if his observations did not correspond with it, bear it out. Yet, such is not the case. The curve which represents the generalization need not pass through any of the points plotted by actual observation. Experiment, in short, is never a process of verification, in the sense of the reference of an idea to an 'objective', 'physical' world, because observations have not (and are never in practice held to have) an absolute, validating authority of this kind. The truth or falsehood of a scientific hypothesis is not a question of its correspondence with or discrepancy from a world of fixed and unalterable objects, because no such world is anywhere to be found. The verification of an hypothesis is a matter solely of ascertaining how far it is coherent with the entire world of scientific ideas, the world conceived under the category of quantity. Nothing whatever is fixed and unalterable except the general character of that world as a whole.

Nevertheless, it will be suggested that the test of the validity of a scientific generalization is its applicability to the future.[1] This view, however, in spite of the weight of the authority with which it comes to us, must be pronounced fallacious; it is a suggestion which conflicts with the character of nature itself. Nature, we have seen, is a timeless world; it neither changes nor evolves; it is static and self-contained and the conceptions of past and future are inapplicable to it. And scientific knowledge, because it is knowledge of a static world of quantitative concepts, cannot be thought of as concerned with past or future. What appears to be prevision in science, is merely the elucidation of what is implied in the character of the given world of scientific ideas. Of course, the capacity to foretell events has been attributed to scientific thought, but since in all cases the events which science was held to have foretold, because they were events, were not scientific facts, the ground of the prevision could not have been scientific knowledge.

There are, however, certain experiments or observations which, whatever our general view of the character of scientific experiment, persist in appearing to be themselves the verification of an hypothesis. And, in order to establish my view that no experiment or observation whatever in science can be held to be a process of verification, I will consider the character of these alleged exceptions. The kind of experiment I have in mind which appears to contravene my view is illustrated by what is spoken of as "the actual observation of the planet Neptune". Owing to the behaviour of Uranus it was inferred that there must be a hitherto unknown planet influencing its orbit, and the direction in which this planet must lie was calculated. "So far deduction. Then came verification. Adams and Leverrier, having each calculated the direction, the planet, since called Neptune, was actually observed through the telescope in that direction. Thus deduc-

[1] 'Future' is here taken to mean something more than 'hitherto unobserved'.

tion was verified empirically."[1] Now, the questions for us are two; What was the character of this observation? And what is the meaning of 'verified empirically'? First, this observation verified no generalization, and it was not an observation in terms of quantitative measurement. And a failure actually to perceive the planet would not itself have invalidated the hypothesis that the behaviour of Uranus could be accounted for only by the presence of some mass in that direction. In short, this observation belongs to the realm of natural history and not to that of scientific experience. And secondly, the observation of Neptune cannot be said to *prove* anything. The failure to observe it might suggest that the previous calculations were mistaken, but it could not prove them mistaken, and if they were mistaken the mistake could be discovered without the aid of any such experiment. And since failure to observe might be a consequence of the mere inadequacy of the instrument of observation, the actual fact of observation cannot, by itself, be said to prove the correctness of the calculation. We must conclude, then, that this is not an example of scientific experiment at all; a single observation is never of any significance in science, and nature, the matter in scientific experience, is not a world of percepts, but a world of pure quantitative ideas.

The method and the matter in scientific experience, the mode of thought employed and the conclusions reached are, we have seen, correlative to one another, and any attempt to separate them, and particularly any attempt to make the method depend upon the matter, is preposterous and will not fail to mislead us. Instead of assuming that scientific knowledge is, as it stands, direct and valid knowledge of the real world as a whole, what we must do is to ascertain the character of scientific knowledge, and then consider in what respect and to what extent it can be maintained to be a complete revelation of the character of reality. And this is what I have attempted. That there must be some relation between scien-

[1] T. Case in *Lectures on the Method of Science*, ed. T. B. Strong.

tific judgments and the real world we may be certain, because all judgment whatever involves the attribution of a certain character to reality. But beyond this general view, we require to know the precise nature of that relationship before a satisfactory view can be said to have been achieved. Scientific knowledge is certainly, in some sense, knowledge of reality, but how comprehensive this knowledge is will depend upon the logical structure of the world of scientific ideas. And to this we must now turn.

## § 4

I come now to consider the logical structure of the world of scientific experience, and hence its validity and the degree of truth attributable to it. I do not, of course, think this degree of truth to be exactly ascertainable, nor (for my purpose) is it necessary for me to ascertain it. What is ascertainable is an answer to the general question whether or not scientific experience is the totality of experience, whether or not the assertion of reality explicit in scientific judgments is a complete assertion of reality. And what I propose to show is that, on account of its general character, scientific experience falls short of the totality of experience, that scientific truth is less than the whole truth, and that the world of science is a world of abstractions. Science, in brief, is real knowledge, and is knowledge of reality; but it is abstract, defective and incomplete, and must suffer supersession. Scientific experience is an arrest in experience.

It will be convenient to consider the logical structure of scientific experience under four heads: induction, statistical generalization, probability and the suppositional or hypothetical nature of scientific generalizations.

Few will engage upon a discussion of induction without reluctance; and only the most confident will leave it without a feeling that somewhere it has betrayed them into absurdity. However, to consider the character of induction itself would be to go out of my way. Induction enters the discussion merely because certain writers have chosen to speak of the scientific method as inductive without having considered the character of induction.

The logical structure of the method of science may be considered from two standpoints. It may be seen as a method of research or discovery, and as a method of proof or verification. The distinction is not, of course, absolute—properly speaking nothing is discovered until it has been proved—but I propose to consider these aspects separately. From the standpoint of discovery, however, not much requires to be said. The scientific method, from this point of view, is supposed by many to be the operation of eliciting general conclusions from particular observations. And those most anxious to recommend this view tell us that wherever such an operation is to be found it will be reducible to one of Mill's four Methods of Induction: Agreement, Difference, Residues and Concomitant Variation. But, setting aside the more general question whether these methods of induction can properly be spoken of as processes of eliciting general conclusions from particular observations, the view I wish to suggest is that the scientific method, as a method of discovery, is not confined to these methods of induction, and that it is not a process of eliciting general conclusions from particular observations.

It is now generally recognized that these methods of induction are not separate and self-explanatory, and that in so far as they are considered in separation their character will be misconceived. They are examples of the discovery of the relationships of observations by a process of elimination. Given situations, between which a general connexion has been postulated or established, are analysed into their components, and by a process of elimination, a specific relationship is established between the remaining components. By an ideal removal of some parts, a definite relationship is established between the parts which remain. Now, that there is something more in the method of scientific research than the mere application of these methods of induction is at once apparent. What is given in scientific experience is not two or more situations between which a general connexion has been established or postulated, but a specific world of ideas in outline, a general sketch of relationships. Moreover, these methods of induction themselves offer no guidance for the formulation of hypotheses, which (we have seen) is an indispensable element in scientific research. In short, they do not become operative in the process of scientific research until the world of scientific ideas has been established in outline and until this outline has been filled in by hypothesis. And further, even when they do become operative in scientific research, it is never these bare methods of induction which govern the process of discovery, but these methods quantitatively modified. The scientific method is a method for establishing quantitative, mathematical relationships between the components of given situations, and unless and until induction is conceived quantitatively it is never of any significance to science. The scientific method, then, is not the mere application of these methods of induction to whatever comes the way of the scientist. And secondly, the scientific method is not, as a method of discovery, a process of eliciting general conclusions from particular observations. What is given in scientific experience is never merely particular observations, but a homogeneous world of ideas. Scientific research never begins with observation; and the importance of observation in science is secondary and derivative. The aim in scientific experience is to elucidate this general concept of the world under the category of quantity: given a world of ideas, what is attempted is to make that world more of a world. And it is only when we take up the process towards the end, and isolate some elements in the process from the process as a whole, that scientific research can be made to appear a process of eliciting general conclusions from particular observations.

Scientific method, then, is not merely a method of discovery, it is a method of inference. Its conclusions are not only general, but valid and certain. It has been suggested that scientific inference is a valid form of inference from particular observations to general conclusions because it involves the complete enumeration of the observations in question. Scientific generalizations are true because they hold of every observation. But we are already aware of the difficulties in which this suggestion involves us. A judgment, the validity of which rests upon a complete enumeration, is not a generalization at all, but a merely collective judgment. And for that reason it must fall short of satisfying the purpose in scientific thought. Moreover, this form of inference is repugnant to science because of the uncertainty of its conclusions; a single contrary observation will overthrow the conclusion. The validity of scientific generalizations is never taken to depend upon the supposition that all possible observations have been made and that among them there is no contradiction or disagreement.

Nor, again, is it true to attribute to science inference in the form of an argument from 'some' (or 'many') to 'all'. There is, of course, no valid inference from 'some' to 'all'; and no appeal to the so-called principle of the Uniformity of Nature will make such an inference valid. But the question for us is not whether this form of inference is valid, but whether it is used by science. From the standpoint of science an inference from 'some' to 'all' avoids many of the difficulties of an inference from a complete enumeration: science observes the 'some', never the 'all'. Nevertheless, any conclusion which might be imagined to follow from such an inference would still be merely collective and not general; and in so far as it insists upon the significance of the bare number of observations it falls short of a generic judgment. In science the relation of observations, the generalization, is not given by the observations themselves—indeed, it is often formulated in contradiction of the precise character of many of the observations—it is judged on the basis of the system or world of ideas which the observations require; and the proof or validity of the conclusion lies in the system itself.[1]

[1] "Repeated observations of ice floating on water, in various times and places, of various sizes and shapes, may lead me to conclude that ice is lighter than water; for as it floats irrespectively

The curve, which represents the generalized conclusion, does not necessarily pass through any of the points plotted by actual experiment or observation. But further, not only is observation in science confined to the 'some', but so are its conclusions. Scientific generalizations are never taken to refer equally and directly to 'all' or even to 'any'. So far as observation is concerned, science knows only the 'some', and so far as a categorical conclusion is concerned, it ends with a generalization of the 'some'. A direct inference from 'some' or 'many' to 'all' is not only logically fallacious, but scientifically useless.

And this leads to what I have taken to be the real basis of scientific conclusions—statistical generalization. Scientific generalization is statistical generalization. Now, statistical generalization is the attempt to give a generalized description of a series of observations, as a series, from a knowledge of the character of the individual observations of the series. A simple example of such a generalization is the determination, from a group of measurements, of the atomic weight of a chemical element, or the specific gravity of a substance. From the observation of the character of certain instances, the character of a series or class, as a series or class, is determined by fixing upon the most stable measurement.[1] Thus,

of size or shape, time or place, I can connect its floating with nothing but a less specific gravity. That it should be lighter, however, remains a brute fact, nowise apparently necessary. But if I could show that water expands in becoming ice, then, though this indeed is still a brute fact, yet, granting this, I see that ice must float; so far, I have explanation, insight into the necessity of the connexion of facts, demonstrative thinking." H. W. B. Joseph, *Logic*, p. 399.

[1] It is misleading to describe this as the 'most accurate' or 'most probable' measurement, because these phrases introduce the erroneous notion of science as knowledge of some absolute 'external' or 'physical' world, as an attempt to come closer to what is fixed and waiting to be known. Statistical generalization, an average, does not aim at eliminating 'accidental errors', there are no such 'errors' to be eliminated, but at producing a *stable* result. The aim of statistical generalization is not to give an 'approximate' result, for there is nothing for the result to approximate to; it is to give a *definite* and *invariable* result.

a statistical generalization refers directly and only to a body or world of observations, as a body or world; it is an attempt to make a given whole of observations significant as a whole. This is sometimes described as presenting an 'outline' from which certain details have been excluded. But a statistical generalization is not the outline of a series or body of observations, it is the character of the series or body as such. The details have not been suppressed or excluded, they have been co-ordinated and superseded. A statistical law or generalization, then, refers directly to a series of observations as such, and never refers directly to the individual observations themselves or any other series of observations.

But scientific experience, we have seen, does not stop there, nor is it required to abandon its statistical character if it goes further. For beyond these elementary statistical generalizations, other judgments may be made by a process of statistical inference. And the most important characteristics of statistical inference are that it deals only with quantitative measurements and their relations, and that its conclusions are always judgments of probability. The first I have discussed already; the second is the corner-stone of all scientific knowledge whenever it goes beyond the mere generalization of a specific body of actual observations. Statistical inference asserts a body or series of measurements to be of such a character that any single measurement in the series, selected at random, approaches the character of the series as a series with an assignable degree of probability. It is an inference from the character of the whole, as such, of observed A's to the probable character of any single A, whether it has actually been observed or not, or to the probable character of all A's whatever, as a whole. Thus, statistical inference can extend the categorical conclusions of ordinary statistical generalization with regard to the character of a series of observations as a series to conclusions in terms of probability with regard to the character of single observations or an entire class of phenomena. These conclusions in terms of probability depend, of course, upon the actual situation, they are always in the form of, 'A has probability *x* relatively to B'. But in so far as the actual situation, the statistical generalization upon which these further conclusions are based, is stable and comprehensive, any extension of it in terms of probability will be equally stable and comprehensive. Judgments will, of course, have different probabilities with regard to different sets of data, and while all are true, not all are equally important. Thus, the validity of a statistical inference does not depend upon the success of its predictions, nor upon the impossibility of discovering any exceptions to its conclusions. It depends upon the stability of the statistical generalization upon which it has been based and upon the accuracy with which the probabilities have been determined in relation to that generalization.

The appropriateness of this form of inference and this form of generalization to scientific experience can, I think, scarcely be questioned. It deals with what we have seen to be the world of scientific ideas, and it deals with no other world; statistical generalization and inference are possible only in a world which is conceived quantitatively. It gives, what the other forms of inference which have been called scientific fail to give, real generalization. From the observation of 'some' we are led to a valid and universal generalization in terms of probability. The significance which it attributes to the mere number of observations, and the weight it gives to any isolated observation is in accordance with the universal practice of scientific research. In scientific experience, we have seen, the mere number of observations is not, in itself, significant; and no single observation is regarded as, by itself, important, and certainly not as conclusive. And the conclusions of statistical inference have the same kind and degree of certainty as scientific conclusions are held to have. It is more important that the conclusions of scientific thought should be valid and definite than that they should be unlimited, for science (once again) is the attempt to find a common, uniform and impersonal world, rather than a world which is absolute and concrete; it is an attempt to abolish superstition rather than establish what is absolutely true. And the conclusions of statistical generalization and inference, though limited to probabilities, are yet certain, and definite and valid. The final validity of statistical inference in terms of probability, when unsupported by any further presupposition, has indeed been doubted, and were I considering the subject from all sides it would be necessary for me to meet other objections which I should find difficult to overcome. Such, however, has not been my purpose. And if I have succeeded in shewing that statistical inference, with all its limitations, is the form of inference upon which all the generalizations of scientific thought (except those which are merely analytical) must be based if they are to be scientific, I have done what is necessary for my purpose. Scientific inference is statistical inference; scientific generalizations are generalizations in terms of probability.

There is, however, an objection which, if it could be maintained, would go far towards wrecking this view of scientific generalization. It is said that not merely the validity but also the usefulness of statistical inference depend upon the existence of a repetition of detail in nature. If nature does not possess the characteristics of atomism and limited variety which this form of inference assumes, then this form of inference can produce neither useful nor valid generalizations. It is suggested, further, that whether or not nature be of this character is a question to be decided only by some kind of statistical enquiry. And the whole process of scientific argument and inference appears thereby to have been convicted of circularity. But this objection is not one which should cause us alarm; it is an old enemy which we have already discovered to be of no account. Wherever, we have seen, the method and the matter of scientific thought are separated, there is nothing we can do to bring them together again. And the objection before us amounts to no more than the assertion that the scientific method can be valid and successful only if and where there is some kind of pre-established harmony between it and nature. Nature is taken to be the world of which we are aware when we open our eyes, 'the universe', and science is taken to be the attempt to discover its character. But the whole puzzle is resolved directly the idea of nature and the scientific method as inseparable correlatives, as aspects of a single whole, is grasped firmly. That atomism and limited variety are characteristics of the nature of which scientific knowledge is cognizant is a principle implicit in the definition of nature, and no experiment or observation can add to its significance or certainty. Nature is, *ex hypothesi*, a world which can be elucidated by statistical generalization.

The fourth head under which I proposed to consider the logical structure of scientific thinking was its alleged suppositional or hypothetical character. The question here is not whether or not in scientific experience we begin with an hypothesis, but whether or not scientific generalizations are themselves hypothetical. In one sense, of course, it is clear enough that any form of experience which begins with an hypothesis can end in nothing more categorical than that hypothesis amplified, unless it could be shown that it is the only possible hypothesis. But scientific thought, by stating its conclusions in terms of a probability, is able to surmount this difficulty. In science a valid conclusion is reached from an hypothesis, not by the mere assertion of the consequent (which would of course involve a fallacy), but in terms of a statistical probability. This, however, leaves on our hands the question whether scientific generalizations are not themselves hypothetical. But we shall have considered the character of scientific generalizations in vain if we are not in a position to offer some kind of answer. We have seen already that scientific generalizations do not refer categorically to particular cases and do not even assert the existence of particular cases. This is true of those generalizations which I have called 'analytic', but (what is more important) it is true also of statistical generalizations. A statistical generalization, in whatever form it is stated, is never in science asserted as an actual observation or as a possible observation; and even if a particular case were found to correspond exactly with the generalization, the value of the generalization as a scientific generalization would not thereby be enhanced. In this sense, then, it appears that all scientific generalizations are hypothetical, and not categorical statements about the real world. The terms of a statistical generalization are not, as they stand, affirmed of reality.

Moreover, scientific generalization always asserts a relation or a consequence, and never the existence of what is related. It is concerned solely with adjectivals. What is asserted is not the existence of the subject or predicate (that is merely supposed), but a relation between the two. And this also indicates the hypothetical nature of scientific judgment. The strict expression of all scientific generalization is, 'If this, then that', or 'Suppose A and B, then C'. And for an illustration of this we need go no further than to the scientific conception of a cause,—the minimum antecedent circumstances sufficient to account for any example of a generalized result. All scientific generalizations, then, may be taken to be hypothetical, and those which are cast in a categorical form, or which refer to permanently presupposed conditions, are no exceptions to this rule. Scientific knowledge is not necessary and unconditional, not categorical, adequate or exhaustive, but abstract and hypothetical.

There are, however, two points which, in this connexion, require remark. First, it is necessary to guard against the misconception that scientific generalizations (except those which are analytic) determine what should or *must* happen when certain conditions are supposed; that is, we ought not to think of scientific judgments as apodeictic as well as hypothetical. Scientific judgments do not take the form, 'Whenever A is, B is also', or 'A must be where B is'; but rather the form, 'If A, then A will probably be when B is', or 'It is probable that, with respect to the character of the observed data,[1]

---

[1] 'The observed data' means, of course, scientifically observed data; that is, facts determined within the limit of the given structure of scientific experience.

A (if A be supposed to be observed) will be $x$'. And secondly, we must maintain the distinction between the hypotheses with which in scientific experience we sometimes begin, and the hypothetical generalizations with which science always ends. It has been said that all supposal is ideal experiment, the application of a particular idea to the world of scientific ideas in order to observe the result. And, in a sense, this appears true both of the initial hypotheses in science and of its generalizations. Of the first it is clearly true. And with regard to the second, no scientific generalization is conceived to be beyond the possibility of revision; it is experimental in the sense that so soon as it is seen to stand in the way of a coherent world of scientific experience it ceases to be held important. But to describe scientific generalizations as ideal experiments is less than the whole truth. For, once a generalization has been established, it always remains true for the world of observations to which it refers. And further, generalizations differ from the initial hypotheses in science because the element of supposal is tacit and not explicit, and no attempt is made to supersede it. It is necessary that the hypotheses with which science may begin should be seen to be hypotheses; but it is not necessary (perhaps not even possible) that the scientist should be conscious of the hypothetical character of his conclusions. The conversion of an hypothesis into a conclusion involves a real change and is no mere pretence. For, while the first hypothesis is a supposal about the world of scientific ideas, the second (the scientific generalization itself) is a supposal about the real world. The so-called 'laws of nature' are hypothetical propositions about the world of concrete reality.

## § 5

Let us consider the position we have reached. Scientific judgment, like all judgment, is an assertion of reality. The world of science is not a separable part of reality; it is the whole of reality. And it demands to be judged as this, to be judged by the criterion to which all experience submits, the criterion of coherence. But, beyond this general character, scientific experience is a specific, homogeneous world of experience, an organized whole. And the question I have undertaken to consider is this: Is the assertion of reality contained in the world of scientific experience a complete assertion? Is scientific experience, taken as a whole and by itself, the concrete totality of experience? This is not, of course, a question the answer to which depends upon the state of our scientific knowledge: it cannot be answered in the negative merely because of the present imperfect integration of the world of scientific experience. And further, my enquiry should not be confused with the question, What degree of truth is contained in the assertion of reality which constitutes scientific experience—if it is not a complete assertion? That question, as I have already explained, lies to one side of my purpose. It is certain (or so it appears to me) that scientific experience cannot be dismissed as having no degree of truth whatever. But the fact that, at worst, scientific experience is not wholly abstract and defective is, so far as I am concerned, irrelevant. For, from the standpoint I have taken up, from the standpoint of the totality of experience, what is relevant is not the degree of coherence which belongs to any world of experience, but whether or not that coherence is complete and unqualified. I wish to consider the world of scientific experience as a whole and by itself to discover whether or not it is the world of concrete reality. And the answer to this question can neither involve nor tolerate any suggestion of a degree of achievement. Moreover, the view I have suggested (and to some extent explained) is that if the world of scientific experience is not the world of concrete reality, then (so far as the totality of experience is concerned) it must be set altogether aside and rejected. There is no way in which an abstract world of experience can, as a world and as such, be seen to be a part of or a contribution to the world of ideas ultimately satisfactory in experience, the world of concrete reality.

The answer to my question is, of course, already clear. The defects of the world of scientific experience, taken as a world and when regarded from the standpoint of the totality of experience, are I think undeniable, and they are also insurmountable. It is impossible to maintain the view that the world of scientific experience is the world of ultimate reality in conjunction with the view of the character of scientific experience I have suggested. On the contrary, nothing is clearer than that the world of science is an abstract and defective world, an arrest in experience. And indeed, the specific characteristics of scientific experience, the characteristics in virtue of which it is scientific, are those which constitute its defect and abstraction from the standpoint of reality. What distinguishes the world of scientific experience from other worlds of experience, the principle of homogeneity upon which this world is constructed, distinguishes it also from the world satisfactory in experience.

The explicit character of scientific experience is a world of absolutely stable and communicable experience: the explicit purpose in science is to conceive the world under the category of quantity. There is, of course, an implicit attempt to establish a world satisfactory in experience, the real world; but it is an attempt governed by the conceptions of communicability and quantity, and these conceptions not only govern, they also limit and modify. The world as communicable is not, itself, the real world. The world conceived under the category of quantity is not, itself, a coherent world of experience. It is the real world from a limited and abstract point of view; it is experience arrested at a point short of what is satisfactory in experience. Science is undeniably an attempt to discover and maintain the real world, but at the heart of it there remains this contradiction: it is a form of experience impotent to achieve the end in experience. And the world of scientific experience is a world of self-contradictions. Science sets out in pursuit of the real world; but it comes home without having achieved its end. Yet it comes home, it achieves a homogeneous and coherent world of experience. But, from the standpoint of the totality of experience, this world is a world divided against itself. Science is

> To wish, but never have the will,
> To be possessed, and yet to miss,
> To wed a true but absent bliss.

And the world of scientific experience, as a world, requires consequently to be set on one side.

The world of science is the world as (or in so far as it is) communicable, it is the world from the standpoint of its absolute communicability, and consequently it is not the world of experience ultimately satisfactory in experience. This, of course, is not in the vulgar sense a self-evident proposition, and it requires to be substantiated. But the inadequacy of the view we get of the world from the standpoint of communicability demonstrates itself by the implications which such a mode of experience involves. The world as communicable is the world conceived under the category of quantity; the judgment of science on that point is certainly not in error. But the defects and limitations of this conception are such that it cries out to be superseded. And further, quantitative conception involves scientific experience in, and confines it to, a world of generalizations. Scientific knowledge is merely generalized knowledge, but nowhere in the whole range of scientific experience is there to be found a generalization categorically asserted. Wherever scientific knowledge passes from generalities it becomes merely probable. And once more, the world of science is a world of supposals about reality. Scientific knowledge is hypothetical knowledge, and its concrete basis lies outside the range of scientific experience itself. The life of science is not its own, but a borrowed life. A scientific proposition is never more than the assertion of the dependence of a consequent upon a condition not asserted to be realized. And the world of science is a world of such judgments. My view is not that the world of scientific experience is a world of mere supposals; for a mere supposal, a supposal that asserts nothing of reality, is contradictory and impossible in experience. To suppose (as also to imagine or to deny) is to assert *something* categorically. To say what *would* be, or what *might* be, or what *may* be, is to say something of what is. And no judgment whatever can avoid this implicit reference to reality. But what is important here is to understand that, whatever a supposal asserts about reality, it never asserts what is supposed. To say what *would* be, is to say something, but not *that* thing, of what is. And consequently a world of supposals is a world of judgments which have some reference to reality, but not the reference represented by their explicit character. Unless we know more about reality than what is explicit in this world of judgments, we know nothing. The world of scientific experience, then, is, in virtue of its explicit character as a world of supposals, an abstract and incomplete world of experience, incoherent, divided against itself and unable to give what is satisfactory in experience. If we set out to find and elucidate a world of absolutely communicable experiences there is no point in the process at which an arrest is justified short of a world of supposals; and a world of supposals is a world of experience which falls short of the character of experience.

Now, if this be our verdict, there can be no doubt about the judgment which must follow. The world of scientific experience is incomplete and therefore incoherent; and unless it somehow passes beyond itself it must remain incoherent. But it can pass beyond itself only by an act of self-destruction: as a world it must perish. There is, in scientific thought, a reference to reality, an implicit reference, and that, of course, cannot perish. But the self-contained world of science must be broken down and abolished, if that reference is to become explicit. It is not by pressing scientific experience to its conclusion that we shall discover the concrete totality of experience, but only by allowing the abstractness of the world of science to assert itself. For wherever a world of experience asserts itself as abstract it has submitted itself to the authority of the totality of experience, it has confessed a limit and a defect in its character. And every world of experience which is abstract and limited must, as a world, be set on one side, if the full character of experience is to be realized. The world of science and the world of reality are, as worlds, exclusive of one another.

I have considered in an earlier chapter the relationship which I take to exist between experience and its modes, between the world of experience satisfactory in experience and any abstract world of experience, and it is not necessary for me to repeat what I have said already. The view that I have recommended involves the conclusion that, if the world of scientific knowledge be of the character I have suggested it to be, it, as a world of knowledge, has no contribution whatever to make to our knowledge of reality. And further, only scientific thinking can elucidate the world of science; no other mode of experience, and certainly not the totality of experience as such, can enter the world of science without irrelevance. Where scientific thought is confined to the elucidation of the world of scientific abstractions, philosophy has, and can have, nothing to say. Philosophy has no criterion wherewith to judge the adequacy of scientific conceptions to achieve the limited end in scientific thought. And so long as scientific thought is engaged with what it can achieve, the organization of its own world, it remains sovereign and unassailable. But wherever an abstract world of experience asserts itself unconditionally, as the world of science asserts itself in Naturalism, wherever a mode of experience represents itself as the whole, there is no longer mere deficiency, mere modification; there is actual error and falsehood. And it is at this point that the authority of the totality of experience is called into play. My view is, then, that the world of science is, as a world, autonomous and self-contained, and that scientific thought, when it is concerned with its own abstractions, when it is confined to the exploitation of its own character, when (in short) it appears to be what it in fact is, secures for itself a position beyond the relevant criticism of the totality of experience. But, on the other hand, since scientific experience is experience, since there is implied in it an attempt to discover a world capable of providing what is satisfactory in experience, it is, from the standpoint of the totality of experience, limited and defective. It is a form (or formulation) of experience impotent to achieve the full character of experience. And where our standpoint is that of ultimate satisfaction in experience, science and the world of science must be pronounced totally incapable.

There are, of course, other views than this of the relation of the world of scientific experience, as a world, to the complete world of experience, to philosophy. But no other, I think, is consistent with the view of experience and of science which I have been maintaining. Some of these I have discussed already, and it is not necessary to pause over them here. The most vicious only need be noticed. "A modern philosophy worth the name", it is said, "must take account of the far-reaching results of scientific enquiry." Again: "In a philosophical study the methods and results of science are the best available evidence". Further: "The laws of science, rather than the original facts, are the raw material of philosophy". And the results of scientific enquiry are spoken of as "the anatomy of philosophy". But I trust it will require no fresh argument on my part to show the absurdity of these views. Where 'philosophy' stands for merely "the most general synthesis of the special sciences", these propositions are either false or tautologous. And a 'philosophy' such as this (which I am unable to distinguish from science itself), since it is something radically different from experience without presupposition or arrest, is not what I have been considering. Why thought should be doomed to the fruitless task of synthesising its own indiscretions; in what sense knowledge can be said to *depend* upon what is seen to be a deficient sub-species of itself; how thinking can hope to construct a coherent world of ideas when it is obliged, not merely to consider, but to adopt *in toto*, as a datum not to be changed, a world of experience which is limited and defective from end to end; and how a mere encyclopaedia of the sciences can, as such, be conceived to be the same as, or to take the place of, a critical examination of scientific experience—are problems I am not called upon to discuss.[1] Any attempt to integrate the fragmentary results of science must be the work of scientific, not philosophical thinking and must itself be stated in the form of scientific generalizations. Philosophy must begin by rejecting alike the method and the results of the arrest in experience called science. For scientific experience must either be avoided or pressed beyond the borders of science, carried out of itself and seen to be an abstract world of ideas, a folly to be fled from, before the arrest in experience which it constitutes can be overcome.

Of the relation between the world of scientific experience, as a world, and other worlds of abstract ideas, other modifications of experience, I will say nothing here. It is a question I have found more convenient to discuss elsewhere. In general, however, we have seen that all abstract worlds of experience are, as worlds, wholly independent of one another, and that it is impossible to pass from one to any other in argument without committing the grossest fallacies.

## § 6

What remains of this chapter I shall devote to a brief consideration of those sciences which fall outside the so-called 'natural sciences', to the scientific study of man and of society. I shall be brief because I am not so much concerned to show that such sciences exist, as to show that they are possible and that wherever they are found they will conform to a certain character. And I take it that these conclusions are already involved in the foregoing discussion. Now that we have ascertained the general character of scientific experience, I anticipate that the scientific study of man and of society, taken as a mode of experience, will afford us no

[1] "If metaphysics is not to work with the data of the natural as well as the philosophical sciences, subject, of course, to logical and epistemological criticism, what is it to work with?" enquires a scientific writer. And from another scientist we have the suggestion that "the philosopher of the future may well be the historian of science".

new problems. In a sense, however, what I have now to say will, I hope, result in the further determination of the character of scientific experience, for it will emphasise the view that science is one and that the so-called special sciences are separated from one another neither on account of special methods nor on account of special subject-matters, but merely fortuitously and on account of present imperfections in the elucidation of the world of scientific experience. And I shall confine what I have to say on this topic to a consideration of economics and psychology. There are, no doubt, other sciences than those which fall outside the so-called 'natural' sciences; but, neither here nor anywhere else, is it my aim to consider all that might be considered.

Economics is a name which covers a variety of intellectual interests, and it may be doubted whether many of these have anything in common beyond this name. But to centre thought upon a mere name not only will never produce a homogeneous world of ideas, but it will tend also to establish in our minds a pseudo-relationship between sets of ideas which do not and cannot belong together; it will encourage argument to pass inconsequently from one world of ideas to another, insensible that every such passage constitutes an *ignoratio elenchi*. Moreover, this is not merely the condition of things we might expect from such a haphazard bringing together of different sets of ideas, it is the actual condition of much economic thought at the present time. Economics, as we find it in the books of many of its most distinguished professors, comprises a meaningless miscellany of scientific, historical and practical ideas and arguments. But it is not my object to attempt to set this world in order, or to suggest in advance what are the lines upon which economists should conduct their thought; that lies beyond my competence. My object is more modest; it is to consider whether there is, coming under the general head of Economics, a mode of experience which may properly be called scientific, and to suggest that, if such a mode of experience be found, it will conform to a certain character and will be as independent and exclusive of other modifications of experience as any other science. My questions are: What must be the general character of a *science* of economics? And, given such a science, in what sense is it scientific?

Economics can be a science only in virtue of conformity with the general character of scientific experience. This, and nothing else, can constitute it a world of scientific ideas. Its conceptions must be of the character of those which belong to science, its method must be that which distinguishes science, and its conclusions will have the same general nature, and consequently the same scope, validity and significance, as those of scientific experience.

Scientific experience, we have seen, is a world of ideas free from the personal idiosyncrasies of particular experients. Science is an attempt to discover and elucidate a world of ideas before all else stable, common, and communicable. And this general end involves science in, and confines it to, the elucidation of a world of quantitative conceptions. Whatever cannot be conceived quantitatively cannot belong to scientific knowledge. The world of science is a uniform world of quantitative ideas, a world, that is, of quantitative generalizations. All forms of scientific thought whatever result in a self-contained, static, mechanical world of ideas. This does not, of course, mean that the ideas of science must always be figures, or that its inferences and generalizations will always be expressed in mathematical symbols. It means that its conceptions must be subject to judgments of 'more' and 'less', 'increase' and 'decrease', 'intensity', 'size' and 'duration'. In any fully developed science the proportions and relations it asserts will always be in terms of definite quantities, they will be mathematical equations; but a form of thought may be considered scientific so long as its conceptions *permit* its generalizations to be stated as definitely assessed relationships. Further the structural concepts of any science will be found to imply certain relationships, to involve us at once in an organized, integrated world of ideas. And these general relationships are the foundation of all scientific thought. They are not, of course, beyond revision or modification; but revision can come only when the characters of the concepts themselves have suffered modification. So long, however, as these remain unchanged (and they will remain unchanged as long as they offer a fruitful source of hypothesis and observation), they constitute the categories in terms of which all hypotheses are framed, all observation or experiment is conducted. Scientific observation is always measurement, the observation of quantities and quantitative change. The generalization of scientific observations is always statistical generalization; and statistical generalization refers directly always and only to the series of observations as a series. Inferences and further generalizations may, it is true, be based upon these statistical conclusions, but they will never be more than probabilities. The relevance of a statistical generalization to a body of phenomena not actually observed, or to any single observation, is always a mere probability. This, then, is the general character, scope and validity of scientific experience, and economics can be a science only in so far as it conforms, in a general way, to this character.

Now, implicit in the arguments of many of those who are accustomed to speak of economics as a science, and explicit in the arguments of those who are disposed to deny this character to economics, there is an attempt to show that, for a variety of reasons, economics is not and cannot be a science in the full sense. I wish now to consider this view. And the conclusion, in general, which I shall recommend is that the reasons upon which it is based are worthless, and that unless others are found we must take it that the attempt has failed. It will be found, I think, that all versions of this view are based either upon a misconception of the character of scientific experience, or upon a misconception of the character of economics, or upon a combination of these misconceptions. All writers who have undertaken to demonstrate the impossibility of a science of economics have failed to produce reasons capable of proving their case; and most writers who desire to show the scientific character of economics base their contention upon grounds which are insufficient to maintain it.

Economics, it is said, whether or not it is or can become a science, certainly can never be an 'exact' science. Its data are too indefinite, and its conclusions are "truths only in the rough". The peculiar indefiniteness of economic data is said to be due to the fact that these are concerned always with human wants, human actions and human satisfactions. "Economics cannot be compared with the exact physical sciences; for it deals with the ever changing and subtle forces of human nature."[1] Any attempt to generalize the variable and uncertain motives, desires and actions of human beings can result only in rough estimates; it can never achieve definite and invariable generalizations. And consequently it must at once be distinguished from science in the full sense. Or again, another argument to the same purpose; science, we have seen and everybody knows, deals with abstractions, but economics is "the study of men as they live and move and think in the ordinary business of life."[2] It is the study of real men, not of fictitious men, or 'economic men'. It is the study of "man as he is", "a man of flesh and blood". Physics, the science *par excellence*, is concerned with what is uniform and measurable; economics is concerned with what is variable, capricious and unpredictable. The one can formulate a system of valid and certain generalizations, the other must be content with generalizations which to-morrow may require revision, not on account of new knowledge but on account of changed conditions, generalizations which apply only to a narrow range of observations and which may at any moment be upset by the capricious action of human beings.

Now, the misconceptions involved in this view are numerous. So far as it concerns physics, or scientific thought generally, it rests upon a misunderstanding. Scientific experience, it is true, is a world of definite and invariable generalizations. But

[1] Marshall, *Principles of Economics*, p. 14.
[2] *Ibid.*

these generalizations, we have seen, refer categorically to the series of observations, as a series, from which they were derived. They refer directly neither to individual observations, nor to unobserved phenomena. Wherever they are taken to be, in the full sense, general they are never more than probabilities. And if the generalizations of economics are only probabilities,[1] they do not differ from those of physics. Here again, as so often before, what has misled us is this word 'exact'. The 'exact' sciences never reach conclusions which correspond without overlap or difference to some event or occurrence, some observation in the perceptual world. The observations and the experiments of science are not the grounds of the validity of scientific generalizations; they are merely part of what is given, incoherent data. The master-conception of science is not 'exactness' but 'stability'; its conclusions are not satisfactory because they represent exactly something actually seen and measured, but because they are stable and general. The analytical generalizations in scientific experience have no meaning whatever when applied directly to the ordinary world of perception, for the conceptions of which they express the necessary relations are not conceptions which have anything correspondent to them in the world of percepts. And the statistical generalizations of science, when referred to the world of ordinary percepts, when referred to the world in which men of flesh and blood live, are mere probabilities. And further, when we turn our attention from the alleged distinction between economics and scientific experience based upon the contention that the conclusions of the one are rough and inexact and the conclusions of the other precise and universally valid, to the alleged distinction between economics and science based upon the view that the data of the one are variable and complex while the data of the other are uniform and simple, we are rewarded with nothing relevant or remarkable. Nothing could be more various than the particular observations of the physicist; the behaviour of a particular electron is not less unaccountable,

[1] Marshall, *Economics of Industry*, p. 24.

not less 'capricious' than the behaviour of a man of flesh and blood. It is not because the particular observations of economics refer to *living* things, or to human beings, or to voluntary actions that their character is complex and obscure and their behaviour variable; complexity, obscurity and variableness are the characteristics of every particular observation by reason of its particularity. And this special handicap which the sciences dealing with organisms or human beings are supposed to suffer is, so far as their scientific character is concerned, a mere delusion. There may be other reasons why biology, psychology and economics are peculiarly difficult sciences, but it is certainly not because they are concerned with *living* things. Moreover, although many economists assert economics to be concerned with men, and voluntary human actions, when we turn to their actual observations and generalizations we shall, I think, find not only that economics *need* not be concerned with these things (that is, that there is a subject-matter in economics apart from these things), but also that economics actually is not concerned with them. But that is another question which I must consider later. For the present, what I have to suggest is that the distinction between economics and science based upon the variability of the data of economics and the inexactness of its conclusions, when referred to the ordinary world of perception, is false; there are no grounds here for a valid distinction.

A second argument in favour of this divorce between economics and science is the view that economics is in some way specially connected with history. The data of economic generalization are, it is said, if not entirely historical, at least partly so. Economic facts are historical facts; and the 'collection of data' for economic generalization is a combination of historical research and the observation of contemporary events. The view implies two things; it implies that the world of economics is a world of historical change, and that economic events, economic actions and behaviour are events, actions and behaviour of a particular kind in the historical or past world, or in a contemporary or practical world. Now, it is true that were economics confined to a study of such a world and such events it would fall short of being a science: there is no science of what is specifically changing or of what is specifically historical. But it is not true that economics need be so confined. And, indeed, wherever economics has freed itself from what is merely empirical, what is merely observable, it has freed itself also from what changes and from what is historical; and it has already achieved this freedom in a considerable degree. Economics, in so far as it can be said to deal with behaviour at all, deals not with a particular kind of action, behaviour or satisfaction, but with a particular aspect of all action, behaviour and satisfaction, and in virtue of this it has quitted a changing world for a static, timeless, scientific world, and has severed itself from all connexion with history. There are no 'economic events'[1]; economics is concerned with an aspect of all events, but an entirely non-historical aspect. The abstractions of economics are not the abstractions of history or of practice, but those of science. If it goes to the past for its data, it always neglects the specifically historical character of what it observes; if it makes observations in the practical world, it always neglects their specifically practical character. The conceptions of economics apply no more to the historical world than to the world of our ordinary perception, and in so far as this is so, economics has become scientific experience.

But again, economics is said to fall short of the full character of scientific experience because it is concerned with, and because its generalizations refer to, a limited world of behaviour. It is suggested, for example, that economics is an attempt to generalize behaviour in a society organized for free competition, in an exchange economy or within a social system in which certain sorts of behaviour are enjoined or forbidden by law or custom. Yet, whatever the truth or the force of these contentions, it is a misconception to suppose that were they all admitted economics would, for that reason, fall short of the condition of scientific experience. Economic

[1] Marshall, *Principles of Economics*, p. 774.

generalizations certainly have a limited range; but so also have the generalizations of every other science. And not until all sciences are seen as one science, not until they have been reduced to one, will this cease to be so. Physics and biology, for example, appear to have separate fields of research, and the generalizations of each appear to be limited to its own field, no less than the generalizations of economics. The view, then, that its limited world of reference places economics outside scientific experience rests upon a misconception of the character of scientific knowledge. And, further, many of the contentions which fall under this general view rest upon a misconception of the character of economics. Economics, we have seen, is not concerned with any particular kind of behaviour, but with an aspect of all behaviour, an aspect which exists and is distinguishable no less in a purely communistic society than in a society of free competition or one ruled by exchange. It is true that certain difficulties will appear in the study of this aspect of behaviour under certain conditions. Outside an exchange economy it may be more difficult to submit this aspect of behaviour to a quantitative treatment, it may be difficult without the concept of price to measure the intensity of demand, but it is not impossible. And whatever solutions economists find for these difficulties, it is certainly an error to suppose either that economics must confine its observations to conditions of free competition or individualistic exchange, or that were they so confined it would for that reason fall short of scientific knowledge. Each science appears to have a separate field of observation; but all sciences are one and inseparable in their character as the elucidation of the world *sub specie quantitatis*.

Two further common contentions in support of the view that economics is not, and can never become a science I will set on one side as scarcely meriting consideration. The impossibility of experiment in economics, and the comparative failure of economics to produce any generalizations to guide present or future behaviour, are both alleged as grounds for this view. Experiment, of course, is not a *conditio sine qua non* of scientific experience; and (as we shall observe in the case of psychology) merely to reorganize a field of research upon an experimental basis will not make a science. And the notion that a capacity to predict future events belongs to scientific generalization is derived from an obsolete and misconceived view of the character of scientific knowledge. Science, as such, has nothing to say about 'events' in the world of perception, and a scientific generalization can no more be vindicated by a demonstration of its applicability to a certain occurrence than it can be called in question because it fails to predict the future. The world of scientific generalization is a world ignorant alike of past and future as such, it knows nothing of historical time, and recognizes time only within its world, as a means of relating its own concepts. Science may announce the probability of the recurrence of a certain measurement within the system of its own observations, but to demand more than this, to demand that a science of economics should predict categorically a slump or a boom in trade, is to demand what, indeed, some economists have pretended to offer, but what an economic science could never afford.

Finally, it has been contended that economics is not a science because among its assumptions there are certain philosophical and ethical postulates; and a science, it is well known, should be free from such assumptions. But here again, the attempt to prove the unscientific character of economic knowledge relies upon what has certainly belonged to it in the past, but what is not necessary to it and what it has in fact largely outgrown. The day when it was thought necessary to assert psychological or ethical hedonism (they are, of course, contradictory of one another) as a basis for economic theory is now long past, though the reasons we are often given for the separation of economics from ethics are certainly invalid. Philosophism in economics is no less fatal and no less irrelevant than in any other science. Economics can become a science only in so far as its world is organized independently of philosophical assumptions; and it has, to a large extent, already achieved this condition.

I conclude, then, that the reasons we are given for believing that economics is not, and cannot be a science, are based upon a misconception of both science and economics. The difficulties in the way of economics becoming a science are certainly not greater than those which stand in the way of biology. But, on the other hand, many of the attempts to formulate economics as a science must be pronounced unsatisfactory; and economics as a science has progressed largely without the aid of any coherent view of its own character. This, of course, is not surprising; a science, in order to maintain its efficiency as a science, does not require to be self-conscious. Nevertheless, although a coherent view of its own character as a science will afford but small assistance to the solution of its own problems, it could, I think, perform the negative service of cutting economics free from some of the other and extraneous ends which have hindered its development as a science. It is not, however, part of my purpose to offer such a view: my business is merely to discover adequate. grounds for maintaining economics to be scientific knowledge.

In its early days economics asserted its scientific character on the ground that it was concerned with what is 'material'. But even if this view could be maintained, it would fall short of establishing economics as a science. Science is not, we have seen, an attempt to discover and generalize the 'material' world, or the 'physical' world, it is an attempt to discover a stable and communicable world of experience devoid of caprice or superstition. And the notion that such a world is, in any relevant sense, material, physical or external must be abandoned as ambiguous and misleading. Again, economics has attempted to establish its scientific character on the ground that its concern is with the behaviour of an abstract 'economic' man. And there can be no doubt that this conception was the means of reducing to order much that had been disorderly in economic knowledge. If economics was to be a science of man, it must certainly show that its concern is with a scientifically conceived man, a scientifically abstracted man. But the economic man of the older economists was never scientifically conceived; he was a pseudo-ethical abstraction. And instead of offering economics an escape from ethical and psychological postulates, this conception ratified the connexion. However, the way out of the difficulty is clear, and economic science has already taken it. 'Man', a man of any sort, is not an appropriate subject-matter for any science; and economics has now come to conceive its material not in the human terms of behaviour, action, desire, satisfaction, etc., but in such quantitative terms as those of cost and price, utility and disutility. Economics is not a science of man; for 'man' is not a scientific concept. It is a science of measurements. Its generalizations do not refer directly to a 'human' world, a world of desires, feelings, wants and satisfactions, but to a world of impersonal quantitative conceptions and their relations. The valuations which form the basis of the observations of economic science are, of course, from another standpoint, human desires, but it is not in their character as human desires that economic science is cognizant of them. A valuation in economics is a quantitative measurement; a desire is a price. Hunger as it is felt is not an economic fact; it is not (as we shall see) even a psychological fact. What concerns economics is a certain possible aspect of hunger, an abstraction, a figure in a scale, a measurement reached not only by rejecting the particularity of this or that man's desires in favour of something more stable and less capricious, a mean, but also by rejecting its specific character as something felt. Hunger, in an economic science, becomes utility or price. Economics is not an attempt to generalize human desires or human behaviour, but to generalize the phenomena of price.[1] And the more completely it leaves behind the specifically human world, the more completely it discards the vocabulary which suggests this world, the more unambiguously will it establish its scientific character.

An attempt, however, has been made to establish the

---

[1] Or perhaps, more generally, the phenomena of scarcity in relation to demand.

scientific character of economics on grounds different from these. It is suggested that economics is a science, and can maintain its position in the world of scientific experience, because it is concerned exclusively with the determination of the necessary relations of certain abstract concepts. All economic generalizations are analytical generalizations; they are reached merely by the 'factorization' of the structural concepts of the science. Economics is a purely analytical science; it neither has, nor has any use for, statistical generalizations, and the attempt to modify economics in terms of statistics is both foolish and inconsequent.

Now, we have seen already that every genuine science will have its purely analytic generalizations. The main structural concepts of a science are always quantitative concepts, and the relations between them can be precisely formulated. And such generalizations are certainly to be found in economic science. The actual quantity of these generalizations may not be great, but it is safe to say that the work of determining the relations between the main concepts of economic science has already gone far. Such economic concepts as supply, demand, scarcity, cost, price and utility are already seen to be mutually implicative and to compose an integrated whole in the same way as the concepts of mechanics are seen to compose an integrated whole. This does not, of course, mean that economic science is bound to its present concepts. In the process of analysis it is frequently found that certain concepts are inadequate or ambiguous, and it is the business of a science to reject such concepts and replace them with others more useful. Thus, economic science may be said to have already rejected the concept of 'wealth' in favour of that of 'price'. And again, economics is not unique among the sciences if many generalizations once considered purely analytic, later prove to be of a different character. Every science is, on one side, purely analytic, an attempt to work out satisfactory concepts and generalize their relations. But no science is merely analytic: a merely analytic science is a sterile science. Thus, for example, physics may be regarded as an attempt to implement the merely analytic and sterile science of mechanics. And again, even so imperfect a science as biology is not content with the enunciation of a merely general view such as the 'theory of evolution', or the 'theory of natural selection'; it must at once set to work upon a quantitative and statistical implementation of these general theories. And economics, as a science, must make a similar attempt. Such an attempt, moreover, is certainly not impossible, and it presents no greater difficulties than those which other sciences have already overcome. The view that economics, like mechanics, is a purely analytic study cannot be considered an adequate ground for calling it a science. And when we discover that this view is based upon no firmer foundation than the fact that hitherto no significant statistical generalizations have been produced in economics, what little there might appear to be in its favour, disappears. No science, I suppose, less than 200 years old has produced statistical observations of any significance. And when we consider the extraneous interests from which economic science had to free itself, it cannot be a matter for surprise that its conclusions are relatively meagre. Economics is a science, then, not only because it works with quantitative concepts, not only because it has already to some extent generalized the relations between these concepts, but also because it has set out to implement this world of concepts by statistical observation and generalization. There is, perhaps, much in the present condition of so-called Quantitative Economics to be regretted and more to be reformed. But there can be no doubt that a scientific economics will be a quantitative economics, or that such an economics can produce valid generalizations.

But this does not mean that all thought, coming under the general head of economic thought, is scientific in character; nothing indeed is clearer than that economics as a science is hindered by extraneous interests and led astray by false pursuits. But in this respect, also, it is not unique among sciences. If economic science is not yet free from the concepts and requirements of so-called Descriptive Economics, a kind of natural history such as is found in the infancy of every science, the same is true of biology and scientific psychology. Natural history and science are, of course, not inimical to one another; but a science must be more critical of its friends and relations, with whom it may become entangled, than with its enemies from whom it is well and securely enough distinguished. Descriptive economics, because of its connexion with the world of practice, is a dangerous companion for an economic science. And it is, perhaps, on account of this connexion that economic science has not yet learned that it can borrow and carry with it into its own world no element of the world of perception which it has not discovered how to transform, that it has not yet learned that a science must make its own material as well as its own conclusions. And again, economic science is more intimately connected with the attempt to apply its conclusions to the world of practice than is healthy in a young science. Physiology has become a science not on account of its connexion with medicine, but in spite of it. This interest in practical life is not, of course, illegitimate; it is merely dangerous from the standpoint of scientific thought. And when we consider the confusion which this connexion with practice has caused merely in the vocabulary of economics— 'economic conditions', 'economic events', 'economic consequences', 'economic needs'—it is difficult to dismiss the danger as negligible. Setting aside the merely misconceived attempts to apply the generalizations of economic science directly to the practical world, this underlying preoccupation with practical life and practical problems can still be seen to lead economics aside from the path of science. And where applicability to the practical world, the capacity to foretell a situation, is taken to be a criterion of the validity of the generalizations of an economic science, what was merely irrelevant turns to actual error.

## § 7

The misconceptions which surround the character of psychology are numerous. A psychological analysis is believed to be the high-road to unconditional truth, and a psychological explanation is believed to be the last refinement of human intelligence. An historian who is no psychologist stands self-condemned, and a philosophy not founded upon the deliverances of psychology requires no other evidence of its futility. Along with these extravagant claims for psychology has gone, however, a determined attempt to place it among the sciences. And it is not easy to understand how these opinions are to be reconciled. The depth and capacity of scientific knowledge are, no doubt, great; but we have seen reason to think that it falls short of being the whole of knowledge, of constituting the foundation of history and of presenting us with unconditional truth. If psychology is a science, then history is not handicapped or philosophy made futile by being ignorant of its conclusions. These difficulties arise, then, from a general uncertainty, in the minds of those most ready to give us their opinions about the nature of psychology, with regard to the character and scope of scientific experience. And the questions I wish now briefly to consider are, What must be the general character of a *science* of psychology? and, What are the limitations of such a science?

As in the case of economics, the first set of views which must be dealt with are those which either assert that psychology is not and can never become a science, or attribute to psychology a scientific character on false or inadequate grounds. The reasons urged against the possibility of a science of psychology are, in principle, the same as those advanced in the case of economics, and I do not propose to discuss them at length. I shall dismiss at once the notion of psychology as mere 'looking within', mere self-knowledge, a direct transcript of an immediate personal experience. Even if such knowledge were possible, it is neither psychology nor is it science. A direct knowledge of mental states as such could never be scientific, for it denies all that science asserts, pursues all that science flees from; but psychology is not, and never has been and perhaps never could be knowledge of this sort.

Beyond this, there are two important views of the character of psychology which assert that it can be a science in only a restricted sense. It is suggested, first, that psychology cannot be a science in the full sense because it is concerned with mental and not physical phenomena; it deals with processes of mind, not those of matter. And, alternatively, we are told that "it is only the possibility of giving a physical expression to mental states which confers on psychology the rank of a science." This distinction between mental and physical processes (and the consequent division of scientific thought into what is concerned with mind and what is concerned with matter) is, however, misconceived; it is a distinction which has no relevance to the matter in hand. For we have seen already that there is nothing in the character of scientific experience which demands the assumption of a 'physical' world as distinct from a 'mental' world. Science is not the attempt to elucidate the character of the 'physical' or 'external' world; it is the attempt to elucidate the world under the category of quantity, and it is this because it is the pursuit of a world of experience above all else stable and communicable. Consequently, if psychology is to be a science in the full sense what is required is to show that it can be conceived as part of this attempt to see the world under the category of quantity; and what is not required is to show that it is concerned (or can be conceived as concerned) with physical in distinction from mental phenomena. It is a perfunctory definition of psychology which relies upon this perfunctory distinction of 'mind' and 'matter', a distinction which, whatever its meaning, has no meaning in science.

This contention that psychology is not in the full sense scientific because it deals with 'mental' and not 'physical' phenomena, and can become a science only when the merely mental is displaced by the physical, has been made a ground for relating psychology to physiology, and even for reducing psychology to physiology. It is said, for example, that specifically mental phenomena exist, but that they cannot, as such, form the subject-matter of a science: psychology can become a science in the full sense only when these specifically mental events and processes are reduced to their physiological accompaniments. This view, however, rests upon the false notion that science is concerned solely with what is 'physical', and it must be rejected. The mere reduction of mental phenomena to their physiological accompaniments will not, in itself, make a science out of psychology. It will result merely in the abolition of psychology. What a science demands is not a 'physical' world, but a world of quantitative concepts.

There are, however, other views about the relationship of psychology and physiology. It is suggested that psychology may be conceived as beginning with physiology and passing beyond it. Psychological conceptions are gradually introduced to eke out the shortcomings of the mechanical interpretation which belongs to physiology. We begin with mechanism, with physiology, and we end with mind, with psychology. But it will be seen that this view, like the other views, suffers from its reliance upon a distinction between mind and matter which is irrelevant and misconceived, and suffers also from the presupposition that what is 'mental' cannot be conceived mechanically or quantitatively.

Or, again, psychology is taken for a kind of developed and extended physiology; it is the science, not of separate organs and of limited systems of reaction, but of the organism as a whole and of its total reactions. The distinction between psychology and physiology is taken to be a matter of degree, and it is hoped that by allying psychology with physiology, psychology will acquire a scientific character.[1] But this view, also, rests upon the false assumption that psychology must work with physiological conceptions and achieve physiological generalizations if it is to be a science in the full sense.

[1] Watson, *Psychology from the standpoint of a Behaviourist*, p. 19.

It belongs to the futile and misconceived attempt to make psychology respectable scientifically by apprenticing it to one of the already established sciences. But those who no longer believe that science is concerned with a 'physical' world or that in order to make a science of 'mental' processes it is necessary to conceive them in physiological terms, will attach little value to this attempt to establish a precise relationship between psychology and physiology. What is important for us to understand are the conditions of a science of psychology and not merely its relation to some other science. No absolute distinction can be placed between any of the special sciences; we have seen already that in all scientific experience there is a common method and a common subject-matter. And the precise determination of a boundary of this particular kind between psychology and physiology is a matter of no significance.

The views, then, that psychology cannot be a science in the full sense because it is concerned with 'mental' as distinct from 'physical' phenomena; that psychology can be constituted a science by making it a study of the physical accompaniments of mental processes; and that psychology must be seen to be allied to physiology, and its conceptions must be formulated in physiological terms,[1] if it is to be fully scientific, must all be pronounced false. They depend upon an erroneous conception of psychology and a confused notion of the character of scientific experience. All that is necessary to establish psychology as a science is to show that it partakes in the purpose of science—the elucidation of the world under the category of quantity.

But there is a second contention about the character of psychology which, if it could be maintained, would involve the impossibility of a fully scientific psychology. Psychology, it is suggested, is concerned with the "intact organism", "the individual"; it is concerned with the total activities of the individual, and the facts of psychology, it is said, "must be

[1] E.g. when Behaviour is conceived as "the integrated responses of muscles and glands".

regarded as having place in, or as being constituent of, *someone's experience*".[1] Now, if psychology were engaged with describing the experiences and the behaviour of 'personalities', 'individuals' conceived under the categories of practical experience, it certainly could not be a science in any sense: there can be no such thing as a "science of individual behaviour". Knowledge of this kind could amount to no more than a species of natural history, that is, a form of experience the character of which is scientific but which falls short of the realization of that character. *Il n'y a de science que du général.* But there is no reason to suppose that psychology is exclusively engaged with a study of this kind, or that it must be so engaged. Much so-called psychology at the present time is, no doubt, of this kind; and psychology as a whole may be said to have emerged only recently from this condition of natural history. But that this emergence has taken place there can be no doubt at all. It has taken place, it is true, under the auspices of physiology, and psychology is still pathetically dependent upon its nurse. But unless we are to ignore all psychological research save that which comes under the head of psychotherapy and (like medicine) deals with actual, living 'personalities', there are no grounds upon which to base the contention that psychology is altogether without a quantitatively conceived world of concepts and that it knows nothing of any world save this world of 'personalities'. And we must dismiss also this view that psychology is and must remain mere natural history and consequently not in the full sense scientific.

I conclude, then, that psychology is a science in so far as it is concerned, not with so-called 'concrete' experience and the behaviour of living 'personalities' as such, but with the elucidation of the character of a world of quantitative concepts. And how far psychology at present has achieved this condition is not a question which requires to be considered here. But a science of psychology is faced with no difficulties which have not already been encountered and overcome by

[1] Ward, *Psychological Principles*, p. 27.

other and more developed sciences. And what hinder the progress of psychology in the direction of scientific knowledge are merely the scientifically undesirable company it has kept in the past—its connexions with both practice and philosophy—and a false conception of the character of scientific experience.

The task of creating a scientific psychology is one which has been seriously undertaken only in comparatively recent years; and there remains, of course, much that is unscientific in the concepts and methods of the modern science of psychology. What, I suppose, is generally taken to be characteristic of the emancipation of modern psychology is the predilection it has shown for the experimental method, and it is even believed that psychology has become scientific because and in so far as it has become experimental. But it is not difficult to detect here a misunderstanding. For what constitutes and defines science is never its experimental character, but its character as an attempt to elucidate experience in terms of a world of quantitative concepts. Nor, again, has the new experimental psychology the capacity to supersede the old psychology which was concerned exclusively with the analysis of certain psychological concepts. Experiment in scientific experience is neither the first step, nor is it a process of verification. All scientific experiment implies hypothesis, which in turn implies an integrated world of quantitative concepts in terms of which the hypotheses are framed. Consequently an experimental study, so far from superseding or excluding other methods of study, wholly depends upon them. It is neither the first, nor the most important business of a science to conduct experiments or observations of any kind. Its primary business is to be clear that it has provided itself with a world of concepts suitable to its scientific character. For the greater part of its history psychology has been engaged upon the elucidation of a world of concepts by means of the analysis of these concepts, and in this it is not unique among the sciences. Nor is it unique because most of the concepts it has been satisfied with in the past have not been quantitative concepts. Indeed, it is doubtful whether psychology can be said to have achieved a world of scientific concepts in outline, to have set up the main structure of its world to anything like the extent and with anything like the success of, for example, economics. Whatever the value of experimental psychology, there can be no doubt that much remains to be done in the way of determining the structural concepts of a scientific psychology and their inherent relations. And the first business of a science of psychology must be to see that its structural concepts are quantitative. It is not true, however, that this business of creating a scientific psychology has yet to be begun. Sensation and attention, for example, are in the main quantitative concepts; what the science of psychology is concerned with is not mere sensations as such, but with their duration, their relation to one another, their 'threshold', their intensity, and with fatigue. The so-called 'confusion' of sensation intensities with the stimulus-values required to produce them (a confusion of which Fechner is accused) is, in fact, no confusion at all, but the condition of scientific observation; it arises from the scientific attempt to conceive sensation quantitatively. Stimuli and reactions are measurable; sensations as such are not, and consequently lie outside the cognizance of a scientific psychology. On the other hand, it cannot be said that such concepts as 'imagination', 'memory' or 'consciousness' are conceived quantitatively in modern psychology, and until they are so conceived or until they have been abandoned as concepts unsuitable for a science, psychology must remain imperfectly scientific.

From its outline world of quantitative concepts, a scientific psychology will proceed to hypothesis, observation, experiment, and the formulation of statistical generalizations. And here also it cannot be said that a beginning has not been made. There are, no doubt, difficulties to be overcome, and it would be foolish to expect from an infant science statistical generalizations of any great significance. But what should be observed is that here also this science is faced by no difficulties which have not been overcome by other sciences, and that in so far as it is a science, its subject-matter is a world of quantitative concepts and measurements, and not a world of 'mental phenomena'. And where psychology is a science, its conclusions will have the same character, significance and validity as the conclusions of any other science. A science of psychology will have the limitations (from the standpoint of the totality of experience) common to all scientific experience, and it will have no limitations peculiar to itself.

The relation of the world of psychology (when it is conceived as a science) to other worlds of abstract experience, and to the concrete world of experience will, of course, be that which belongs to any world of scientific experience. Nevertheless, it is a common view that psychology should issue, in the end, in a kind of synthetic knowledge of human personality, that it should pass from the world of science to the world of practical life and give us a *Menschenkenntniss* which will enable us to understand both ourselves and others. This notion, however, that a science of psychology completes itself by applying its generalizations to the practical world and to actual human character is self-contradictory. It involves a denial of all that scientific experience asserts. In so far as psychology is a science, it has nothing to offer us in the way of a knowledge of human life. The psychologist is not one who "understands human nature"; the world of quantitative abstractions in which he moves is a world without any direct relation to practical life, and the generalizations of psychology do not and cannot refer to human personalities as such, or to the practical world. Psychology in becoming scientific ceases to be practical.

With history, also, the case is the same. It is not psychology which is of assistance to the historian, but a knowledge of human character, a little natural sagacity. History is concerned with abstractions, but never with the abstractions of science. And the view that "the chief instrument for the study of past history is a knowledge of psychology" implies a total denial of the scientific character of psychology or a misconception of the difference between the world of history and that of science. The presuppositions, the categories, the concepts, the method and the matter in psychology are not those of history; the world of history is not that of psychology; and any argument or inference which attempts to pass from one of these worlds to the other is at once convicted of irrelevance.

Of the relation of the world of psychology as such and the world of concrete experience little requires to be said. If psychology is a science, its world of scientific abstraction is without relevance to the world of experience unhindered by presupposition or arrest. Psychology, at one time, seemed to be closely linked to philosophy; to a large extent they shared the same concepts and seemed engaged upon the elucidation of the same problems. But this condition of things, needless to say, could not be maintained when psychology showed signs of constituting itself a science. For the world of scientific experience, as a world, has no contribution whatever to make to the absolute world of ideas satisfactory in experience; and psychology cannot be supposed to be more nearly related to philosophy than any other science. From the standpoint of the totality of experience, a science of psychology is a mere arrest; it is a mode of experience which falls short of the full character of experience. And to pass in argument from the world of psychology to that of philosophy, or *vice versa*, or to subordinate either world to the other, cannot fail to involve us on every occasion in *ignoratio elenchi*.

There remains, however, to notice one further question. In my view there can be no doubt as to the status of the world of experience of a scientific psychology and of its relationship to other worlds of experience. And there can be little doubt that such a scientific psychology to some extent already exists and is in the course of development. But in what sense this science can properly be called psychology, and whether psychology must be scientific or nothing at all, are questions I have not so far considered. But since to consider them in detail lies to one side of what I have undertaken, I will remark only that, in my opinion, a science of psychology does not exhaust the conception of psychology and is perhaps even a contradiction in terms. A psychology which is not scientific certainly exists, and certainly would not be superseded by a science of psychology, however fully developed that science might become. Nevertheless, such a psychology would fall short of constituting a world of ideas satisfactory in experience. It would be a pseudo-philosophical form of experience—a form which I shall discuss in a later chapter.

§ 8

The conclusions of this chapter which I take to be important are, briefly, (i) that scientific experience is a single, specific mode of experience, distinguished by a single method and a single subject-matter, and the world of scientific ideas is a single, homogeneous (but fortuitously divided) whole: (ii) that scientific experience is defective experience, it is a mode of experience which falls short of the totality of experience, and scientific knowledge is abstract, conditional, incomplete, self-contained but not self-sufficient: and (iii) that the characteristic of this modification of experience, in virtue of which it must be considered incomplete, is its attempt coherently to conceive the world, under the category of quantity; the explicit purpose in science is the elucidation of a world of absolutely communicable experience. The second and third (the more important) of these conclusions I have considered already in detail, but on the first I wish now to make a few observations.

My purpose, I have said, was to exhibit all sciences as one science and to discover its character, and I ought to give my reasons for supposing that the character of scientific experience is to be found in its unity rather than in its diversity. For, to the casual observer, nothing could be clearer than the distinction between physics and biology, between chemistry and economics. Briefly, I take the unity of scientific experience to be more significant than its diversity because I take it to be logical, while the diversity of science appears to me merely a misconception due to the historical circumstances of the growth of the scientific interest and to the intrusion of an interest extraneous to that of science.

The view is commonly held that the unity and the diversity of scientific experience are of the same character and of equal significance. Science is believed to consist of a number of attempts to discover 'nature', each attempt being directed towards the elucidation of the character of some particular department of nature. These are the special sciences. And while they are believed somehow to 'interlock', it is never supposed that their independence can legitimately be broken down. Unity and diversity are alike taken to be logical characteristics of scientific experience. There is, indeed, something called the 'scientific method' which, in a general way, is believed to be the common property of all the special sciences; but it is believed also that these sciences are effectively and permanently distinguished from one another on account of a difference of subject-matter.

Now, this view, it will readily be seen, conflicts at every point with the view I have undertaken to defend. Scientific experience I have taken to be a world of absolutely communicable experience, science is the attempt to conceive the world under the category of quantity; and beside this unifying principle the divisions in scientific experience must sink into insignificance. And, from my standpoint, these divisions are the product of historical circumstance and of the intrusion of an extraneous, non-scientific interest. Historically, this attempt to conceive the world under the category of quantity has appeared to be an attempt to discover the 'facts of nature'. But if (as might well have been the case) science had, from the beginning, been conscious of its character as the pursuit of a homogeneous world of quantitative experience, instead of the attempt to elucidate separate worlds of 'facts' about 'matter', 'life', 'sensations', etc., there would have been no opportunity for the exclusive development of the special sciences. These separate sciences might still have existed, but the apparent difference of subject-matter would not have been mistaken for the principle of separation. And, from the other point of view, the differences between the special sciences may be seen as the result of the intrusion of a practical interest into the world of scientific experience. The special sciences have been created by connecting this scientific attempt to conceive the world under the category of quantity with different classes of phenomena which have been determined, not scientifically, but by our ordinary, practical experience. Thus, biology is scientific experience connected with a class of phenomena, not conceived under the only category relevant to science (that of quantity), but under the practical category of 'life'. And the connexion is, consequently, of minor importance when we are considering scientific experience as such. The more firmly the explicit purpose in scientific experience is grasped, the less significant will these differences appear. My view is, then, that science, like every other form of experience, must create its own subject-matter, determine its own internal divisions; and that the present separation of the special sciences is the result, not of scientific determination, but of an unwarranted inter-ference on the part of practical experience in the world of scientific ideas.

Nevertheless, this view should not be taken to imply that the present division of the sciences is meaningless, or that it may not in the future be extended. An undisciplined in-crease in the number of special sciences is, perhaps, evidence of febrile activity rather than of real advance in scientific experience; but there is nothing to prevent, and much to encourage it. But when we turn to the actual development of the scientific interest itself, we discover how small has been the influence of this division upon its destiny. Sciences, distinguished in this non-scientific way, are continually coming into being and suffering transformation and super-session. These sciences die natural deaths. Interest wanes, a particular set of quantitative concepts proves fruitful and attracts attention, a more stable method of measurement is, perhaps, discovered, and hitherto separate sciences are drawn together and coalesce. And whenever this practical division of the sciences is met by the force and pressure of the unitary purpose in scientific experience, it is incapable of defending itself successfully. On the other hand, the day when it will be no longer permissible to make any distinction between (for example) the 'physical' and the 'social' sciences is, no doubt, distant, and on the view I have suggested it is not necessary that it should ever arrive. The notion that the true path of development calls for the immediate reduction of sociology to physics is, of course, absurd. The logical unity of science does not depend upon the achievement of formal uniformity among the sciences; it is there already, the life and inspiration of every science. And the diversity of the sciences, due to the circumstances of their growth, due to our ignorance and to the convenience of having some perfunctory and not too ambiguous method of farming out this attempt to conceive the world under the category of quantity, is dangerous only when its character is mistaken.

Finally, I must disclaim any intention to dictate the course or mode of advance in scientific knowledge: to do so would be an absurd pretension on my part. What I have offered is neither a history of science, nor a classification of the departments of science, nor an opinion about the future of science, but a view of scientific experience and the world of scientific ideas from the standpoint of the totality of experience, from the standpoint of what in experience would afford complete satisfaction.

# V

## PRACTICAL EXPERIENCE

### § 1

The worlds of history and of science, in spite of the testimonials to the completeness and perfection of their character with which they come before us, have turned out on examination to be abstract and defective. They are modes of experience which fall short of the totality of experience. And it is time now to consider the character of a world of ideas, different from these, which to many who have considered the matter has appeared to offer what these have failed to provide,—I mean the world of practical experience.

Writers are not wanting who conceive the totality of experience in terms either of history or of science; but those who thrust forward practice as the criterion of experience have at least the satisfaction of finding themselves in a majority. Indeed, when we consider the force of the temptation to reduce all experience to practical experience, to find in practical experience not merely the criterion of historical and scientific truth, but the criterion of all truth, it is not the prevalence of this belief which should surprise us, but the fact that it is not universal. This form of experience is (we may suppose) at once the most primitive and most general of all forms. And it is difficult to avoid the presumption that, if we embrace it, it will prove to be the world of concrete reality itself. The reduction of the whole of experience either to scientific experience or to historical experience has found general consent only upon rare occasions and in peculiar circumstances. But anyone who, at any time, comes forward with the suggestion that the world of practical experience is itself what is absolutely and finally satisfactory in experience; that it belongs to the character of thought to be for the sake of action, is assured in advance of the concurrence of the majority of mankind. Indeed, it is a common opinion that both history and science are modes of experience merely auxiliary to practice; they have been understood and explained as departments of the world of practical experience. History, we have seen, has been, and still is, almost wholly obscured by the confusion which exists with regard to its relationship with practical experience; and the emancipation of science from the despotism of practice is both slow and uncertain. And it is not to be expected that a form of experience which can so easily subdue and enslave such extensive and dissimilar worlds of ideas, will not find advocates to urge its claim to the sovereignty of the entire realm of experience. Our very instincts appear to concede to this world of practical ideas the presumption that here, until some ingenious philosopher shall prove the contrary, lies the world of concrete reality. For the practical world is the most familiar of all our worlds of experience, the practical attitude our most constant mood. Unless we make some conscious effort to step outside, it is within this world that we pass our lives. Unless we are persuaded to the contrary, this world is the world to which we submit all experience. Nor can it be denied that this practical attitude is, in fact, a powerful solvent of many of the puzzles and sophistications of both science and history. It cannot, then, be a matter for surprise that such a form of experience should appear, not as a determinate and limited mode of experience, but rather as what is absolute and satisfactory in experience.

Nevertheless, the character of this world of practical ideas must suffer examination: a reputation is valueless where the power to maintain it is lacking. And I propose in this chapter to consider the character of practical experience from the standpoint of the totality of experience. I wish to enquire into the validity of practical experience as a form of experience, and to discover what truth, if any, there is in the contention that, where history and science have failed, practice can succeed.

The difficulties which surround an attempt of this kind are, of course, great. They are, I believe, greater than those encountered in the case of history and science. For, whereas the difficulties there were comprised mainly of the prejudices and preconceptions of the historian and the scientist as such, who find it troublesome to conceive their worlds except in terms of the abstractions of those modes of experience, the difficulties here lie in the prejudices and preconceptions of the larger part of mankind, who find it impossible to entertain the idea that this practical world, within which they are confined as if in a prison, is other than the universe itself. We shall, then, expect that the practical man's view of the world of practical experience will be different from the view I am proposing to develop in this chapter. And we ought not to allow this discrepancy to alarm us. Indeed any serious attempt to consider the character of the world of practical experience from the standpoint of the totality of experience must collide with the practical man's view. What may be called a philosophy of practical experience cannot expect to have anything whatever in common with a so-called practical philosophy. This, at least, is the view which appears to follow from what I have already committed myself to, and it is the conclusion I wish to recommend.

The view of the character of practical experience which I wish, in this chapter, to maintain may be conveniently formulated in four propositions. I intend to show, first, that practical activity is a form of experience and that the world of practice is a world of ideas: secondly, that (when the detailed character of this world of ideas is considered) it will be found to be abstract and defective from the standpoint of the totality of experience: thirdly, that (consequently) it is without any direct relationship with other abstract worlds of experience, such as those of science and of history: and fourthly, that, from the standpoint of the totality of experience it must be rejected. And since each of these pro-positions has been denied, on more occasions than one, it is not to be expected that in considering them I shall be able altogether to avoid controversy.

§ 2

The notion I am to defend—that practical activity is a defective mode of experience, an abstract world of ideas—implies, of course, the wider view that practice is a world of experience, and that the difference between it and other worlds of experience lies not in what is attempted in it but in what is explicitly achieved; lies not in its implicit character, but in its explicit assertions. And the most elementary objection which this notion has to meet will be a general denial of its truth in the form of a denial of this implication. Practical activity, it will be said, is not itself a form of experience; it lies outside the region of experience: the world of practice is not a world of ideas. It is true that, could this view be substantiated, it would afford a short and easy way of disposing of some of our difficulties. If practical activity be a tissue of mere conjunctions and consequently situate outside experience, it can have neither truth nor reality, and would not require even to be considered if what we are looking for is a coherent world of experience. Nevertheless, it is, I believe, a false view. And our first business must be to consider the reasons which make it untenable and compel us to accept practical activity as a form of experience.

That the world of science is a world of experience is a notion upon which we found no considerable body of disagreement. Those only were found to deny it who had failed to understand it. What was contentious was the character and degree of the modification which scientific experience introduces into experience. In this respect the case of history was different. We had there to consider not only the belief that the world of history is itself the world of concrete experience, but also the contrary contention that history (so far from being a world of experience) is a world of 'pure facts'; and further, that history (so far from being a world) is a tissue of mere conjunctions and more often falsified by an excess than by a defect of thought. And when we turn to practical experience, these objections are pressed upon us with even greater insistence. We are offered the view that practical activity is not a world of ideas; and together with this, the view that it is not a world.

Practice, it will be said, is activity and not thought; and the world of practice is a world of actions, not of ideas. Indeed, 'practical thinking' is a contradiction; what is practical is (for that reason) not thought. This view, however, is one we have already met with, and having disposed at some length of the principle upon which it rests, it is unnecessary to reconsider it in detail here. Since there is nothing whatever which is not experience, and since there can be no experience which does not involve thought or judgment, practical life cannot be supposed to be other than a world of experience. 'What happens' in practical life is not the material of thought, it belongs itself to the world of thought; 'action' is not the product of thought, it is itself a form of thought. An 'external' or an 'objective' world of doings and happenings which is not a world of ideas, is a mere fiction. Events and actions, if they are to fall inside the world of experience, must conform to the character of that world; and to remain outside is an acknowledgment of nonentity. The view, then, that practice is not thought because it is action, and that the practical world is not a world of ideas because it is a world of actions and events, cannot be entertained in conjunction with the view of experience and of reality which I have recommended.

And further, it is impossible to accept the view that practical life, because it is concerned with volitions, is therefore not a world of thought. For such a view is meaningless unless we are to believe that the will is a faculty independent of the intellect, and that volition is experience, yet not judgment; and there is nothing to encourage us in these beliefs. We have seen already that, whatever its defects as experience, volition nevertheless is a form of experience; and because it is experience it must be judged as an assertion of the real world. Volition is itself thought and not the mere result of thought. In so far then as experience in practical life is volition, practice is itself a form of experience, a world of ideas.

There is, however, the other and more weighty contention to be considered. Among those who do not deny that practical life is experience, there will be found some who contend that, nevertheless, it is not a *world* of experience, but a tissue of mere conjunctions. They assert that practical activity is, perhaps, a collection of ideas, but because it falls short of the condition of a world, it falls short of the condition of knowledge. Practical activity, for them, is defective from the standpoint of the totality of experience, not because it is an abstract world of ideas, but because it is not a world at all. Where others discover a world (and therefore, knowledge), they find only instinct, intuition, or mere opinion. And it is clear enough that, were this view to be established, practical activity could scarcely maintain itself as experience.

The more elementary difficulties involved in the notion of a collection of ideas which neither is, nor can be transformed into, a world of knowledge, I have considered already, and they need not delay us here. I have discussed the notion of intuition as a separate and determinate kind of experience, and have found it wanting. Intuition cannot, in any connexion, sustain the character of a form of experience independent of judgment, a mere collection of ideas not subject to the criterion of coherence and consequently incapable of becoming a world of knowledge. Nevertheless, it is a common opinion that practical experience is a collection of intuitions incapable of being transformed into a world of knowledge. 'Practical knowledge' is not the conclusion of reason, but of intuition, not of reflection but of instinct. Some writers (such as Hume) have used these and similar expressions to indicate the disparity between practical experience and philosophy and not to assert the impossibility of practical knowledge, and with these we are not concerned. Our business is with those who contend that practical activity is a collection of immediate intuitions in the sense that it is not, and cannot become a world of knowledge. The position, as I understand it, is this. Many of our practical experiences, it is asserted, are immediate intuitions, easily distinguished from what we take to be knowledge. They are instinctive, random, irrational and beyond control. "The rules of morality are not the conclusions of our reason"; and it is not reflexion, but intuition which tells us what in particular is right and wrong. We feel distrust independently of any knowledge of dishonesty; we do not suppose a man to be dishonest merely because we distrust him; and a knowledge of innocence often will not allay our suspicion. It must, however, be observed that these feelings and intuitions are not radically immediate; for what is radically immediate must fall outside experience altogether. They are not completely isolated and wholly groundless; they belong to a world the principle of which is one of coherence; and, so far as it goes, it cannot avoid the character of a world of knowledge. These intuitions, which certainly constitute a large part of our practical experience, are equally certainly not immediate in the sense of belonging to no world; and wherever there is a world of experience, it is not merely capable of integration, but is actually integrated and calls out for further integration. Nor are these feelings, properly speaking, irrational—feelings in the sense of being other than judgments. To suppose a wholly irrational element in practical experience is to suppose a mode of experience which not merely falls short of, but which explicitly contradicts, the character of experience. And whatever defects this 'irrational' world of intuitions may suffer from, they are defects which belong to a world of experience capable of becoming a world of knowledge. In short, a collection of mere intuitions ignorant of the criterion of experience is a contradiction, and practical experience is not a collection of intuitions of this kind.

But there remains a yet more formidable contention. It is believed that practical activity is not a world of knowledge because it is a mere collection of opinions. The view is that there is nothing in practical experience beyond a multiplicity of separate opinions, into which no sort of unity or principle can be introduced. Some people think one thing, and some another; some desire one thing, and some another. Moral judgments, for example, are personal or social estimates of value, and as such never rise above the condition of mere opinion into a world of knowledge. Nothing, it is said, is more frequent than a difference of opinion on these questions of moral value: what one judges to be good, another considers bad; what one believes to be right, another thinks wrong; what one holds to be admirable, another finds despicable. The most elementary lesson of life is the necessity of recognizing these irreducible differences; a life passed in an attempt to reconcile them would indeed be febrile and fruitless. And what is true of moral judgments is true, no less, of all practical judgments whatever; they belong to no world and recognize no criterion of coherence. This view, however, in its extreme form, is open to a fatal objection. If anything were a matter of *mere* opinion there could be no difference of opinion. It belongs to the character of a mere opinion that it can never be contradicted: in the region of mere opinions, what one asserts the other never denies. Yet not only does this view of practical experience assert the possibility of a difference of opinion, but it is obliged to assert it. A 'mere opinion', in this sense, must fall outside possible experience. Everywhere there is the possibility of contradictory opinions, and where these are possible we have left behind a collection of mere opinions and have, at least, entered a world of opinions. Now, it is not denied that much of our practical experience borders upon the condition of mere opinion. Nowhere is the criterion of judgment more negligently applied than in practical experience, nowhere else does the full character of judgment more frequently remain unrealized. But to pass from this, to the position that in practical experience no such criterion exists or is recognized, is to take a step which even the most foolish will quickly regret. A collection of mere opinions certainly falls short of a *world* of experience, but it falls short, also, of experience, for everywhere in opinion there is implicit assertion, reference to reality.

Nevertheless, it will be suggested, the defects of this view may be repaired without requiring us to assent to the proposition that practical experience is a world of knowledge. For, it will be said, practical experience is not a collection of mere opinions, but a collection of true and false opinions; and its final condition is not a determinate world of knowledge, but a collection of true opinions. Now, if the distinction of true and false be admitted into this collection of opinions, it is certainly impossible for it to remain a mere collection; indeed, it becomes at once a world, an organized system. Nevertheless, the view that practical experience is, at most, a world of true opinion, is not without its difficulties. It implies an absolute distinction between knowledge and true opinion, and this, I think, is impossible to maintain. Opinion is not the negation of knowledge, it is merely unorganized, immature knowledge. True opinion differs from knowledge, not absolutely, but in degree. And wherever there is true opinion there can be knowledge; for a world of true opinions is merely an imperfectly integrated world of ideas in which the principle of knowledge, inherent in every world of ideas, remains implicit. And if it be the case, as will doubtless be suggested, that the world of practical experience never, as a matter of fact, realizes itself as a world of knowledge, we must not mistake this incidental defect for an absolute or characteristic deficiency. Practical experience shares this failure to realize its full character with every other actual world of experience whatever. It is a world of knowledge, not in spite of, but because of the fact that it is often only a world of true opinions.

I conclude, then, that practical life cannot be supposed to be other than a world of experience. And further, this world of practical experience is a world of knowledge, and its character and criterion are those common to all worlds of knowledge; the principle of this world, as of every other, is one of coherence. The world of practical experience is a world of judgments, not of mere actions, volitions, feelings, intuitions, instincts or opinions. Practical truth is the coherence of this world of practical experience. And practical activity, because it is a world of experience, must be content to be judged from the standpoint of the totality of experience.

§ 3

The general character of practical activity (we have found) compels us to accept it as a world of experience, and to accept the world of practice as a determinate world of knowledge. Practical life (whatever it achieves or fails to achieve) is an attempt to make coherent our world of experience as a whole. Our business now is with the particular character of practical experience which distinguishes it from other worlds of experience. Our business is no longer with the implicit character of practice as experience; but with its explicit character as a determinate degree of experience. And I propose to offer a view of practice which, in spite of its defects, has, I believe, something to be said in its favour. To present it fully will require some space, but here (as elsewhere) what I am attempting is to establish a point of view rather than the detailed exposition of a system.

We may say, in the first place, that what distinguishes practical activity from all other worlds of experience is that in it the alteration of existence is undertaken. Practical life comprises the attempts we make to alter existence or to maintain it unaltered in the face of threatened change. It is both the production and the prevention of change, and in either case it is not merely a programme for action, but action itself. Our practical world is the totality of such actions, together with all that they imply. Practice comprises everything which belongs to the conduct of life as such.

Now, it must be admitted that this view of practice carries us beyond what is ordinarily considered to be practical; but that should not, I think, disconcert us. A man who, as Rousseau says, makes love "la grande affaire de sa vie", a poet, a religious mystic or an evangelist are not commonly considered 'practical' persons, and yet their lives are certainly active and consist wholly in attempts to change or maintain existence. And it appears impossible to confine practice to what is, in the vulgar sense, practical. For what is in this sense practical is no more than a particular kind of practice, which has achieved the monopoly of the name merely on account of the restricted tastes and defective genius of the majority of mankind. He who determines to do away with his life is no less conducting his life than the man who spends it in satisfying his ambitions: and the man who seeks satisfaction in imagination or devotion to God requires to be no less active than he who looks for it in conquest or an empire. Indeed, we cannot deny the name of practice to the life of one who, following some creed of quietism, passes his unproductive existence in contempt of all that the world holds active and practical, for here also is involved the change or maintenance of existence. Practice is activity, the activity inseparable from the conduct of life and from the necessity of which no living man can relieve himself.

But further, it may be observed, practice everywhere implies and depends upon an unrealized idea, a 'to be' which is 'not yet'. For activity involves a discrepancy between 'what is' and what we desire shall be; and practice is activity. And this is true not only when practice takes the form of explicit change, but also when it appears to be confined to the maintenance of 'what is'; because, in fact, practice is strictly never so confined. Such maintenance is undertaken always and only in the face of threatened or proposed change, and this threat or proposal belongs no less to the situation, to 'what is', than the existence which it is desired to maintain. To maintain is always to change. There is here, as everywhere in practical activity, an unrealized idea, an unfulfilled desire, a 'to be' discrepant from 'what is'. And always in practical activity this discrepancy is felt and essential. Action, then, implies change, and involves a world in which change is both possible and significant, a mortal world.

This view of the character of practice may, perhaps, be presented in another form and from a different standpoint. In experience there is always the pursuit of a coherent world of ideas. But in practical experience what is distinctive is not the end pursued, but the means followed to achieve this end. In practice a coherent world of experience is achieved by means of action, by the introduction of actual change into existence. And the aspect of mind involved is the will. Practice is the exercise of the will; practical thought is volition; practical experience is the world *sub specie voluntatis*.

The elementary misconceptions of the character of volition which might stand in the way of our accepting the view that practice is experience and, at the same time, the world *sub specie voluntatis*, need not at this stage be reconsidered. Volition implies neither mere caprice, nor the exercise of an isolated faculty; it is a form of experience. And, in virtue of this character, it must be accepted as involving an assertion of the real world. But beyond this, there are to be found among those who maintain the view we are considering, or any view which brings together practice and volition, some who assert that, since the will is concerned in all judgments whatsoever, it follows that all judgments are practical. It is contended that by associating practice and volition we destroy practical experience as a determinate form of experience. All experience, it is said, presupposes and involves volition and therefore all experience is practical. But it will be readily observed that this line of argument is preposterous. To conclude that what is common to all judgments, for that reason, constitutes the *differentia* of judgment, or to argue that what is always present is, for that reason, constitutive, involves us in some gross, if elementary, fallacies. Because volition is the *differentia* of practical judgment, and is present in all judgment, it does not follow that it is the *differentia* of all judgment. Whether or not it is true that volition is the *differentia* of practical experience, it is certainly false to conclude, from the assertion that it is, that it also is the *differentia* of all experience, and that consequently all experience is practical.[1]

The other important misconception of what is implied in the view of practice as the exercise of the will is the notion that practice, because it is the exercise of the will, involves an external or finite world. The realization of the idea in volition is believed to consist in its being translated from a world of mere ideas into an external world of things. To 'put into practice' is to transform an idea into an action. But, whether or not this is what we feel ourselves to be accomplishing in volition, it is certainly not what actually takes place. For this world of mere ideas and this purely external world of 'things' are alike fictions. A purely external world of this kind is no less embarrassing and no more necessary in practice than we have found it to be in science. What volition requires and presupposes is a world in which change is possible and significant, a finite world in *this* sense, and not in the sense of a world which is not a world of ideas. And any view of volition and action which depends upon the assumption of a purely external world must end by regarding action itself as something other than experience, and must (for that reason) be dismissed. Volition and action are experience; and in experience there is never the realization of a mere idea in an external world, but always the coordination and completion of a given world of ideas.

I suggest, then (as others have suggested before me), that the *differentia* of practice is the alteration of existence; and that this implies a felt discrepancy between 'what is' and what we desire shall be, it implies the idea of a 'to be' which is 'not yet'. And practical experience is, in this sense, the world *sub specie voluntatis*. Yet, even allowing for its mere

[1] A more elaborate refutation of this fallacy will be found in Bradley, *Logic*, ch. i, § 15.

generality, this cannot, I think, be maintained as an entirely satisfactory account of the character of practice. And what in particular it lacks is a precise view of the presuppositions involved. Practice as activity presupposes, it appears, two worlds which are somehow to be reduced to one. It presupposes a present world, which I have hitherto spoken of as 'what is' or 'existence'; and beside this, another world, so far represented as a mere 'to be' or 'not yet'. The detailed character of these presupposed worlds of ideas must engage our attention in a moment, but first it is important for us to understand that they *are* presupposed and that practice depends upon them.

Practice is action, the alteration of existence. But what is to be altered, and what is the character of the alteration? In practice there is never the assertion of a reality merely discrepant from an existing world of ideas; there is always the attempt to make coherent a given world of ideas. To think of it as a system of judgments about what merely does not exist in the present world is to deprive it at once of its character as experience and as activity. Volition and action move always within a given world of ideas; and this given world of 'what is', no less than the will to rearrange it, belongs to, and qualifies the character of practice. Practice, that is, implies a world of ideas not itself directly qualified by action, but which—quite apart from a will to change or maintain it—is a world of practical ideas. And further, when action (so far as it can) has achieved its end, has created a world of facts in agreement with its idea, that end does not cease to be practical; it is the world of practical experience. Practice implies the notion of a 'to be' discrepant from 'what is', but never from the whole of 'what is': the 'to be' is always of the same general character as 'what is'. Whatever can be transformed by action, for that reason, falls within the world of practice; and whatever cannot be transformed by action, for that reason, lies beyond practice. In short, the *differentia* of practice is not simply the alteration of existence, but the alteration of *practical* existence, or (more comprehensively) the realization of the practical self. Wherever there is action there is presupposed a world which action may modify, but which it can never wholly and in principle transform. And the alteration in practice is the attempt to make coherent this given world of practical ideas.

But besides this world of 'what is', practical experience presupposes a world that is 'to be'. And it is important to observe how the character of this world which is 'to be' qualifies the character of the action which is distinctive of practice. Practice, because in it there is a movement towards what is coherent, is never mere activity; and this world that is 'to be' is never merely 'not yet'. Change is never merely for the sake of alteration; nor is maintenance merely for the sake of preservation as such. The 'to be' of practice is never a world merely discrepant from 'what is'; it is always and everywhere considered, not merely a 'not yet' or a 'not here', but, in some sense, more coherent than 'what is'. And since, in practice, coherence is conceived in terms of value, the 'to be' of practical experience is not merely that which is 'to be', but also that which it is believed is valuable or 'ought to be'. This, indeed, is implied in the view of practice as the satisfaction of the will, when that view is freed from the misconceptions which commonly surround it. For volition lies always within a system and is the attempt to make that system more systematic. What we will is always a world, perhaps a self; and the criterion of volition lies not in the mere fact of willing, but in the coherence of the world that we will. And this coherence is conceived in terms of value. This presupposed world of 'to be' (which we have hitherto seen merely as discrepant from 'what is') is, then, a world of value; and severed from the presupposition of a world of value there is no practical experience. The world of value is not itself the world of practical experience, and when valuation enters practice it has always passed beyond mere valuation. Nevertheless, the practical world and practical judgment, separated from the world of value and valuation, become a world of mere activity and a vicious abstraction.

§ 4

We have seen generally that practice is the alteration of practical existence so as to agree with an idea of what ought to be, it is the world *sub specie voluntatis*; and our business now is to determine more precisely the character and content of 'practical existence', this world of ideas presupposed in activity.

It will be remembered that in considering the nature of scientific and historical experience we discovered that each was a mode of experience in which a world, or an existence of a certain character was presupposed. Each, we found, was confined within a world of conceptions which was neither criticised nor modified. And in practical experience also a world, or existence of a certain character is presupposed. It would, of course, be a mistake to think of this presupposed world as itself independent of and entirely unqualified by practical activity. Practical activity and its world of presuppositions (like science and its world of presuppositions) are inseparable; they constitute a single world of ideas. And in examining the presuppositions by themselves we are considering merely a certain aspect of the world of practical experience; we are considering, in fact, the general principle of that world, a principle which remains wholly unchanged. Practice is the transformation of a given world of ideas; but the principle of this world, which distinguishes it and in virtue of which it is the world of *practical* ideas, remains always unchanged. And in discussing the world of practical experience from this standpoint I intend to confine my attention to the explicit conceptions of fact, of truth and of reality which belong to it, conceptions which, of course, cannot be kept separate.

(i) Practical activity presumes a world of practical facts, an existence to be changed. And what, I take it, distinguishes practical fact and severs it from all other fact is its instability. The world of practical fact is the world of 'what is now', as such. And consequently, what is a practical fact to-day, may to-morrow be no fact at all. All fact, of course, is present; we have seen already that a past or a future fact is a nonentity. But practical fact, beside being present, consists in what is present as such. And hence arises its instability. Scientific and historical experience presuppose a world of fact which does not change or move; practical activity assumes a world of facts which is not merely susceptible of alteration, but which has change and instability as the very principle of its existence. And severed from this assumption, there could be no practical activity. The world of fact in practice is the world of 'what is' at this moment; it is the present as such. What cannot change cannot, for practice, be a fact. In both scientific and historical experience to deprive something of its factual character is to assert that it never was a fact; in practical experience a fact of yesterday may lose its place in the world of 'what is now' of to-day without at the same time surrendering its factual character. Science assumes a world of stable, unchanging, quantitative fact; history assumes a world of unchanging past fact; practice assumes a world of mutable, transient fact.

Nevertheless, practical fact conforms to the general character of fact. It is both given and made, a datum and a conclusion. It belongs always to a world, and maintains its factual character, not merely because it is a conclusion, much less because it is a datum, but because it is required to make that world coherent. What is fact in practical experience is, in the end, the world of practical experience as a coherent whole.

(ii) It will readily be understood that in my view practical truth can be nothing else than the coherence of the world of practical ideas. And the only view in opposition to this which need be considered is that which suggests that the criterion of the truth of a practical idea lies in the consequences or results which follow from it. Nothing more is required to establish its practical truth than that it should be shown to be followed by consequences of a particular kind; or, if an idea can be shown to 'work' in the practical world, its practical truth has thereby been established. And in examining this view it will be convenient to consider separately the notion that the criterion of the practical truth or falsehood of an idea lies in the results or consequences which follow from it, and the notion that the consequences in virtue of which an idea can be shown to be practically true are comprised in the 'workableness' of the idea in the practical world.

Now, the view that the truth or falsehood of an idea lies in the consequences which follow from it has frequently been held, not merely in respect of practical truth, but of all truth. And those who have undertaken to defend it as a general view of the character of truth have chosen the name of Pragmatists. But in this wider aspect it does not concern us here. At present we are considering neither the view that the universal criterion of the truth of an idea lies in its consequences, nor the view that the universal criterion of all ideas lies in their practical consequences, but the view that the criterion of the practical truth of practical ideas lies in their practical consequences. A view of this kind is, I think, closely associated with Utilitarianism, and its general character is well known. And for this reason (and because it is impossible for me to consider it in all its forms) I propose to pass over the defects peculiar to each of the various elaborations of this view, and examine only those general defects which appear to me to belong to it in whatever form it is held. The view is, briefly, that the criterion of the truth or falsehood of a practical idea lies not in the self-evidence of the idea itself, nor in any intuitive certainty or doubt we may have concerning it, nor (again) in the fact that it is required to make the world of practical ideas as a whole coherent, but in the results which actually follow, or which may follow from it. And this truth or falsehood can be established only by investigating the situation which follows from the adoption or rejection of the idea. Thus, truth and falsehood are sought always and literally ahead, in the consequences which follow the idea as distinguished from the idea itself, and never behind, in the idea itself, in the circumstances of its generation, or in its situation in the present world of practical experience. Truth, falsehood and the future are thrown together, and it is only by ascertaining what is literally consequent, in the practical world, upon an idea that we are able to determine its truth.

It may be said at once that, since the only truth relevant to practical ideas is their practical truth, if the truth (or falsehood) of a practical idea lie in the consequences which follow from it, then these consequences are certainly and always practical consequences. A practical idea can have effect only in the practical world, and the practical world can be qualified and changed only by specifically practical ideas. It is true that, for example, scientific ideas sometimes appear to have practical consequences, but there is never any difficulty in showing that this appearance is an illusion. A scientific idea must be transformed, taken out of the world of scientific experience, before it can establish itself in the world of practice, just as a practical idea must be radically transformed before it can become relevant in scientific experience. The only consequences, then, which are relevant to practical ideas are practical consequences. But, beyond this, we have to enquire what is implied in the notion that these consequences are the criterion of practical truth. And I may say at once that I can discover no alternative to the conclusion that this notion contradicts simultaneously the character of experience and the character of truth. For in so far as the criterion of truth and falsehood is sought in the consequences of an idea, the conception of experience as a world of ideas and the conception of truth as the coherence of a world of ideas have been implicitly rejected. Truth is sought in what is 'other' than what is given, and not in what is a whole. Thinking has become the construction of a chain or series of ideas; and truth, not merely difficult of attainment, but inherently unattainable. And both these views I believe to be radically perverted. In experience there is never the construction of a mere series of ideas, but the elucidation of a world of ideas; and truth which is unattainable is a contradiction, a romantic fantasy, and no truth at all. Whether the criterion of the truth of practical ideas be sought in the actual consequences or in the possible consequences, whether it be sought in the total consequences or in the consequences which have been observed so far, the same insuperable difficulties present themselves. Truth is the mere agreement of an idea with a developing body of miscellaneous 'experiences', and the particular condition of that body which is taken to guarantee truth remains unspecified. If the consequences of an idea are 'satisfactory', the truth of the idea is established. But how are we to determine what is satisfactory? And until we have determined what is satisfactory, have we any criterion at all? The defect of this view, then, does not lie in its recognition of the instability of any truth, however well established, nor in its conviction that fresh truth will be discovered in the future; these, indeed, are its merits. It lies, rather, in the fact that the future *as such* is selected as the criterion of truth, and that when this criterion is considered it turns out to be no criterion at all. The problem has been postponed, not solved. In place of system, we are offered consequences; in place of a whole or world of ideas, we are offered a series; in place of logical implication, we are offered temporal sequence; in place of the coherence of a world of ideas, we are offered the agreement of an idea with results of a certain character—a character left undetermined. And perhaps the best that can be said for this view is that it seems to be an appeal to the principle of wholeness or coherence, but imperfect because it fails to take this principle seriously and press it to its conclusion. Where the conception of truth as a system is seriously entertained, the notion of results and consequences has been implicitly rejected. And moreover, when an attempt is made to remove the ambiguity of this notion that the truth of a practical idea lies in its consequences, by specifying the character of consequences, it is impossible to stop short of the principle of coherence. 'Satisfactory' consequences, or consequences which 'work' provide, in fact, no specification at all unless what is meant is that the idea and the whole world of practical ideas, taken together, form a coherent whole. For, if the 'working' (and therefore the truth) of an idea signify merely its agreement with what follows upon its realization in action, then we have embraced a theory of truth which relies upon a conception of correspondence and is, for that reason, false. While, if by saying that an idea 'works' in the practical world we mean that it is required to make that world coherent, we have implicitly abandoned the notion of consequences and all that it involves.

My view is, then, that practical truth conforms to the general character of truth; it is the world of practical experience as a coherent whole, the world of practical fact. But the world of practical fact, like all worlds of fact, is, from one standpoint, a conclusion, the result of practice; it is a world of ideas made and maintained by means of the principle of coherence. And, from another standpoint, it is no less a datum, a world of ideas given in order to be changed. Seen as the world of practical fact, it is the conclusion of practical activity: seen as the world in which action takes place, it is a presupposition, a datum, and practice is the process by which it is changed. Yet, though every action constitutes a modification of the actual content of this world, its general character remains unaltered. For what is constant, and what distinguishes this world of fact from all other worlds of fact, is the possibility of change. Here, and here only, can what was true yesterday be false to-day. Scientific and historical experience involve processes of abandoning truths which were never true in search of a coherent world of facts; practice involves a process in which the achievement of a coherent world of facts is merely preliminary to its transformation.[1]

---

[1] One implication of the character of practical truth should, perhaps, be noticed at this point. I mean the connexion between practical truth and freedom. Freedom, I take it, is a practical idea, an idea which has relevance in the practical world of activity and nowhere else. It is true that the notions of freedom and necessity are often referred to other worlds than the practical world. We hear

(iii) The question What in a mode of experience is real? I have preferred to consider in the form, What is in this or that mode of experience an individual or a thing? And, in considering this question in connexion with practice it may be remarked, first, that the thing or individual in practical experience, like that in both science and history, is presupposed. Practical experience is without a critical conception of reality. The world of practice is a world of things and individuals which are designated, not defined. And, consequently, the explicit criterion by which the individual is determined is that of separateness, rather than of completeness: what is fixed upon is that which is self-contained, and not that which is self-complete. Whatever is required, in the conduct of life, to be separate and to be treated as separate, this (in practice) is a thing and is real. It is, of course, real because it appears to be complete and a whole; but to press an enquiry into this appearance beyond the point at which separateness is established is no part of our business in practical experience. To do so would defeat our own end. Often, for the purposes of practical experience, that which is separate in perception is taken to be real and a thing; and where such a conception of reality satisfies the requirements of practical life, where it introduces coherence into the world of practical experience, it would be stupid and irrelevant to question its validity. But even where practical experience

of them not only in so-called scientific discussions, but also in the writings of those who pretend to offer us a philosophy; but we must not allow ourselves to be misled by this misappropriation of ideas. Freedom and necessity are conditions of the mind which has achieved (or has failed to achieve) practical truth. They are conditions of the practical self. They have neither meaning nor relevance for the self in scientific experience or in history, and are certainly meaningless when attributed to the universe as a whole. If a man thinks to set himself free, in any save a vague and metaphorical sense, by the study of science or of history or by the pursuit of philosophy he is grossly mistaken. The only truth that makes a man free is practical truth, the possession of a coherent world of practical ideas. Indeed, practical truth and freedom seem to me inseparable; wherever the one is, the other will be found also.

passes beyond the individual of perception, as (for example) in the conception of a society or a community, at no point does it require or understand more than a designated reality. In practical life it is more important to appreciate separateness than completeness, because separateness rather than completeness is the explicit criterion of reality. In short, the assumption in practical activity is of a world of discrete realities.

But the conception of reality which is presupposed in practical experience is to be seen more clearly when we turn from the idea of an individual thing to that of an individual person. For the conception of the self or personality assumed in practical experience, is at once the most important and most characteristic of all the conceptions which go to make up the world of practical ideas. Indeed, this practical conception of the self is doubly important; the practical self is both the self which thinks practically, the practical I, and, at the same time, the self which practical thinking recognizes in others. The world of practical experience is the world of the practical self and also, to a large extent, a world of practical selves.

Practical experience, then, the conduct of life, involves a certain conception of the self or person. And this conception is not so much a construction of practical thought, though it is that, as a presupposition of action. Now, any conception of the self or personality must first provide a principle by means of which the unity or individuality of the self may be established. And the principle upon which practical thinking establishes its conception of the self is a principle of separation or distinction: the process is one of designation. The self, in practical experience, is what is separate, unique and self-contained. "Nicht als Gattungswesen, sondern individuell bestimmt tritt der Mensch in das *Leben* ein." The explicit problem of reality or individuality for practical thought is not, Where is there to be found a person or thing which is self-complete? but, Where is there to be found a person or thing which is distinct, separate and unique? The practical self, then, is known, in the first place, as something contrary to and exclusive of its world. And this contrariness is selected as the principle of its individuality. It is determined, not by the inclusion of all that belongs or is related to it, but by the exclusion of all that can be shown to stand outside an arbitrarily separated centre. It thus appears, first of all, in opposition to an environment of things and other selves, determined upon the same principle. The practical self is surrounded by a world of 'others'; but it is real and individual because it can maintain its independence and separateness. And again, the practical world, because it is a world of activity and change, is a world of oppositions to be balanced (because they cannot be unified), of contradictions which (because they cannot be resolved) must be co-ordinated. The practical self and its interests can never give way before the interests of 'others'; the relationships into which it enters are external to itself; and, since in practical experience the practical self is the very embodiment of reality, its dissolution is a contradiction and inconceivable.

In short, it may be said that the practical self is the will; for the will is inherently free and self-determined.[1] The self presupposed in practical activity is a self-determined self. And in practical experience it is not required to demonstrate the freedom of the practical self (just as in scientific experience it is not required to demonstrate the 'mechanical' character of 'nature'); this freedom belongs to it by definition. The practical self is an 'end in himself' for no other reason than that in practical experience he must be presupposed to be of this character. Whatever be our principle of reality or individuality, that which is real or individual is, for that reason, an end in itself; and where the principle of reality is taken to be separateness and uniqueness, that which has demonstrated its separateness and uniqueness, has demonstrated also its character as an end in itself.

[1] Here again, of course, there is mere designation and not definition. We have seen already that the will is certainly not isolated and that the self as will cannot be a merely separate self.

It appears, then, that without such a self as this, action would be impossible: activity involves the existence of this self; they are inseparable. The will operates in a world of wills; and to deny the integrity and reality of the will is in practical experience a self-contradiction. And it must be observed that this is true of the entire realm of practical life. Wherever an attempt is made to break down the separateness and uniqueness of the practical self, wherever its 'freedom' is denied and wherever it is replaced by an idea of the self based upon some other principle of individuality than separateness and distinction, the seeds of disintegration have been sown in the practical world. And the necessity, for the conduct of life, of maintaining the integrity and separateness of the self, which to a dramatist like Hebbel, a novelist like D. H. Lawrence, or a moralist like Kant is a matter of psychological observation or moral conviction, for us is a matter of definition. The practical self and the conduct of life are correlatives; deny the one, and the other becomes impossible.

This view of the character of the self and the reality presupposed in practical activity is not, of course, without its difficulties. It cannot be denied that there are moods and actions in the conduct of life which seem to point in a different direction. It is true, for example, that the self which each of us experiences within himself is thought of as unique. "Si je ne vaux pas mieux, au moins je suis autre." The principle and criterion of its reality lies in its separateness and self-determination. The self for introspection is alone. My soul is with myself and beyond implication in the world. To close up the gulf which is fixed between my self and another is to violate the integrity of the self, to qualify its reality. The reality of the self is a function of its invulnerability. But often, in introspection and in practical activity, we cannot rest there. This practical necessity of preserving the self, this instinct for which reality is identified with the maintenance of separateness, does not remain unqualified. The attempt to lose oneself, to find oneself in another, to preserve oneself by abandoning oneself, to become oneself by surrendering oneself appears to imply a conception of the self somewhat different from that which belongs to ordinary practical activity. And the self which is separate, the self as the will, the self whose identity is situate in the body, appears to be (in these moments) replaced by another, distinguished by some principle other than that of its mere separateness from 'others'. And again, even where we still recognize the separate self, we are often aware of a self which, though it be unique, is anything but a unity. We are aware of a thousand selves within this single self; and what we are least able to do is to persuade ourselves of our practical identity. There are moods and there are activities in the conduct of life when it is scarcely an exaggeration to say that the separateness of the self is qualified, and its singleness is destroyed.

Yet, on the other side, it must be observed that we cannot go far in this direction without passing outside a world in which action is possible, outside the world of practical experience. If the separate and single self, the self as will, appears sometimes to be an illusion,[1] it is an illusion to which, however often it be shattered by our inner experience, we always insist upon returning. To take the self as separate, single and unique, and to take it to be real because it is separate, single and unique, is an absolute necessity in practical experience. And it is never the philosopher, persuading us that this separate self is an abstraction, who will succeed in ridding us of this obsession; it is the lover who momentarily convinces us that it is an illusion. Yet even in satisfied love, when we come nearest to breaking down and desiring to break down our too separate selves, and when the world seems least incomprehensible, the last word is, I suppose,—

> Let me confess that we two must be twain
> Although our undivided loves are one.

[1] And, of course, from the standpoint of the totality of experience it is, if not an illusion, at least an abstraction.

And we find ourselves asserting our separateness because we know that it is at once the guarantee and the criterion of our existence. There is no point in the conduct of life at which this assumption that the self is what is separate and self-determined, that the self is the will, can with impunity be abandoned.

Practical activity, then, presupposes a world of fact and of reality the determining characteristic of which is that it can be changed. Unlike those in history and science (which assume a fixed and unchanging reality), the explicit concept of reality in practical experience is that of a mutable reality. In practical experience reality is asserted under the category of change. And there are those, no doubt, who will take me at this point to have abandoned philosophy for poetry. That

> Nought may endure but mutability

is, I suppose, the most constant of all themes in poetry; but one does not require to have been a close reader of the poets in order to have become aware of its truth. Mortality, I take it, is the central fact of practical existence; death is the central fact of life. I do not, of course, mean merely human mortality, the fact that we must one day cease to be; I mean the far more devastating mortality of every element of practical existence, the mortality of pleasures and pains, desires, achievements, emotions and affections. Mortality is the presiding category in practical experience. Some have gone further and have seen this as a fatal defect in life, as a poison polluting life and making it insufferable; and perhaps this universal mortality must make life insufferable unless, somehow, we can ally ourselves with it. But, whatever our views on this point, the world presupposed in practical experience is a mortal world, because it is the world of what is here and now, of what is present as such; and the actual content of this world is determined by practical judgment. This practical judgment, which constitutes a world of here and now, is, however, never in practice conceived to be an end in itself; it is always preliminary to the activity which belongs to practical experience. Practice is never the mere assertion of the present; it is essentially action, the alteration of 'what is' so as to make it agree with 'what ought to be'.

## § 5

We have seen that the 'to be' in practical judgment is always more than a mere 'not yet'; it is conceived always as what is valuable or what ought to be. Without valuation, I have suggested, there is no practical judgment, no activity. Nevertheless, where practice is identified with action, the alteration of practical existence, the world of value is in the nature of a presupposition. It has a character of its own, for practice and valuation are never identical. And it is our business now to consider the character of this presupposed world of value. The view I have to suggest is, briefly: (i) that the world of value is a world of experience, it implies an assertion of reality; (ii) that valuation is thinking, the attempt to make coherent a world of ideas; (iii) that value is a world of being, and a judgment that 'This is valuable' is, in the end, a judgment that 'This exists in a certain way'; and (iv) that the world of value is a mode of experience, an abstract world of ideas, an incomplete assertion of reality. And in discussing these propositions it will be impossible to keep them entirely separate.

(i) That the world of value is a world of experience follows, of course, from the general view I have already recommended. Unless it be a world of experience it is nothing at all. And it is only necessary here to point out the implications of this general conception, to point out what other views of the world of value it excludes. The world of value is a world of experience, consequent y it is a world of ideas and it is not a world of mere ideas. First, then, the world of value is a world of ideas; and this excludes the view, frequently to be met, that values are radically 'objective', that they exist independently of any relationship with consciousness. Valuation, it is suggested, is the mere recognition of the character of certain objects or actions, and the world of value is a world of 'objective' existence unmodified by thought or judgment. This view, however, may be dismissed at once. It involves a conception of experience contrary to that which I have made my own. A world of things which is not a world of ideas is a self-contradiction. In the sense suggested there are no 'objects'. And the function of consciousness is not to 'recognize' or to 'interpret' the character of wholly independent 'objects'; it is to determine the character of what is given—a world of experience.

But secondly, the world of value is not a world of mere ideas, because a world of mere ideas falls short of a world of experience. Nevertheless, it has been suggested that the appreciation of value is 'subjective' in some sense in which nothing else in experience is subjective. Fact, we are told, imposes itself upon us; value is what we impose upon things. And the criterion of value lies in the state of mind itself: my judgments of value refer to my condition of mind as such. Of this view there are, of course, several varieties, but they differ only in respect of the particular state of mind selected to serve as the criterion of value. The most elementary variety, perhaps, is that which asserts that we find valuable whatever interests us or claims our attention, and we find it valuable solely because it interests us. The value of anything consists in the fact that somebody takes, or could take an interest in it. And the degree of value is commensurate with the degree of interest. But there are other less elementary views belonging to this class. There is the view, for example, that we find valuable whatever we desire, and we find it valuable on account of our desiring it. To have value is to be desired. And "the strength of the actual desire corresponds to the value attributed". This view is sometimes confused with another, which asserts that what is valuable is what is desirable, but (apart from the fact that this gives us no information at all) it should be clear that the two views have nothing in common, unless we are to consent to Mill's regrettable suggestion that "the sole evidence it is possible to produce that anything is desirable, is that people do actually desire it ". A third and important variant of this view asserts that we find valuable whatever gives us happiness, that we find it valuable because of the happiness it gives, and that the degree of value is commensurate with the degree of happiness. But, for all these views alike, the world of value is a world of mere ideas, and for this reason they must be rejected. No judgment whatever is, in the sense suggested, purely subjective, for subjectivity is never more than an aspect of any judgment, and an aspect which cannot stand alone. And further, these views imply that valuation is a matter of 'mere opinion', and this is contradictory of what is involved in every judgment of value. All judgments of value demand to be universally recognized; but if they were no more than assertions of mere opinion this would be impossible. And assertions of value would not differ from assertions of preference. The question whether or not a man was correct in asserting something to be valuable would resolve itself into the question whether or not he had correctly assessed his condition of mind. And a dispute about judgments of value would be not only futile, but meaningless and impossible.

The view, then, that the world of value is a world of experience implies the rejection of the view that it is not a world of ideas and of the view that it is a world of mere ideas. And it implies, also, that in valuation there is always an assertion of reality. For, wherever there is judgment there is assertion of reality, and wherever there is experience there is judgment.

(ii) It is a common opinion that valuation is a form of feeling rather than of thought; and this, for psychology, may be a significant distinction. But the view of experience to which I have bound myself makes it impossible for me to hold that valuation is feeling in any sense which precludes it from being thought. Nevertheless, if by calling it feeling, it is intended to assert that valuation is often an elementary and unselfconscious form of thinking, no dispute is likely to arise. For most of us valuation is an almost unreflective process; many of our judgments of value are vague and inexplicit; often they must be inferred from our actions. This, doubtless, is due partly to the formation of habits and settled ways of thought; our values quickly become, in the vulgar sense, instinctive as our lives degenerate from experiment to routine. But the unreflective character of valuation does not imply that it is intuitive, immediate, a matter of feeling and not of thought, or that it is merely the expression of opinion. No experience is immediate in this sense. Valuation is thinking, and it issues in knowledge. It is true, of course, that for the most part our judgments of value are presented indirectly, in the form of actions and not of propositions; and we are rarely conscious of a continuous attempt to make our world of values coherent. But we have seen already that the absence of explicit judgment is no evidence for the absence of implied judgment, that the absence of explicit assertion does not mean the absence of assertion altogether.

And further, the view that valuation is thinking must be taken to exclude the view that it is the pronouncement of a 'sense of value'. There is, I believe, nothing whatever to be said in favour of the cruder forms of the view that what is valuable is what our 'sense of value' tells us is valuable, and it is valuable because our 'sense of value' asserts that it is. And I find the somewhat similar view that the consciousness of value is immediate, absolute, underivative and indefinable no less unsatisfactory. This notion has the advantage of that which appeals to a 'sense of value' in that, while affording no explanation of value and valuation, it asserts that none is required or possible. But beyond this it has no merit. No experience whatever is isolated, immediate or inexplicable. And the assertion that something is isolated and underivative can render definition unnecessary or impossible only because it implies that there is nothing to define.

Valuation, then, is thinking; and it is subject to the criterion common to all forms of judgment and all worlds of ideas. The criterion by means of which we distinguish what is valuable among the things we take to be valuable, the criterion by which we determine the truth or falsehood of our judgments of value, is not correspondence with some external standard, but the coherence of the world of value itself. The reason why anything is taken to be valuable is because to do so appears to make our world of values coherent; and the reason why anything is valuable is because the coherence of the world of value depends upon its acceptance. Valuation, because it is thinking, is the attempt to make coherent, to make more of a world, a given world of ideas; and in this process each given value is qualified and modified by every other value. I do not mean, of course, that in every judgment of value this criterion is present in our minds. I mean that whatever *is* present in our minds as a criterion of value—whether it is the idea of an external authority or the notion of conscience—can be shown to depend finally upon the principle of coherence. 'What ought to be', should be, because the coherence of the world of 'what ought to be' requires it to be in that world: and to this there is no exception. And consequently, there is no value, no judgment of value, nor anything valuable which, taken by itself and on its own account, may properly be spoken of as absolute. Whatever virtues there be, whatever judgments of value, each must submit itself (and does submit itself in the mind of anyone who leads an "examined life") to the world of value as a whole, and from this it derives both its status and its truth. For here, as everywhere, absoluteness belongs solely to the coherent world as a world and as a whole.

(iii) As I see it, the question in valuation is, 'Ought, or ought not, this to be?' What is judged to be valuable is, *eo ipso*, judged to be worthy of being in the practical world. And conversely, whatever we think ought to be in this world, we think of as valuable. I do not, of course, mean that what is valuable is so *because* it ought to be, or that what ought to be, should be, *because* it is valuable. I mean merely that the idea of value is always an idea of what ought to be in the practical world, and that valuation is incompletely understood unless it is seen to be a judgment, an assertion of reality.

Such an identification of the ideas of 'ought to be' and of value is not, of course, novel; and there are objections ready to hand. It will be said, first, that we do not, as a rule, when we think of a thing or an action as valuable, go on to think, also, that it ought to be; and that if we do think that it is both valuable and that it ought to be, we do not consider these two ideas to be but a single judgment. But, since the view I am advocating is not concerned with what we think, in the sense of what we are conscious of thinking, but with what is implied in what we think, this objection appears to me beside the mark. The proof of the necessity of certain ideas has never been supposed, by anyone who knew what he was about, to rest upon the fact that everyone was aware of having them, for the force of such a proof would be at the mercy of a single ill-considered denial.

But secondly, it will be objected that the conception of ought refers to actions and to actions alone, and that while it may be true that some of the actions we think valuable we feel also obliged to perform (though this is questionable), it is quite misleading to refer this notion of obligation beyond the world of actions. Now, if the idea of 'ought to be' is taken always to assert an obligation to act, to assert a duty, if the judgment, 'This ought to be', is taken everywhere to mean only, 'I ought to realize this here and now', then some distinction between the notion of 'ought to be' and that of value would certainly seem to be required. But the reasons which would compel us to hold this view appear to me obscure. I can see no good reason for supposing that the judgment, 'This ought to be', can mean nothing save, 'I ought to do this'. Not only do we frequently judge that things ought to be without implying that we feel, or should feel, any obligation (duty) to realize them, but also we assert, of things which are already in existence, that they ought to be; and when we so judge we are judging them to be valuable. And this distinction, which we certainly make, between what ought to be and what is obligatory or a duty (for ourselves or for another), is not, I think, illusory or misconceived.

What, no doubt, is at the back of the minds of some who assert that the notion that 'this ought to be' implies always the notion of an obligation to act, is the idea that God ought to realize it here and now. But, if they were to consider their position, they would readily allow that the attribution to God of a duty or obligation, in the ordinary sense, is not what they intended.[1]

Thirdly, it will be suggested that, since the notion of 'ought to be' implies the notion of a discrepancy from 'what is here and now', what is valuable (if it be identified with what ought to be) can never be what exists in the practical world. And this is clearly in conflict with many undoubted judgments of value. We often judge to be valuable what exists in our world of practical experience. This suggestion introduces the difficult question of the precise character of the existence implied in the notion of 'ought to be', a question which I must consider in a moment. But for the present it will suffice to point out that it rests upon a

---

[1] I do not propose to consider here in detail the relation of what is obligatory to 'what ought to be'. Briefly my view is that what makes an action obligatory is the apprehended superior coherency of the state of things which the action would produce. Yet this, by itself, is not enough. The apprehension of a merely other perfect world, standing over against our world of what is here and now, carries no obligation with it. It becomes a duty, an obligation to realize what is judged to be valuable, not merely and only because it is seen to be valuable, but when and because it is seen to be necessary for the completion, the coherency of 'what is here and now'. "What ought to be' must be seen as the 'ought' of this particular 'is', this particular 'here and now', and must be seen also as fitting within the competence of my volition, before it becomes obligatory to realize it. And it is this which distinguishes obligation from a mere judgment of value.

Also, I should say that although I have written as if I believed that there are no values save moral values, I have done so merely in the interest of brevity. There can, in my view, be no ultimate independence of different values within the world of value; but whether all values are, in the end, forms of moral activity is a question upon which I do not wish to commit myself. And truth, of course, may be considered 'a value' only when it is conceived as practical truth.

misconception. The notion of 'ought to be', although it implies a mode of being different from that implied in 'what is here and now', does not necessarily imply a total discrepancy, a discrepancy in every sense, from 'what is here and now'. The absolute discrepancy lies only between 'what is here and now' *as such*, and 'what ought to be' *as such*. And while the mode of being signified by 'what ought to be' is certainly discrepant from that signified by 'what is here and now', 'what ought to be' may without contradiction occupy the same world as 'what is here and now'. In short, it belongs to 'what ought to be' to be affirmed, as well as to be desired or willed. And where the notion of 'what ought to be' does involve a will to bring it into being in the world of 'what is here and now', it need not also involve an obligation to do so. It is perhaps true that the notion of obligation usually implies the notion of a total and absolute discrepancy, a discrepancy in every sense, between 'what ought to be' and 'what is here and now'; but we have seen reason to distinguish between the idea of 'what ought to be' and the idea of duty or obligation. And wherever there is a felt obligation there is a modification of the simple judgment of value.

From the standpoint of the world of practical fact, then, the world of value is 'what ought to be'. But this standpoint is abstract and incomplete. Value cannot be left as a mere 'ought to be', because a mere ought is something meaningless. This world of value must be seen to be a mode of being if it is to be seen fully. But in considering the question, What is the character of the existence involved in 'what ought to be'? it must be understood that we are not considering, What notion of being (if any) is present in our minds when we venture upon a judgment of value? It is probable that no such notion is present at all; it is probable even that, on those occasions when we actually make a judgment of value in terms of, 'this ought to be', we are unconscious of any precise reference to a mode of being. Judgments of value, from the point of view of consciousness, may be emancipated altogether from any reference to existence. But all this is beside the point. Our question is, What mode of being is *involved* in the conception of value or 'what ought to be'?

The view has been suggested that, so far from 'ought to be' signifying a mode of being, it signifies precisely what does not exist at all.[1] And this view must be met before going further. From the standpoint of the present argument it is enough to say that, since it involves the separation of 'what ought to be' from 'what is valuable', it must be dismissed as untenable. What is valuable is, certainly, sometimes considered to exist; and if what is valuable is what ought to be, what ought to be cannot mean merely that which does not exist. But, from a wider standpoint also, the notion breaks down. The idea of the merely non-existent is one to which no meaning can be attached; it can enter experience only as an idea of a mode of being, as "existence after a fashion". This I have discussed already. And any attempt to define (or designate) a mode of thought, such as that implied in the judgment, 'This ought to be', in terms of the bare and absolute not-being of the 'this', involves the contradiction of a 'this' which nevertheless in no sense exists, of something which both is and is not. I take it, then, that 'ought to be' does not and cannot mean merely what does not in any sense exist.

The first observation to be made in considering the character of the existence involved in the judgment, 'This ought to be', is that 'what ought to be' may be discrepant from 'what is', where 'what is' means 'what is here and now', the world of practical fact. The nature of this world of fact has been before us, and we have already seen enough to know that it is different from anything which could maintain itself as the concrete world of real existence. Hence, when I say that 'what ought to be' may be discrepant from 'what is', I mean no more than that it may be discrepant from what itself falls short of the full character of existence.

[1] "Unter Sollen verstehen wir gerade das, was nicht ist oder nicht existiert." Rickert.

And by 'discrepant' I mean that judgments of value may refer to a subject which has nothing to correspond with it in the practical world. That this is so I have already attempted to demonstrate. It is a matter of common observation that not all judgments of value need refer to what has existence in the present practical world. Indeed, we often take to be valuable much that we cannot imagine realized in that world: though we never judge to be valuable what we know could not exist in that world. In short, judgments that, 'This ought to be', where the 'this' is a 'not here' or a 'not yet', are both possible and frequent. But, on the other hand, it is equally clear that many of our judgments of value refer to what is here and now, refer to what has existence in practical experience. 'What ought to be' is not necessarily discrepant from 'what is here and now'.

Nevertheless, although 'what ought to be' may be, but is not necessarily, discrepant from 'what is here and now', the mode of being signified by the one is necessarily and absolutely distinct from that signified by the other. That is to say, 'what ought to be' or what is valuable as such, can never be reduced to 'what is here and now' as such. The judgments that 'This is valuable' and that 'This is here and now', are never identical. And it is, on the whole, more urgent that we should observe this distinction between our judgments of value and our judgments of practical existence, than that we should insist upon the apparent identity of the subject referred to in those judgments. What is important is that no attempt should be made to substitute a judgment of practical fact for a judgment of value, or a judgment of value for one of practical fact.

In separating 'what ought to be' as such from 'what is here and now' as such, we are, then, separating 'what ought to be' from one mode of being, but not from all modes of being. The view has, indeed, been suggested that every attempt to define the notion of 'ought to be' in terms of any mode or conception of 'what is', in terms of any world of being whatever, must be misleading because the conceptions of value and of fact are radically and absolutely disparate. But since it implies that 'ought to be' is something other than a mode of being, I am unable to accept it. What I wish to maintain is that the world of value and the world of practical fact are two worlds, and to pass directly from one to the other, or to attempt an explanation of one in terms of the character of the other, must always involve an *ignoratio elenchi*; but that the world of value is, nevertheless, a world of fact (though not this world of fact), and 'what ought to be' signifies a mode of being (though not this mode of being). *Was sein soll, ist in der Tat auch, und was nur sein soll, ohne zu sein, hat keine Wahrheit.*[1]

Valuation, then, is thinking, the attempt to make coherent a given world of ideas. This world of experience which valuation qualifies is not the world of 'what is here and now', the world of practical existence as such. Nevertheless it cannot be a world of mere ideas, for that would force valuation outside experience. Every judgment, no matter what its explicit form may be, is, in the end, an assertion of reality. But judgment, we have seen, need not assert reality directly; what is explicitly judged need not be what is asserted of reality. And although a judgment of value (as we shall see) does not assert reality directly, yet it cannot avoid an assertion of reality. And it must be equally misleading to suggest that the world of value is a world of mere ideas and that valuation is devoid of reference to a world of being, either because it does not qualify the real world directly, or because it does not qualify the real world by means of the world of 'what is' for practical experience.

But valuation (we have seen) is the judgment that 'this ought to be'; and consequently, what ought to be, because it is excluded for the qualification of reality which belongs to 'what is here and now' (judgments of practical existence), qualifies reality through a world of its own. To exclude an idea from one reference to reality, to exclude it from one world of ideas, forces it into another; for every idea is more

[1] Hegel, *Phänomenologie des Geistes* (Lasson), S. 168.

than a mere idea and belongs to a world which, though it be abstract, yet has a *locus standi* within reality. And when we judge that 'this ought to be', in asserting something totally different from that it is here and now, we are asserting it to be real, to be a fact, in a world of its own. In short, 'what ought to be', although it is never, as such, a fact in the world of 'what is here and now', is a fact in another world. And when we say, 'This ought to be', we imply that, in this other world, it *is*. To be valuable is to be worthy of being in the world of practical fact, and whatever in this sense 'ought to be', belongs already to a world of being, disparate from the world of 'what is here and now', but nevertheless a world of being and not a world of mere ideas.

(iv) The world of value is, then, a specific world of experience, unlike any other world so far as concerns its explicit character. No other judgment can take the place of a judgment of value; valuation is a unique assertion of réality. And the question arises, What is the character of this world of value from the standpoint of the totality of experience? Is this the world of concrete experience? And is valuation an unlimited and absolute assertion of reality? Or, is this an abstract mode of experience? And before we go further some answer to this question should be provided. We must, however, have clearly before our minds the question we are to consider. What we are to deal with is not the question of the relation of 'what ought to be' (the world of value) to 'what is here and now' (the world of practical fact). It is not the old, and often misconceived question whether 'what ought to be' can be reduced to actual fact, the question which Naturalism answers one way and philosophy another. We have seen already that 'what ought to be', as such, has an existence independent of the world of 'what is here and now'; and what we are concerned with is the character of that existence, not in relation to 'what is here and now', but in relation to ultimate reality. 'What ought to be', as such, is certainly different and discrepant from 'what is here and now', but it cannot, on that account, be said to be different and discrepant from what ultimately is, from the world of concrete reality. Let us, then, consider the view that the world of value is, not a mode of experience, but experience itself, that the world of value is the world of concrete reality.

But first, we may notice a modified form of this view which, although it must be dismissed at once, is sufficiently influential to require consideration. It has been asserted that values are facts, that value is an aspect of reality, and that these facts and this aspect must be "taken into account in interpreting reality". Value-experiences must not be neglected when we are considering experience as a whole. If value is not the whole of reality, at least it is a too often neglected aspect of reality. The fatal weakness of this view lies, of course, in the defective notion of experience which it implies. Values are, no doubt, facts, value-experiences are, no doubt, experiences, but what such 'facts' as these demand is not to be "taken into account" (as if their shape and character were fixed in advance and what was required was merely to put them in place), but to be criticized; and what these experiences demand is not merely to be accepted and given a place in the world of experience, but to be interrogated. For the factual character of these so-called facts depends upon their place in the world of concrete fact; and the totality of experience is not a mere collection of everything which comes to us in the form in which it comes, but a coherent world of experience. And everywhere in thought is involved a transformation of what is given. The given as such has no place in the real world of experience. Our question, then, is not, How can we incorporate these value-facts in our view of reality? but, What is the character of these value-facts when they have been submitted to the concrete totality of experience? In short, nothing in experience is 'real' just because, and just as, it is given: its reality depends not upon its being given, but upon its coherence when seen in the totality of experience. Every experience is real—so long as we do not take it for less or more than it is. What we have to decide is not whether value, as such, is a part of reality (for it can never be that), but whether the world of value is itself the world of concrete reality, or whether it is an abstract world of experience which (consequently) requires, as a world, to be transformed and superseded. And the weakness of a philosophy which, from start to finish, takes no account of value and valuation is not that it has (or may have) "left out" something that is (or may be) required in order to make up the totality of experience, but that it has failed to consider a form of experience which, because it is experience, itself claims to be the whole.

The world of value, when compared with some so-called worlds of fact, appears to be fixed, certain and invulnerable. Valuation gives, at least, an intelligible universe. And this appearance of completeness has led to the assertion that the world of value is the world of absolute experience. The meaning of a thing is its value, and this is its ultimate and final meaning; this is what it really *is*. What is fact in the world of 'what ought to be' is fact in the real world. And the discrepancy between 'what ought to be' and 'what is here and now' is the discrepancy between 'what is here and now' and what really and absolutely is.

This view I believe to be untenable: the world of value is not the world of concrete experience, but is an abstract mode of experience. But since it lies to one side of my main purpose to consider fully the character of value, I will offer only a brief suggestion of the line of argument which would lead to the establishment of my view. First, there is nothing in the character of the world of value as it comes before us to suggest that it has the capacity to supersede all other worlds of experience, or indeed any other world of experience. Valuation does not, for example, supersede either historical or scientific judgment; it has the capacity neither to criticise nor to destroy them. It may be that this world is a less restricted world of experience than those of science or history; but there is nothing to suggest that it is without restriction. The valuable as such never even appears to be the whole, nor the universe as such to be valuable. And the *ignoratio elenchi* apparent whenever, for example, a judgment of value is set over against a scientific judgment, is what we have learned to expect whenever two abstract worlds meet. But secondly, we have seen that nothing can be valuable which either does not, or could not exist in the world of 'what is here and now', in the world of practical fact. The world of value is inseparable from the world of practical existence. 'What ought to be' is not postulated *a priori* in respect of practical experience; it is governed and limited at eveiy point by the necessity of having to conform to the structural concepts of the world of practical experience. Consequently, the world of value can have no higher degree of coherence or reality than the world of practical experience. And we may postpone our judgment upon it until we have ascertained the status of practical experience in the totality of experience. From the point of view of the totality of experience, these two worlds stand or fall together, and whatever conclusion we reach with regard to the world of practical experience must, on this point, be our conclusion with regard to the world of value.

§ 6

The presuppositions of practice are before us. I have considered the world of practical fact which activity presupposes. And I have undertaken, with considerable misgiving, an examination of the world of value. And with the results we have achieved, we may return to consider again the character of practical experience.

Practice, we have seen, is the alteration of practical existence. And practical existence is a determinate world of ideas never, in practice, wholly to be transformed. "In my practical attitude I experience myself as something contrary to the object. I do not merely receive the object and feel it as mine, although other than me, but I also feel myself as something which is opposite and struggles to change it." Thus, practice is not merely the alteration of 'what is here and now'; it is the alteration of 'what is here and now' so as to agree with an idea. Practice is the alteration of one given world so as to make it agree with another given world. And it is, therefore, qualified and governed at every step by the character of the two worlds it presupposes and the character of the alteration it attempts.

(i) 'What is here and now', the world of practical fact as such, I have spoken of as a presupposition of practical activity, but we have seen, also, that from another standpoint it is a constant; for, on the one side there is no world of practical fact known in experience which is not the product of activity, and on the other the alteration which practical activity produces is never absolute. The given is always and only relatively given; there is no absolute beginning. And the world of practical fact which activity creates, though it may and does differ in detail and content from the given world of practical fact, is a world of the same kind of fact; and this general character remains always unchanged.

(ii) That which practical activity attempts to realize is not something merely 'not here' or 'not yet', it is what is both 'not here' and at the same time what is valuable as such, 'what ought to be'. Practical activity is prefaced by the distinction between 'what is here and now' and 'what ought to be', between what exists for practice and what is valuable as such; and it is an attempt to alter 'what is here and now' so as to agree with 'what ought to be'. Thus, the world of value is, from the standpoint of practice, a presupposition. Nevertheless, there is no ultimate priority, much less separation. 'What ought to be' is not a world entirely independent of 'what is here and now'; the facts of the one are of the same kind as the facts of the other. Valuation is involved in practical activity as a necessary implication. And that it can and does exist independently of practice does not lessen the necessity which binds practical activity to it.

(iii) With regard to the character of the realization involved in practice, practical activity goes further than mere valuation which (we have seen) distinguishes between 'what is here and now' and 'what ought to be', but implies no attempt to reconcile them. Practice is the world *sub specie voluntatis*, and the will is not satisfied with mere valuation. What it attempts is the reconciliation of 'what is here and now' and 'what ought to be'. Its business is to realize in the world of practical fact what exists and is already real in the world of value. But practice is activity, the actual alteration of 'what is here and now', and consequently it has no choice of the manner in which this transformation of its given world must be achieved. 'What ought to be' can be realized in the world of practical fact only by means of action, by means of specific change. Presupposing a discrepancy between 'what is here and now' and 'what ought to be', the business of practice is to break down that discrepancy, but to break it down in one direction only. Any attempt to resolve this discrepancy generally or theoretically must be made without the sympathy of practice. The only means which practice recognizes for this purpose is action, the actual, point-by-point qualification of 'what is here and now' by 'what ought to be'. For practice, then, no theoretical reduction of 'what is here and now' to 'what ought to be', no demonstration that 'what ought to be' exists and is fact in a world other than that of the present as such, will achieve its purpose. Indeed, such a demonstration must always appear irrelevant, or worse, in practical experience. Even to consider it, if it do not seduce and make flaccid this will to realize 'what ought to be', must at least divert our attention and dissipate our energies. And for these reasons, practical experience cannot tolerate the suggestion that 'existence' may signify being in any world save its own world of practical fact. Practice sees 'what ought to be', not as a world of existence, but as a world waiting to be born. This, from a wider standpoint, might be called a prejudice; but then, practice is itself the world of ideas involved in the acceptance of this prejudice. Practice sees its given world of fact as there, always in order to be changed; and 'what ought to be' remains, consequently, always discrepant from 'what is here and now'. Thus, the resolution of this discrepancy which practice undertakes, can never finally be accomplished. No sooner is it realized at one point in the world of practical existence, than a new discord springs up elsewhere, demanding a new resolution, a fresh qualification of 'what is here and now' by 'what ought to be'. A theoretical resolution would be, if it were successful, a final resolution. But, since practical activity undertakes not this general resolution, but the particular resolution of all instances of this discrepancy, it undertakes what, from its nature, can never be brought to a conclusion. And even if we suppose a condition in which everything was as it should be, that could never be more than a momentary condition. For every achievement brings with it a new view of the criterion, which converts this momentary perfection into imperfection. Indeed, we may find that even the 'ought not' of one moment is the 'ought' of another. Nowhere in practice is there uninterrupted progress or final achievement.

Or again, practice is thinking, the attempt to discover and elucidate the real world. What is given is a world of ideas; what is achieved is a coherent world of fact. But, for practice, action is the only means by which this coherent world of fact may be achieved. And action is the qualification of 'what is here and now' by 'what ought to be'. And this qualification is, thus, itself the establishment of practical fact, the road to a coherent world of fact. 'What is here and now', though from one point of view it is fact and established, is, for practice, merely what is given, given in order to be changed. And the criterion of this change is always the principle of coherence. Practice, then, going beyond mere valuation (which judges merely, 'This ought to be'), going beyond the abstract practical judgment (which says merely, 'This is here and now'), transforms in detail its given world of practical existence by making it agree with 'what ought to be', by making it coherent. Practice is the alteration of one given world of ideas so as to make it agree with another given world of ideas, and this alteration is, in fact, the making coherent of the world of practical experience.

It lies beyond my task to consider in detail particular examples of practical activity. Nevertheless, it may be of interest to indicate here how this view is illustrated by practical life in its most concrete mood, by religion. But such indication must necessarily be brief. Practice is, in general, the assertion of reality by means of action, and in particular it is the attempt to make coherent the given world of practical existence by qualifying it by 'what ought to be'; and religion I take to be the form of practical activity in which this attempt is carried furthest. Religion, indeed, as I see it, is not a particular form of practical experience; it is merely practical experience at its fullest. Wherever practice is least reserved, least hindered by extraneous interests, least confused by what it does not need, wherever it is most nearly at one with itself and homogeneous, at that point it becomes religion. And in what I have to say on this topic I may confine myself to considering two propositions: That religion is practical activity, and religious experience is practical experience; and that in religion practical experience realizes its full character, religion is the consummation of practice.

I take it that there will be few who wish to deny the view that the general conduct of our life and our religion are inseparable. It is true that our religion, in this sense, may be different from what we profess, and that what we profess may be better or worse than our way of living. Nevertheless, what is important for religion has always been the profession which is contained in the actual conduct of life. A man who is 'religious' and does not behave in accordance with his 'religious' beliefs may be said to profess one 'religion' and to follow another. And there is no doubt which of them should be spoken of as his religion. But the view of religion I wish to recommend goes further than the mere assertion of the inseparableness of the conduct of life and religion: religion is, itself, the conduct of life. All religions are ways of living, and our religion is our way of living. And, since whatever is a way of living is itself activity and belongs to the world of practice, religion and practice are, in the end, one. The conduct of life, we have seen, is a mode of experience; a way of living is (and not merely implies) a way of thinking; and consequently religion is at once a way of thinking and a way of living.

Over against this view of religion there stand two others, both of which it must be taken to deny. Religion, it will be said, so far from being identical with the conduct of practical life, often involves a complete retirement from such life. Quietism certainly cannot be denied the name of religion; and if in quietism the practical world and all that belongs to it is not abjured, it is difficult to understand what it may mean. But with such a view as this we are driven back to the abstract (and meaningless) conception of practice which we have already seen reason to abandon. Quietism is no less a way of living, a method of conducting life, than the most febrile activity. And a religion which involves a retirement from 'life', even that which leads to suicide, is not less practical than one which requires the conversion of mankind. And secondly, it will be said that religion is not a body of practical ideas but of theoretical (or, at least, semi-theoretical) ideas; that religion is not merely a world of practical, but of ultimate knowledge. The ideas, for example, of God and of immortality are not practical ideas, subject to the limitations of practice; they belong to the world of concrete truth and reality. A full reply to this view of religion (if it be taken to imply more than merely a confusion between religion and theology) would clearly involve the discussion of many topics which lie far beyond my subject, and it must not be attempted here. With many who hold this view, the ultimate truth of religious ideas is not more than a prejudice, which (regardless of the contradiction) they maintain by an appeal to the criterion of practice. 'If these be not *true*', they will say of their religious ideas, 'then religious belief is mere delusion. What is not finally true can neither guide nor console; and what guides and consoles does so by reason of its ultimate truth'. Like the lover, they believe that what is true for their mood must be ultimately true or not true at all. But there are others, whose thinking is more candid and less confused, who yet are willing to associate themselves with this view of religion. They believe that what is true in religion must be true ultimately, because they believe that what is true in practice must be true ultimately. But we have found little in the character of practical experience to lead us to believe that it is concrete and absolute experience. And the reasons why this view must be rejected will appear in a moment. I shall be content here with the assertion that religion is practical experience (which is not seriously denied), and that, *prima facie*, there is no reason to assume the identity of what is true for practice and what is true ultimately. Religion, then, certainly belongs to the conduct of life: it is the alteration of practical existence so as to agree with an idea. It is the qualification of 'what is here and now' by 'what ought to be'. It cares nothing for what lies beyond the world of practice; if it looks to 'another' world, it is for the purpose of determining what shall be our conduct in 'this' world. And a theoretical reduction of 'what ought to be' to 'what is here and now', which in practical experience must be regarded as a misleading and extraneous enterprise, in religion is shocking and blasphemous.

Yet religion, I have said, is not merely a form of practical experience, it is practical experience at its fullest, and is the consummation of all attempts to change or maintain our practical existence. Valuation alone is, we have seen, without force or motion. It exists in a world which, though it is self-contained, is yet impotent to satisfy its own demands and looks outside itself for its own completion. And this force and motion, which it lacks, belongs to practice, the comprehensive transference and transformation of what is real in the world of 'what ought to be' into the fact of the world of 'what is here and now'. But, in actual experience, the conduct of life as a whole (in which each separate attempt to maintain or change our existence has its place, and from which each takes its meaning) is not everywhere and at all times discharged with the same degree of integrity, the same completeness, intensity and coherence. Indeed, it is a rare and peculiar genius which enables a man to see clearly what belongs to his life and to follow it without reserve, unhindered by the restraint of prudence or the impediment of doubt. And to most men it will come only as an intermittent experience, which they have neither the courage nor the energy to make permanent. Nevertheless, the tendency of all practical activity is towards this integrate state of mind, which holds nothing worthy of consideration that hinders the achievement of practical satisfaction. Each point in the process which offers itself as a stopping-place, so soon as it is reached, reveals its own inadequacy, and compels us to go forward. And whenever the seriousness with which we embrace this enterprise of achieving a coherent world of practical ideas reaches a certain strength and intensity, whenever it begins to dominate and take possession of us, practice has become religion. There is no exact point in the conduct of life at which religion can be said to begin. Religion differs from other forms of practical activity, not in kind, but in degree; it is characterized everywhere by intensity and strength of devotion and by singleness of purpose. Thus, we are forced by the nature of practical experience to religion, and there is no point at which an arrest in the process can be justified. For to be satisfied with anything less than what is, for practice, comprehensive and complete, is to be satisfied with what is less than practical. More may, of course, be said of religion than that it is the consummation of practice, the achievement of what practice demands, or that it is distinguished by the intensity and strength of its devotion for whatever is selected as its object, but these are, I think, characteristics the importance of which would not be modified by a more extended view. Religion finds its place in the world of practical experience and nothing must be attributed to it incompatible with that station.

§ 7

I have now set out my view of the character of practice as clearly as I can. Practical experience is the most familiar form of experience. We depart from it but rarely, and such departures are always excursions into a foreign country. Practice is the conduct of life. But, I must repeat, in interpreting the meaning of the practical we should not allow ourselves to be bound by the prejudices which commonly surround the conception: it comprises far more than is ordinarily attributed to it. It comprises all that we mean by a 'moral' life, a life directed by an idea of the right and the good; it includes all that we mean by beauty; it comprises the religious life; and it comprises a conception of truth and reality—a life directed by an idea of fact, of system and of coherence. The practical life is neither a mere miscellany of disconnected desires, random hopes, and casual actions, nor is it confined to the attempt to satisfy vulgar ambitions. The most thoroughly and positively practical life is that of the artist or the mystic. For the complete exemplification of this life we do not, I think, require to turn to the life of primitive men. That life, certainly, is immersed in practice, the intellect there directly subserves practice. But there, also, the possibilities of practice remain undeveloped, and it would be as misleading to confine our view of practical experience to this rudimentary example, as to confine our view of scientific experience to the mixed and ambiguous deliverances of natural history.

And, again, we may think it proper for us to confine ourselves to what is offered in this practical mood; we may think that all thought which is directed away from the realization of these practical ends is mistaken. To live at home in the universe and to satisfy, somehow, their desires are ambitions enough for most men, and they are essentially practical. Science, history and philosophy may (and indeed, I think, should, from this standpoint) be regarded as attempts to escape from the conduct of life, attempts to throw off the responsibility of living. In them we hope to find a more radical and more complete escape from life than that which art, music and poetry can offer. For in these, in the end, we are wholly taken up with practical life.[1] And if what we dream of is an escape which shall not itself be a fresh attempt at the conduct of life, we shall find it only in these non-practical modes of experience, and find it most fully in philosophy. But in so far as science and history and philosophy are undertaken in order to satisfy such or any desire, even though it be a desire to escape from life, they also must be thought of as, in origin and impulse, practical. Yet these worlds of experience, as worlds, are wholly independent of the world of practical experience. And when we seek in them the achievement of some practical end, when we approach them from the standpoint of practice, we misconceive their character. Anything may be perverted, but what is perverted is *ex hypothesi* false to its own character.

But my present business is not to consider what we ought to think about these engrossing questions; it is to draw together what we have discovered about the character of practical experience and to consider it from the standpoint of the totality of experience. Practice, we have decided, is experience, and consequently it is reality. Practical judgment is the assertion of reality, the attribution to reality of

---

[1] This may appear a hard saying; but it would be going out of my way to attempt to amplify it here. Instead, I will put this passage from Rilke. "Art is childhood. Art means not to know that the world already exists, and to make a world: not destroying what is found already existing, but simply not finding anything ready to hand. Nothing but possibilities and wishes. And then, suddenly, fulfilment, summer, the sun. Involuntarily, without making any words about it. Never completing, never having the Seventh Day. Never seeing that all is good. Dissatisfaction is itself youth....A song, a picture which you treasure, a poem which you love, all this has its value and significance. I mean for him who creates it for the first time, and for him who creates it the second time; for the artist and for him who really appreciates." *Werke,* VII, 280.

a certain character. It is not merely the attribution of a certain character to a part of reality, but to the whole of reality. And the question we have been considering is, Is the world of practical experience the world of concrete experience? Is the assertion of reality explicit in practical judgment, a complete assertion? We are not concerned with the general fact that practice is experience; our business is with the specific character of this particular form of experience. And our standpoint is that of the totality of experience.

Now, we have seen that the specific character of any form of experience is its character as a world of experience. Every determinate form of experience is a homogeneous world of experience, and the explicit and immediate end in every form of experience is to make its own world coherent. What and all that is given in a form of experience is a co-ordinated world of experience; and we must accept this world as a whole and as a world. We must accept it for what it is. Thus, the question we are concerned with may be reformulated; Is the world of experience given us in practical experience, as a whole and as a world, the totality of experience, or is it not? That practical experience provides what is in some degree satisfactory in experience cannot be doubted. But it is not the degree of achievement in practical experience upon which we have to decide: that is a question I have set on one side. Ours has been the simpler enquiry, Is the world of practical experience, as a whole, the world of complete and concrete experience, the world of reality, or is it not? And I must insist, once more, that this is a question which must be answered with an absolute affirmative or an absolute negative. From this point of view the world of practical experience must be accepted or rejected as a whole. The question we have set ourselves is a question of absolutes, and an answer in terms of degrees must be impertinent. Practical experience may be said to be a world of experience with some degree of truth; but what we wish to discover is whether or not this world is the world of absolute truth, the world of concrete reality.

Any one who has followed my argument so far will be in no doubt about the answer which must be given to this question. To examine the character of the world of practical experience in detail is to become convinced of its abstractness and inadequacy from the standpoint of the totality of experience. And I have no hope of convincing any one who has not already convinced himself. But it is important that the reasons upon which we maintain this conclusion should be valid, and I propose to offer now a brief summary of the grounds on which I base the view that practice is experience, but an arrest in experience; that the world of practice is a world of experience, but not the world ultimately satisfactory in experience.

Among those ready to believe that the world of practical experience is incomplete from the standpoint of the totality of experience there are some who maintain this belief on the grounds of the obvious insufficiency of our practical experience and the lack of system which distinguishes our way of life. Even the wisest could be wiser; and we shall look in vain for the man whose life is altogether rational. But it will easily be recognized that these are not valid grounds for asserting the incompleteness (in the sense of the abstractness) of the world of practical experience. We have seen that the present incompleteness of our scientific knowledge is not a valid ground upon which to maintain the abstractness of scientific experience as such, and similarly the incompleteness of its present content is inadmissible as evidence of the inadequacy and abstractness of practical experience from the standpoint of the totality of experience. Nevertheless, it is so commonly believed that practical experience is inadequate solely on account of the actual incompleteness of our practical experience that we ought to consider, for a moment, the misapprehensions upon which this view rests.

The assertion of the disorganized and unsystematic character of practical experience comprises, I think, two notions which it will be useful to distinguish. And both these notions rest upon a misconception. First, what is in the minds of those who make this assertion is that our own practical experience, and that which we judge others to possess, is full of irrationality, prejudice and contingency. We hope one day for what we fear the next. What gave us pleasure yesterday causes only pain to-day. We desire what does not bring us satisfaction. We love what we hate, and hate what we love. Neither our desires, nor our hopes nor any other mood in practical experience can be persuaded to compose a consistent whole; the random, unguided element is on the surface for all to see. And, if we turn to our specifically moral experience, this element is emphasized rather than diminished. Our particular attempts to convert 'what is here and now' into 'what ought to be' are governed by no general rules. Nobody not forced to do so by some moral or spiritual tyranny—tyranny of education or of command—conducts his life according to a set of absolute principles, unmodified by the common-sense, intuition or insight which interprets such principles. And, though we may discover in another a more organized world of practical experience than we can discover in ourselves, we shall find nowhere a completely integrated world of practical experience, a life which is a perfect system: that is something which lies beyond, not only our actual experience, but our imagination also. Now, it is clear enough that, whatever general truth this view of practical experience may contain, it is not a truth relevant to the determination of the character of practical experience from the standpoint of the totality of experience. In deciding the character of practical experience from that standpoint, what we must consider is not the character of the practical experience of which we are conscious, but the character of practical experience which is implied in our actual experience. And our unawareness of the systematic and organized world implied in our random experiences is no argument whatever against the existence of such a world. It means merely that we are not ordinarily conscious of its existence. We must then, look elsewhere for a demonstration of the absolute inadequacy of the world of practical experience.

But, secondly, what may be in the minds of those who assert the incompleteness of practical experience is not only that we are aware of it in our own personal experience, but that it is an essential characteristic of practical experience. This unsystematic character is not only incidental, but inherent in the nature of practical experience. It is to be preserved rather than suppressed, fostered rather than restrained. A life like that of Don Quixote, regulated entirely by what he had read in the books of chivalry, a life cluttered up with doctrinaire precedent, is a life devoid of vitality, a contradiction. And this, perhaps, is most keenly felt in connexion with what is thought of as the specifically moral life. The moment morality is identified with the mere observance of a rule it ceases to be moral. And further, so soon as moral action is reduced to mere reasoning, the calculation of chances, the forecasting of results, or the application of general rules, it has surrendered the very characteristic which most distinguishes it. Law is the enemy of the moral life; casuistry the grave of moral sensibility. But this prejudice against the realization of the consistent world of experience which I take to be implied in practical experience is also misconceived. It suffers primarily, I think, from careless specification; for in it two separate notions are confused. There is, first, the notion that it is repugnant that the practical experience of any man should be a perfectly consistent whole, integrated in every detail, an organized system. And, secondly, there is the notion that it is repugnant that a man's practical life should be governed by a set of ready-made and absolute principles or rules which come to him either by way of command or advice. A man's practical experience should consist of something more than the application of a system of rules to what life offers him. But, whatever truth there is in the second of these views, the first is by no means involved in it. Yet, unless the first can be established, we are still without any reasonable ground for supposing that practical experience does not imply a world of experience in the full sense. And the obstacles in the way of establishing this supposition seem to me insuperable. For what is repugnant is not that a man's life should be a perfectly consistent whole, but that it should be an incoherent collection of isolated desires, hopes, fears and achievements. I do not mean that this is *morally* repugnant (though to some it may very well be that), I mean that it is contradictory of practical experience itself to select incoherence as a satisfactory state of a man's world of practical experience. And I believe that any other view, any view which supports the notion that disorganization is inherent in practical experience, rests upon a conception of 'intuition' or 'insight' (which is taken to represent practical experience) which I have already considered and dismissed. There are those whose life is ruled by what appears to be a happy instinct, who do not require to do what has been called "laying in a stock of light for our difficulties" (for, living extemporally, they have no difficulties); they

> rely
> Upon the genial sense of youth.

But it is not these whose practical life composes no system or whole, whose practical experience is most nearly removed from the condition of a coherent world of knowledge. That, rather, is the condition of the practical experience of those who pass a futile and feverish existence endeavouring to make their random desires and capricious hopes conform to some preconceived system of general maxims. For, what is characteristic of a world of experience is not that it is the product of prolonged argument and reflection, but that it composes a coherent whole. But, if reflection be required to weld our practical experience into a world, it is not less a world on that account. The division between intuition and thought we have already seen to be misconceived; and this instance of it is no exception to our general conclusion. It is one thing to say that a man should live as he feels and not according to some extraneous and preconceived theory of life, but it is quite another to say that his feelings should be disorganized and capricious. And there is no reason why he should be denied the use of reflection if that be required to co-ordinate his experience. It is one thing to say that there is a kind of reflection, that there are modes of thought, which will paralyse moral sensibility and make a man less, rather than more capable of conducting his life, but it is quite another to say that the less a man thinks about how he is acting the more satisfactory will be his way of living. There is a difference between the "unexamined life", which Plato said no man would wish to lead, and a life devoid of a philosophical or speculative interest. Though it is, perhaps, the major defect of Plato's philosophy that it fails to recognize this difference.

I conclude, then, that those who assert that practical experience is an abstract and defective mode of experience because it is, not a world of experience at all, but a mere collection of miscellaneous experiences, have (indeed) discovered a defect which is common to the practical experience of most persons, but have presented us with no ground whatever for supposing that a fully coherent world of experience is not implied and involved in practical experience as we know it. They have discovered an incidental defect, but they have not discovered a radical and absolute deficiency. And if the world of practical experience, as a world, is to be convicted of abstraction, we must look elsewhere for evidence and an argument to serve our purpose.

The essential abstractness of the world of practical experience may, I think, be shown to arise, neither from the present incompleteness of our practical experience, nor from its apparent lack of organization (which is sometimes mistaken for inherent chaos), but from the terms in which the attempt in practice to achieve what is ultimately satisfactory in experience is conceived and executed. Practice is the reconciliation, in detail and in practical fact, of 'what is here and now' and 'what ought to be'; it is this and all that it presupposes and involves. It is not the reconciliation in principle of the discrepancy between what is valuable and what is practical fact, but the reconciliation of each instance of this discrepancy as it arises. And such a reconciliation can never be finally achieved. For, no sooner is it executed in one instance, than a fresh example is presented. We have at each moment in practical experience a partially integrated world of experience, but that integration (on account of the character of the experience involved) can never be finally completed. The assertion of reality in practical judgment must remain always partial and inadequate. The presupposition of practical experience is that 'what is here and now' and 'what ought to be' are discrepant. And practice is not the reconciliation of these worlds as worlds, but the reconciliation of particular instances of this discrepancy. To reconcile these worlds generally and absolutely would involve the abolition of the discrepancy, the denial of what is presupposed throughout. 'What is here and now' and 'what ought to be' must be continually reconciled and as often left discrete; they must be brought together, but always held apart. Practice is the healing of a division between two modes of existence, a division which the lapse of time perpetually remakes. Permanent dissatisfaction (no matter how satisfied we may be with ourselves and our achievements) is inherent in practical experience; the explicit assertion of reality in practical judgment is never complete and consequently the world of practical experience as a world, is, from the standpoint of the totality of experience, abstract and incoherent. It is an abstract mode of experience, an arrest in experience. Practical experience is the world *sub specie voluntatis*; and the will is not a separate faculty, volition is not a separate kind of experience, but an inadequate mode of experience.

Furthermore, practice appears to undertake and to execute an actual change in the real world: practical experience is experience which claims to be creative in the largest sense. It is the world conceived under the category of change; its explicit assertion of reality is in terms of change, and the purpose in it is the transformation of reality. And on account of this, practical experience must be considered to contradict the character of experience, and the world of practical experience must be considered a world of self-contradictions. In experience, we have seen, what is undertaken is the modification, the transformation of a given world of experience on account of the incoherence of that world; but a form of experience in which achievement is represented as the modification of reality, the transformation of the real world, convicts itself of contradiction. The modification or change of reality is a meaningless conception. And the world of practical experience, in so far as it adheres to what is explicit in its character, must renounce the capacity to achieve what would be satisfactory in experience; and if it surrenders its own explicit character, it surrenders itself. Practice is a mode of experience the validity of which is denied by the character of experience. Like history, which threw reality into the form of the past only to discover that 'reality' and 'the past' are contradictory, practice purports to throw reality into the future, into something new and to be made, only to discover that this also is a contradiction of the character of experience.

And here we might leave the matter. The world conceived *sub specie voluntatis* and conceived under the category of change, is an abstract world. But there are some who will mistake a feeling of satisfaction for evidence that practical experience is not, in the end, an abstract, defective, mode of experience. There are others whose solid achievements will have blinded them to this aspect of practical experience. And there are many who, because they are unaware of any other experience than practical experience, will find it difficult (perhaps humiliating) to admit that this experience is not, and can never be the concrete whole of experience. The inherent unsatisfactoriness of practical activity is *felt* probably only by those who are temperamentally despondent, and these (regardless of the irrelevance of their conclusions) will require no persuasion that practical experience is ultimately and necessarily defective. But those who have not lost the "feeling of immortality", who are still on the high tide of hope and consequently deaf to the suggestions of any who do not sail with them, will not easily be persuaded that the world they live in is not the world of reality, that their world of experience is abstract, and that even though they "drink life to the lees", or "sail beyond the sunset", they will not succeed in discovering the real world in its total reality. And for them, if for no others, a more detailed and precise argument will perhaps be required.

Practice, we have seen, presupposes a world of 'what is here and now', it presupposes a world of 'what is valuable', and it is the reconciliation of these worlds. Let us, then, reconsider the character of each of these worlds, and of this reconciliation from the standpoint of the totality of experience.

The world of 'practical existence' is, in the first place, a world, not merely susceptible of change, but a world determined by change. Change is the concept or category under which reality is known in the world of practical existence. What is not transient is, for that reason, not real for practical experience. And further, this world of 'what is here and now' is a world of the present as such. Reality, in practical experience, is a momentary and absolutely present reality. In one sense, we have seen, all reality is essentially present; but what distinguishes reality in practical experience is that it is the merely present, what is present as such. And it is real because it is present. And, again, fact and reality in practical experience are the product of designation. The individuals of practical experience are merely designated individuals. And on account of each of these characteristics this world of 'what is here and now' cannot be considered to be the real world. A world determined by the category of change lacks the coherence which belongs to reality: a world which is merely present, is no less abstract than one which is merely past or merely future: and a world constituted by designation is a world of individuals which fall short of complete individuality; for designation is itself an arrest in experience, it is definition falling short of itself. We must conclude, then, that the explicit assertion of reality in the world of 'what is here and now' is incomplete and abstract.

The second presupposition of practical activity is a world of value, a world of 'what ought to be'. This also, we have seen, is a world of existence: and value is a form of experience. But the explicit experience in valuation, the explicit assertion of reality in a judgment of value, falls short of completeness. In valuation there is the whole of reality, but from an abstract point of view; there is a partial, abstract experience. And a judgment of value, though it asserts something of reality, falls short of asserting what it judges, and in this respect it classes itself with imagination, with supposition and with denial. So far as its explicit content is concerned, every judgment of value has meaning and relevance, truth or falsehood with reference only to a confined and special world. Reality as a whole is neither valuable nor worthless. Every belief in the value or the worthlessness of life, every attribution of value whatsoever, signifies an arrest in experience. And, further, the world of value, the world of 'what ought to be' is qualified and controlled by the world of 'what is here and now'; nothing can be valuable which cannot belong to the world of practical existence. And the abstract character of the world of value is involved in the abstract character of the world of practical existence.

Practical activity itself is the reconciliation of the world of 'what is here and now' and the world of 'what is valuable'. It is not the reconciliation of them as worlds, rather it is the modification of the world of practical existence in terms of the world of value. Practical activity, then, is experience which involves the presupposition that two different and discrete worlds are both real, though not equally real. It is permanently divided between the reality of 'what is here and now' and the reality of 'what ought to be'; sometimes one and sometimes the other will appear in practical experience to possess the superior reality. And, again, practical activity is the transformation of the given world of 'what is here and now', but it is not the total transformation of that world. The transformation to which practical activity subjects this world does not touch the main structure of that world;

it is a transformation merely of content. The principle of transience lies, for example, beyond the reach of practical activity itself. And, consequently, the world achieved in practical experience does not differ in principle from the given world. If what is given, if this world of 'what is here and now' is abstract, what is achieved will be no less abstract. For what is achieved by practical activity is always a world of 'what is here and now'. And, once more, everything is subordinated by practice to the will. Practical experience is the world *sub specie voluntatis*, and this experience is an abstract and incomplete experience.

On all sides, then, practical experience reveals its inherent unsatisfactoriness from the standpoint of the totality of experience. It is an arrest in experience, a modification of experience. And the world of practical experience, as a whole and as a world, must suffer supersession. Practical truth is not ultimate truth; and what is real, or what is asserted of the real in practice is not ultimately real. What contributes to the coherence of the world of practical experience is, of course, true for practice; and from that standpoint there is nothing more to be said. Every truth is true in its own place. But practice cannot confine itself to itself, it cannot separate itself from the totality of experience. For in practice there is necessarily an attempt to find and assert the totality of experience, the real world, and practical experience demands to be judged from this standpoint. And when judged from this standpoint it is found to be abstract and incomplete. And consequently the world of practical experience, as a world, has no contribution to make to the totality of experience.

Practical truth is the truth that we can live by and act upon; it is the truth which can give freedom. And similarly, the errors of practice are those which enslave, which mislead our conduct and endanger our lives.[1] And in this connexion, what belongs to practice in general, belongs also

[1] "Generally speaking, the errors of religion are dangerous; those of philosophy only ridiculous." Hume, *Treatise of Human Nature*, I, iv, 7.

and particularly to morality and religion. "The common prejudice in favour of the ultimate truth of morality and religion" still exists, though perhaps less strongly than before: nevertheless, if the view I have suggested be true, the grounds upon which, among the so-called 'enlightened', this prejudice is rejected are usually irrelevant and often inadequate. To base such a rejection upon the variety of moral and religious opinion, the instability of moral and religious custom or the development of moral and religious ideas is entirely to misconceive the situation: it is but to replace one prejudice by another. What alone requires us to reject this prejudice is the abstract character of the mode of experience to which morality and religion belong. And this compels us to assert at once the sovereignty of moral and religious truth in the practical world, and the abstract and defective character of moral and religious truth from the standpoint of the totality of experience. Religion, we have seen, is practical experience pressed to its conclusion; in it all subordinate attempts to establish the harmony, unity or coherence of the world of practical experience—attempts such as politics and morality constitute—are swallowed up and superseded. Religious truths are those which are necessary to practical existence, without which practical existence falls short of coherence; they are those which attempt to satisfy the furthest claims and largest needs of practical life. Yet religion, in the persons both of its defenders and those who have attacked it, has claimed more. It has claimed that its truths are not merely practical, but belong to the world of concrete truth. But, were this so, their practical value would at once disappear. And the business of establishing both the practical and the ultimate truth of religious ideas is a task which any one who is aware of the conflict involved is not likely to undertake. If religion has anything to do with the conduct of life, then the ideas of religion—ideas such as those of deity, of salvation and of immortality—are practical ideas and belong to the world of practice. And an idea which serves this world can serve no other. So far from it being the case that nothing less than ultimate, concrete truth will serve the purpose of religion, those who have any conception of what they mean by such truth know well enough that where it is not irrelevant to religion it must be inimical.

My conclusion, then, is that the world of practical experience turns out on consideration to be abstract and defective throughout. The pursuit of coherence in it must lead us further from, not closer to, concrete truth and reality. The homogeneity of this, as of every abstract world of experience, is the homogeneity of death. Its truth is true so far as it goes, but, because it stands in the way of our going further, it must be rejected *in toto*. Practical experience, to gain the whole world, must lose its own soul. Not until we have become wholly indifferent to the truths of this world of practice, not until we have shaken off the abstractions of practical experience, of morality and religion, good and evil, faith and freedom, body and mind, the practical self and its ambitions and desires, shall we find ourselves once more turned in the direction which leads to what can satisfy the character of experience.[1] For, since the

---

[1] This, perhaps, is the meaning, or one of the meanings, of the passages in the *Phaedo* (and elsewhere) in which Socrates asserts that those who engage in philosophy "study only dying and death". For, to be dead to the world of practice, as also to all other abstract worlds of experience (and Socrates is thinking particularly of the world of 'sensation'), is the beginning of philosophy. Religion begins with the renunciation of one abstraction which it calls 'the world', in order to devote itself to another abstraction; philosophy begins with the renunciation of all abstractions whatsoever. *Der echte philosophische Akt ist Selbsttötung*, says Novalis. But it should not be supposed that every one who engages in philosophy must be expected to make a beginning by committing suicide. Suicide, in the vulgar sense, is an attempt to solve practical difficulties and belongs to the world of practice; it will solve no philosophical problems. It merely replaces one practical abstraction, life, by another practical abstraction, death. Nor should the fact that the philosopher is an exile from the practical world be taken to mean that he not only is but ought to be a fool in practical affairs. It is philosophy itself which must be free from the abstractions of living; and no man is merely a philosopher. *Es ist nichts Herabwürdigendes darin, dass jemand lebt*, remarks Hegel; nevertheless, from the stand-

world of practical experience is abstract and defective, a modification of experience, it cannot be considered a necessary form of experience. However unavoidable it may be, it is not, from the standpoint of the totality of experience, necessary. From that standpoint, indeed, it is no more than a *cul-de-sac*, a regrettable mistake, perhaps a youthful folly, which, if it cannot be avoided, must be superseded.

## § 8

It will not be necessary for me to consider in detail the relationship of the world of practical experience with the two other worlds of abstract ideas the characters of which I have discussed—the worlds of history and science. I have shown, in principle, that all abstract worlds of experience are wholly independent of one another. Between them there can be no passage of argument whatever without the grossest fallacy. What is true for one of these worlds can be neither true nor false for any other; it is merely irrelevant. To carry a practical attitude into the world of science or history, or to carry a scientific or an historical attitude into the world of practice, must, in every case, turn what is significant into nonsense, turn what is valuable into something worthless by dragging it into the wrong market: and this, I take it, is the essential character of *ignoratio elenchi*. Nevertheless, there are a few remarks which must be made under this head.

(i) I have considered already the necessity which scientific thinking is under of freeing itself, at the outset, from the conceptions which belong to the world of practice. The importation of these conceptions into the world of science is the source of almost every departure of scientific thought

point of the totality of experience, it is a defective (though not degraded) existence to remain in front of this "painted veil which those who live call life". And, after all, this freedom from extraneous purpose and irrelevant interest is the sign of all seriously undertaken thought. Philosophy is remarkable only because the interests which are extraneous to it are those which engage the sympathies and attention of the majority of mankind.

from its true path. In the past the attempt to limit the methods and conclusions of science to those acceptable, not only to the particular religious beliefs of the time, but to religious beliefs in general, has always bred false science. It has resulted either in confusion or sterility. And at the present time there would appear to be some danger that science, in attempting to become 'popular', in attempting to translate its conclusions into the language and conceptions of practice, should do for itself what it had previously suffered from other antithetical modes of experience.

But we have now to consider the consequences of an incursion of scientific thought into the world of practical experience. And my view is, of course, that such an incursion causes no less error and confusion in the world of practice than that which follows, in the world of science, from a similar incursion of practical thought. No other conclusion is possible on the view I have taken of the character of these worlds of experience. Nevertheless, it is not easy for the modern mind to accept this view. We have too long been accustomed to the notions that science is a guide to life, that science is the only true guide to life, and that the world of practical experience (and particularly moral and religious ideas) must submit themselves to the criticism of scientific thought, for any other view not to appear false or reactionary or both. But there is little in the history of folly to which one may compare the infatuation which the modern mind has conceived for 'science'.

I do not propose to consider in detail the various attempts to construct a 'science of life'. These attempts follow, in the main, the character of the attempts to construct a science of history, which I have already examined. My conclusion then was that in so far as each of these attempts involved genuine scientific thinking, it must fall altogether outside the world of history; and that in so far as they involved a way of thinking which was not genuinely scientific, no good purpose could be served by attributing to them a character they do not possess. And, I think, wherever a 'science of life' has been attempted its relation to the world of practical experience will be found to be similar to that which exists between a 'science of history' and the world of historical experience. That is, in so far as economics, or psychology or biology belong to the world of scientific experience, they must surrender all claim to be a guide to life; and in so far as they are not scientific, it is misleading to say that a 'science of life' is produced when they are connected with the world of practical experience.

Now, the grounds of the confusion which attributes to science the capacity to organize our world of practical experience lie equally, I think, in a false conception of science and in a false conception of practical experience. For example, the conception of science and the scientific method which takes it to be the only gateway to a true knowledge of the universe has been made the foundation of the view that the world of practical experience can be made coherent only with the aid of scientific thought. But this view is false both in what it asserts and in what it implies. For we have seen already that we grossly misrepresent the character of scientific thinking when we take it to be the only gateway to a knowledge of the universe. The world of scientific experience is a world of abstract ideas; and scientific experience is a defective mode of experience. But even if we suppose the world of scientific experience to be the world of concrete reality, scientific knowledge could not be considered necessary or relevant to the organization of the world of practical experience unless that also were taken to be the world of concrete reality. We have seen, however, that practical experience is abstract and incomplete; and ultimate truth must always be irrelevant to an abstract world of experience as such. This argument in favour of a 'science of life' must, then, be considered wholly fallacious, a congeries of misconceptions. There are only two circumstances in which scientific truth could be relevant to practice. First, if the worlds of science and of practice were abstract and equally abstract, if they constituted the same arrest in experience, and were consequently indistinguishable. And secondly, if both science and practice gave us the world of concrete reality, and were for that reason indistinguishable. But neither of these conditions is satisfied. And again, so long as scientific experience is not set free from the presuppositions and conceptions of practical experience, it will appear to have some connexion with practice. But genuine scientific experience begins only with the attainment of this freedom: not until the scientist as such has discarded "the world which spontaneously appears to him when he opens his eyes", does his thinking begin to be scientific. And so soon as this freedom is attained, the apparent connexion between science and practical life at once disappears. Scientific ideas are seen neither to work nor to fail in the practical world; they are seen merely to be irrelevant. Of course, it is possible to relate certain pseudo-scientific ideas to the world of practice, but the relation is itself a removal of them from the world of science to that of practical life, and with this removal they cease at once to be—or rather, even to seem to be—scientific ideas. It appears, then, that practical experience is not under the necessity of submitting itself to the criticism of scientific thought. Popular science no doubt has its place as an intellectual interest, and the application of pseudo-scientific ideas to practical life has, perhaps, increased the happiness of our existence; but it can procure nothing save error and superstition when it leads us to recognize no truth but that abstract and attenuated mode of truth which belongs to the world of science.

My business is not to point out the detailed implication of this view, but I may be forgiven for remarking that it is not unlikely that some of our ideas about morality and religion would require revision were we to take it seriously. Those who have undertaken to consider the nature and grounds of our moral judgments have long ago faced this problem of the relationship between the scientific and the moral world, and with what success it is not for me to say. But those responsible for our theological thought have not, I think, been equally successful in distinguishing the roots of the problem. A practical interest has usually intervened to put an end to serious discussion; the philosophical problem has been abandoned in favour of a merely political dispute; on both sides, the assertion of prejudices and opinions has taken the place of argument. But my view is, in short, that practical, moral and religious beliefs must submit themselves, not to the criticism of science, but to that of life. And a science which ventured to take a hand in organizing the world of religious beliefs would be a science which had ceased to be scientific without becoming anything else. "It is better", as Epicurus said, "to follow the myths of the gods than to become a slave to scientific truth."

(ii) In considering the effect upon the world of historical experience of an invasion of practical thought I was led in an earlier chapter to discuss also the effect of an incursion of history into the world of practice. And to that discussion little requires to be added. My conclusion was that the invasion of either by the other is a disaster followed on every occasion by the disintegration of both. Neither can enter the other without suffering the loss of its own character. Neither can submit to the other without surrendering itself entirely. Between the worlds of history and of practice, as specific worlds of experience, there is an impassable gulf. Both in history and in practice there is an attempt to find and elucidate a finally coherent world of experience. But since in both cases there is a failure to achieve what was undertaken, and since the failure is at different points, they must be regarded as logically exclusive of one another.

In view of the way in which science and religion have been set over against one another, it is, however, a matter of some surprise that more has not been heard of a collision between history and religion; there are certainly grounds for such a conflict. The notion of deity is one which both history and science must reject or neglect. No conflict, of course, can arise between history and religion so long as each mode of thought confines itself to what it is competent to conclude.

Science, history and practice, as such, cannot collide; they are merely irrelevant to one another. Yet it might be supposed that the invasion of religion by historical thought, and the consequent error and confusion, is not so rare that we should expect them to pass unnoticed. And Christianity, for example, has perhaps suffered more and has more to fear from the incursions of history than from those of science.

But perhaps it is in the field of politics rather than in the fields of religion and morality that practical experience is most often in danger of perversion by the irrelevant intrusion of history. Both the active politician and the writer on politics, both the reformer and the conservator invoke the oracle of history and interpret its answer according to their predisposition, giving out their conclusions as the lessons of history. But history itself has neither the ideas nor the language wherewith to teach practical conclusions. And those who assert themselves to have learnt something from history, may have learnt what they assert, and it may be true, but they certainly have not learnt it from history.

## § 9

It may, perhaps, be thought that I have reached my conclusions in this chapter without taking sufficient account of other and contradictory views. I am aware, of course, that there are views different from that which I have recommended, but a detailed account of what I have thought about them would be out of place here, where I am concerned to state a view of my own rather than to give an account of what others have thought. And besides, a theory cannot satisfactorily be maintained merely by disposing of certain objections to it; and I have thought it necessary to discuss objections to my view only in so far as this would enable me to make clearer the full character of the theory I am defending. Nevertheless, our grasp of that theory must remain incomplete and insecure so long as we do not appreciate what it denies as well as what it expressly asserts. And I wish to conclude by considering a few of the notions which this theory requires us to abandon.

The general view of the character of practical experience which stands in direct antithesis to the view I have suggested is that which sees in practice the complete and absolute realization of experience. All thought exists for the sake of action; action is the consummation of experience, and we try to understand the universe only in order to learn how to live. The activity which realizes the full character of mind is that which is connected with the will. To realize the will is itself to realize the mind as a whole: all other experience, every other attitude and mood, is subordinate to this. The real world is the world *sub specie voluntatis*.

Now, a view of this kind is, I know, common enough among those who have not considered the matter very deeply, and I scarcely expect any one who holds it to be persuaded by my arguments. Nevertheless, when we turn to those who have given the question some thought, this view is not so common as it might, at first sight, appear. And I think that wherever a writer is found asserting this view, he will be found also to have mistaken the character of what he believes himself to be denying. Practice is set over against what is spoken of as 'theory'; and when 'theory' is interpreted in its most abstract sense and is then represented as the only competitor, it is not difficult to show the relatively more complete coherence of the world of practice. But this alternative between practice and theory is false and misleading, because, when we have abandoned practice as the final satisfaction in experience, we are not obliged to concede this character to what is represented as 'theory'. Kant, for example, found it necessary to subordinate theoretical reason to practical because the former, as he conceived it, was limited to 'phenomena'; that is, it was not unlike what I have spoken of as scientific experience. It was a dissatisfaction with what appeared to be the only alternative which drove him to assert the primacy of practical experience. And in this he has been followed by a large body of thinkers. Others have identified 'theory' and 'rationalism' or 'intellectualism', and have set their belief in the finality of the will over against what they call 'mere intellectualism'. A rationalism of this sort, it is true, is an abstract mode of experience. Indeed, there is little or nothing to be said in its favour. Where it is not a confusion of scientific, historical and practical thought, it will be found to be an attempt to replace science, history and practice by an attenuated and falsely conceived 'philosophy'; and its result is distinguished only by its inconsequence. But to think of this as the only alternative to a belief in the finality of practice, and to conclude, from the obvious abstractness of the one, the completeness of the other, is a form of argument which might be expected to appeal to none but 'rationalists'.

Or again, what is called Pragmatism might be taken to assert the finality of practical experience. But this, I think, would be a mistake. It is true that we are still waiting for an unambiguous statement of the pragmatist position; but later writers, in an attempt to repair some of the weaknesses of William James' position, have directed our attention away from his doctrine of "practical consequences", and pragmatism can no longer be considered as the assertion of practice as the criterion of experience. Pragmatism in its early days had much to say about practice as the criterion of truth, and so far as it is possible to ascertain, 'practice' stood for what we should expect—the ordinary conduct of life. The "pragmatic method", we were told, was "to interpret each notion by tracing its respective practical consequences". And whether or not a notion were true would depend upon its practical consequences. There were, of course, difficulties; and it was not always clear whether a notion was to be considered true if it had *any* practical consequences, or only if its practical consequences were "satisfactory". But, on the whole, the early pragmatist position seems to have been, in effect, the assertion of the view that there is no truth save practical truth, that all thought is for the sake of action, and that the real world is the world *sub specie voluntatis*. And this is clearly in direct opposition to the view I have been suggesting. Later writers, however, have withdrawn the emphasis which pragmatism first placed upon 'practical' consequences. On the one side there are those whose pragmatism is almost confined to the view that the truth of an idea lies in its consequences—a theory of knowledge I have already considered. And on the other side there are those who have derived their theory of truth from considering thought from a 'biological' standpoint. An idea is true if and because it is biologically efficient. But these, it will be seen, are theories of knowledge rather than of practice, and in so far as pragmatism has taken up with such ideas as these, it cannot be supposed to assert that what I have called practice is, not an abstract mode of experience, but itself the totality of experience: and consequently it is not among the views which, adherence to the conception of practice I have suggested, requires us to abandon.[1]

The view of the character of practice from the standpoint of the totality of experience which I have been defending, and the view which, if mine is adhered to, must be rejected, may be stated in another form. The contrast may be presented as a contrast between practice and philosophy. And those who wish to represent practical experience as itself the totality of experience may be expected to identify it with philosophy. There is, perhaps, nothing fresh which may usefully be said on this topic, save to emphasize what I have already suggested. Philosophy I have taken to stand for experience which is critical throughout, experience without presupposition, reservation, or arrest. And if practice be what I have contended it is, it cannot, as such, afford any contribution to, or offer any relevant criticism of, philosophical propositions. Life as a guide to philosophy is worse than useless—it is misleading. And wherever an attempt is made to force the

[1] It need scarcely be remarked that these are theories of knowledge which conflict at every point with the theory I have recommended, and for that reason I must reject them.

entry of practical thought into the world of philosophy, nothing but error and confusion can follow. Johnson's celebrated refutation of Berkeley is an attempt of this sort; but he was not the first, nor will he be the last to commit this *ignoratio elenchi*. It is committed daily not only in the name of common-sense, but also in the names of religion and morality. Indeed, it is still true that "there is no method of reasoning more common, and yet none more blameable, than, in philosophical disputes, to endeavour the refutation of any hypothesis, by a pretence of its dangerous consequences to religion and morality".[1] Nevertheless, it is meaningless alike either to accept or to reject a philosophical proposition for a practical reason.

But what I have to insist upon is, equally, the necessity of keeping philosophy unencumbered with the mood and postulates of practical experience, and the necessity of a world of practical experience without the interference of philosophy. In its explicit character, practice is the tireless pursuit of a more satisfying way of life; and in serving this purpose it must relinquish all capacity (though not, of course, the implicit attempt) to serve a less abstract and more complete purpose. Yet it is not to be expected that practice will think nothing of philosophy, and there can be no doubt what it must think. In philosophy there is the explicit pursuit of what is ultimately satisfactory in experience, and, *ex hypothesi*, this must be irrelevant to practical experience; and wherever it enters practical life, that irrelevance must turn to error and falsehood. From the standpoint of practical experience there can be no more dangerous disease than the love and pursuit of truth in those who do not understand, or have forgotten, that a man's first business is to live. And life, we have seen, can be conducted only at the expense of an arrest in experience. The practical consciousness knows well enough what is inimical to its existence, and often has the wisdom to avoid it. *Pereat veritas, fiat vita*. It is not the clearsighted, not those who are fashioned for thought and the

[1] Hume, *Enquiry concerning Human Understanding*, § viii.

ardours of thought, who can lead the world. Great achievements are accomplished in the mental fog of practical experience. What is farthest from our needs is that kings should be philosophers. The victims of thought, those who are intent upon what is unlimitedly satisfactory in experience, are self-confessed betrayers of life, and must pursue their way without the encouragement of the practical consciousness, which is secure in the knowledge that philosophical thought can make no relevant contribution to the coherence of its world of experience. The world of concrete reality must, indeed, supersede the world of practical experience, but can never take its place.

> The splendours of the firmament of time
> May be eclipsed, but are extinguished not.

# VI

## CONCLUSION

It is, I suppose, the ambition of everyone who thinks to understand himself, and of every writer to be understood; whether the writer can also convince and persuade is a matter upon which he is wise to be indifferent. But, in order to be understood he will set out his view as completely and as clearly as he is able. For what is either partial or confused will at once be ambiguous. It is difficult, however, in a long argument to preserve a continuous emphasis upon the view as a whole; it is difficult to be certain that what is taken for the whole is actually complete. I propose, then, in this conclusion to offer a brief restatement of the general view I have been defending, and to show also how this general view is capable of meeting difficulties which any view of the character of experience should be prepared to meet, to show how (though incomplete as it stands) this view might be completed.

### § 1

My view is, in the first place, that experience (by which I mean the single and indivisible whole within which experiencing and what is experienced have their place) is always a world. Not only must we say that with every experience there comes a world of experience; we must say that every experience is a world. What is given in experience is a world, and what is achieved is this given world made more of a world. What is given in experience is single and significant, a One and not a Many.

Secondly, experience implies thought or judgment; it is always and everywhere a world of ideas. Sensation, perception, intuition, feeling and volition are never independent kinds of experience, they are different levels or degrees of judgment. What is given in experience is a world of ideas, and what is achieved is that world of ideas made more of a world. There is no experience which is not an idea, and no idea which is not a world.

Further, truth is the world of experience as a coherent whole; nothing else is true, and there is no criterion of truth other than this coherence. Thus, truth and experience are given together, and it is impossible to separate them. Truth is what is given in experience, because what is given is given as a coherent world of ideas; without truth there can be no experience. And truth is what is achieved in experience, because what is achieved is a coherent world of ideas, a world of ideas at once single and complete.

And again, no separation is possible between experience and reality. Reality is nothing but experience, the world of experience as a coherent whole. Everything is real so long as we do not take it for more or less than it is. Nothing is real save the world of experience single and complete. Thus, reality is a world, and is a world of ideas.

Moreover, in every experience there is the whole of reality. That is, experience or reality is not divisible into parts or departments; there are no distinct and separate areas of experience, no separate fields of knowledge. In every judgment whatever something is asserted of the whole of reality. And neither denial, nor supposal, nor imagination, nor opinion, nor any other form of judgment in which this positive assertion of the whole of reality is not explicit can be admitted as an exception. Wherever anything is denied something else is asserted; and wherever anything is asserted, it is asserted of the whole of reality.

Nevertheless, it is not true that in every experience the whole of reality is given explicitly and as a whole; it is not true that in every judgment the whole of reality is asserted directly and as a whole. But, wherever in experience reality is not given explicitly and as a whole there has occurred what I have called an arrest in experience; the full obligations of experience have been avoided, its full character surrendered. Now, these arrests in experience may take place at different points; and each one is a determinate falling short in experience, differing from every other by reason of the degree of deficiency it represents. Again, each arrest is a determinate world of ideas, distinguished from every other world of ideas in respect of the precise assertion of reality it embodies. And I have called these arrests in experience, modes or modifications of experience. But it is important to notice that a mode of experience is not a distinct kind of experience; it is a distinct level or degree of experience. And a mode of experience, from the standpoint of the totality of experience, is a world of abstract ideas. But here again, it is important that this category of abstraction should be taken fully and seriously. A mode of experience is not an independent stage in experience; in the end, a mode has no independence, because its character depends upon the totality of which it is a modification, the concrete whole of which it is an abstraction. The totality is not made up of its modifications, the concrete whole is not a collection or a system of abstractions. For what is genuinely abstract is not a part of the whole, it does not contribute to the wholeness of the whole, and certainly it is not prior to the whole; it is the whole as a whole falling short of its full character.

This view provides us with three different standpoints from which we may consider experience. From one point of view there is in every experience the whole of reality: every judgment is the assertion of reality as a whole. Of course, every judgment is not equally the assertion of reality as a whole. But every judgment is alike in respect of its being an assertion of reality as a whole. Thus, from this standpoint, experience is single, and a kind of equality can be maintained between every item in experience. This is the pure generality of experience, its abstractly universal character. And because this is an abstract point of view, it must be superseded. From another standpoint, experience is always a homogeneous world of ideas. To be a world is the form of every experience. And the experience of each one of us, in so far as it is our experience and from that point of view, composes always a single, homogeneous world. Experience is always somebody's experience, and on account of this it is a world, it is single and homogeneous. This is the pure particularity of experience, its abstractly particular character. And because this also is an abstract point of view it likewise requires to be superseded. The third point of view from which experience may be considered is the standpoint of the significance or validity of experience. From this point of view experience is seen to have specific content and significant form. For in each experience there is seen to be a specific reference to reality, and the question of the adequacy of that reference is, for the first time, considered and determined. And each experience, in virtue of the specific assertion of reality contained in it, assumes a specific form. The form of experience, that is, is no longer determined by the mere fact of experience, but by the quality of experience, and consequently it is, for the first time, significant. The world of experience is judged no longer from the standpoint of its bare singleness and homogeneity, but from the standpoint of its coherence. Thus, experience is seen as a differentiated whole, a diverse unity; and the question of the character of the diversity and of the character of the unity is at once presented. And this, I take it, is the concrete point of view, which, because it is complete, requires no supersession.

Now, the first thing to be noticed with regard to the diversity appearing in experience is that it is a significant, and not a merely capricious or contingent diversity. Each mode of experience represents a specific level or achievement in experience. The diversity is never mere diversity, for there is nothing separate and independent, nothing which does not derive its character from its relation to the totality, nothing which does not submit to the single principle of subordination. The criterion of coherence is universal; and where there is a universal criterion there can be no mere diversity, no contingency. But these modes of experience, these abstract worlds of experience may be seen from two standpoints. We may regard them as they are in themselves, regard them, that is, from the point of view of the specific achievement in experience which they embody. Or we may regard them from the standpoint of the concrete totality of experience itself. And it is, I think, important to distinguish between these two standpoints.

From the first of these points of view each abstract world of ideas would be seen as the achievement of a certain degree of coherence in the world of experience, it would be seen to contain an assertion of reality, true so far as it went, but falling short of completeness. What would come into view would be the specific achievement or degree of achievement characteristic of each mode of experience. And further, experience would be seen as a kind of hierarchy of modes. Each mode would be subjected to the criterion of coherence and assigned its place according to the degree of its achievement. But this point of view, as I see it, is abstract and defective; the view of experience it gives is incomplete, for the standpoint is not that of the totality of experience as such. And if our view is to throw off this abstraction, it must take its stand upon the concrete totality of experience; it must, that is to say, be a genuinely philosophical view. And from this standpoint, what is apparent is not the relative achievement in each mode of experience, but the fact of abstraction, the fact of modality itself. Experience is no longer seen as a hierarchy of abstract worlds of ideas, but as a single concrete whole in which every modification represents an arrest, and every arrest a failure.

Our standpoint, then, is that of the totality of experience; and the problems we have to consider are, (i) the relation of modes of experience to one another, and (ii) the relation of modes of experience to the concrete totality of experience.

(i) Each mode of experience is a homogeneous world of abstract ideas. And what distinguishes one such world of experience from another is the degree of completeness belonging to the assertion of reality which it contains, or the degree of failure to achieve a complete and absolute assertion of reality. It is clear, then, that these worlds, as worlds, are exclusive of one another. Of course, since all are modifications of a single, concrete whole they have a general character in common: but as specific and abstract worlds they are independent of one another. What, from the standpoint of one world, is fact, from the standpoint of another is nothing at all. What, from the standpoint of one, is reality, from the standpoint of another lies outside experience and is no reality at all. Each world (and I am speaking only and always of worlds of experience distinguished and constituted by specific differences in the degree in which they achieve or fail to achieve what is satisfactory in experience) is a homogeneous whole which can neither recognize nor admit anything disruptive of its homogeneity; and *ex hypothesi* what belongs to one such world would necessarily disrupt the homogeneity of every other. Between these worlds, then, there can be neither dispute nor agreement; they are wholly irrelevant to one another. And an argument or an inference which pretended to pass from one world to another would be the pattern of all forms of *ignoratio elenchi*. An idea cannot serve two worlds. And although it may be difficult, or even impossible, to determine the exact degree of coherence attained in each or any of these modes of experience, the fact that two worlds are distinguished by different explicit principles of homogeneity, indicates that they are arrests in experience at different points and that they are consequently exclusive of one another.

(ii) From the standpoint of the concrete totality of experience, a mode of experience is a world of abstract ideas. The relation between the totality and the mode is the relation between what is concrete and complete and what is abstract and incomplete. And what that relationship is we have considered already. Since a mode of experience is an abstraction, the totality cannot be conceived as made up of modes; indeed, it is impossible for a mode as such to contribute to the totality. A mode, from the standpoint of the totality, is a failure; and no collection or system of failures can make up a concrete whole. What is not itself the whole is incomplete; and it is irrelevant to suggest that after all what is incomplete possesses a certain degree of completeness. If a mode of experience is what I have asserted it to be, a world of abstract ideas, then, on the one side, such modes depend for their existence upon the totality from which they are abstracted, severed from the concrete whole they are meaningless; and on the other side, the concrete whole, as a whole, must, where it recognizes such modes, supersede them, for as modes they serve, not to fill out the totality, but merely to disrupt it.

This perhaps is a difficult doctrine, and I have no intention of concealing its difficulty; but to make certain that it is not misunderstood I will restate it in a fresh form. What I have called a mode of experience is, as I see it, a contradiction; it contains the element of self-contradiction inherent in all abstraction. On the one hand, a mode of experience, in virtue of its character as a world of ideas, comes before us as that which is satisfactory in experience, a coherent world of ideas; but, on the other hand, in virtue of its modality, it must fall short of a fully coherent world of ideas. Thus, no mode of experience is merely a mode, for no abstraction can be a mere abstraction. And consequently its modality actually and continuously contradicts its character as experience. From the standpoint, then, of the concrete totality the modality of these modes must be destroyed. For it is in respect of their modality that they fail to achieve what is satisfactory in experience; it is their modality as such which is negative, non-contributory, disruptive and contradictory. But what is the modality of a mode of experience? What must be rooted out if we are to expel the modality itself? There can be no doubt, I think, how we must answer these questions. The modality of a mode of experience is its character as a homogeneous whole, its character as a world of experience. It is its character as a world which is negative, non-contributory, disruptive, contradictory and which must consequently be destroyed. Every world of abstract ideas is explicitly the assertion of its own incompleteness; in asserting its character as a world, as a homogeneous whole, it is asserting its pure abstractness. Of course, every such world of ideas is more than merely abstract, but its abstractness lies in its character as a world; and the destruction of this bare abstractness (which the concrete totality of experience demands) is the destruction of the world as a world. And since it has no specific character save its character as a world, when that is destroyed nothing distinctive remains.[1] So far, then, are these modes of experience from having the capacity to contribute to the totality of experience, that all that is specific or distinctive in them—their character as determinate, homogeneous wholes of experience—is exactly what requires to be destroyed. And while every mode depends for whatever meaning or significance it may have upon the concrete totality, that totality is in no sense whatever dependent upon the modes.

One further aspect of this relationship may, perhaps, be noticed. Each world of abstract ideas, we have seen, so long as it is content to mind its own business, is unassailable. None but historical thinking can achieve historical truth. And in this respect every mode of experience is free from the relevant interference both of every other mode and of the concrete totality itself. If what we want is history, or science, or practical experience—if, that is, what we want is an arrest in experience—it is useless to go for it to the concrete totality of experience. Philosophy, no more than science, is able to take the place of historical experience. Actual error, then,

---

[1] 'But', it will be objected, '*something* must remain. Since in every mode there is something present in different degrees, they must in virtue of that sameness at least be relevant to one another and to the whole.' Yes; all this is true, and I have said it myself. But *what* remains is a bare abstract universal, experience in its pure generality. When, for example, the modality of history and of science has been superseded, there remains nothing to distinguish the one from the other; and so long as there is anything to distinguish the one from the other, there is failure, modality and mutual exclusion.

appears, and appears only when what is asserted in a mode is asserted also beyond the mode, is asserted absolutely and without qualification. All this we have noticed already. But what we have now to notice is that this actual error is, in fact, unavoidable so long as the modes remain. It is one thing to say that *if* a mode does not put itself in competition with the concrete totality it is sovereign and unassailable; but it is quite another thing to show that this condition is, or can be satisfied. And, as I see it, in the end it is impossible for a mode of experience not to assert itself absolutely and so sink into actual error. Every world of experience whatever asserts itself as coherent and demands to be taken for and judged as concrete reality; that is what it means to be a world of experience. And this is true, *inter alia*, of every arrest in experience. An arrest in experience knows no better than to assert itself absolutely; it is impossible that it should not be ignorant of its own defect, for to be aware of its defect would be to have overcome it, to have ceased to be this arrest. Thus, a mode of experience cannot fail continuously to put itself in competition with the concrete totality of experience, continuously (that is) to bring itself within the power of the totality. In short, in experience what is incomplete cannot avoid asserting itself as complete; and when it asserts itself as complete, it cannot avoid the destructive force of the criticism of what actually is complete.

This, then, is my general view of experience and its modes. And in applying this general view to actual experience, I have reached the conclusion that those forms of experience called respectively history, science and practice are modes within the meaning of my view. All that I have taken to be true of a mode of experience is true of history, science and practice. Each of these is an arrest in experience, a world of abstract ideas; and in each what is distinctive (from the standpoint of the concrete totality of experience) is its failure to provide what is satisfactory in experience, a coherent world of ideas. We sought in each a full assertion of reality, but found nothing better than an incomplete and abstract assertion. We looked for birds and found only nests. And, from the standpoint of the concrete totality, each of these worlds of ideas must be superseded, each as a world must be destroyed.

§ 2

I have nowhere pretended that the whole actual or possible modification of experience is confined to the three modes which I have chosen to consider in detail. History, Science and Practice were selected, not because between them they comprise the total possibility of arrest in experience, but merely because they appeared to be the chief among the more highly organized worlds of abstract experience at the present time. Indeed, my view is that there can be no limit to the number of possible modifications in experience. And the business of philosophy, in so far as it is concerned with these modes at all, is not to anticipate or suggest arrests in experience, but to consider the character of those which actually exist. And my picture of experience is thus far incomplete.

But, besides the fact that I have considered only a selection from all the possible modifications, there is a further incompleteness in my presentation of experience. For it appears that the whole of what lies beyond this region of actual or possible specific arrest in experience, this region of expressly formulated, homogeneous and self-contained worlds of abstract ideas, is not concrete and complete experience. In experience there are not only arrests which constitute homogeneous and self-contained worlds of experience, but also arrests which compose no such worlds; there is not only abstraction as a special process, but abstraction as a mere inadvertence. The failure to achieve what is satisfactory in experience may be merely implicit as well as explicit and formulated. There may be mere falling short as well as determinate arrest. And account must be taken of the one as of the other.

We have seen already that it belongs to the nature of an abstract world of experience to be self-contained, sovereign and to lie beyond the relevant interference of any other world of experience, so long as it confines itself within the limits which constitute its character. Of course, if it oversteps itself, an abstract world of experience immediately becomes vulnerable, and of course, in the end, it must overstep itself, demand to be judged as embodying a complete assertion of reality: but so long as it remains faithful to its own explicit character, even the concrete totality of experience itself cannot compete with it upon its own ground. History, Science and Practice, as such, and each within its own world, are beyond the relevant interference of philosophic thought. But where an arrest in experience is merely inadvertent, a mere falling short, but with no precise formulation of the failure, a different situation arises. For, since such an arrest does not constitute a homogeneous and self-contained world of experience, it remains unprotected against interference. Since this is a mere falling short in experience, a failure at once to achieve what is satisfactory in experience and to achieve a self-contained, homogeneous world of experience, it lacks specific identity, and is consequently unable to defend itself against the concrete totality of experience. The strength, indeed the character, of an explicitly abstract world of experience lies in its homogeneity; in spite of its incompleteness it has an identity to defend. But where in experience there is both failure to achieve complete coherence and failure also to achieve a specific world of experience, the result is incompleteness, abstraction, deficiency, but without homogeneity or determinate character.

Arrest in experience may, then, be divided into the determinate and the indeterminate modification of experience. And I shall call the indeterminate modification of experience pseudo-philosophical experience. For this, I think, indicates its general character. It is 'pseudo' because it is abstract. But its relation to philosophical experience, though not necessarily closer, is different from that of a determinate modification of experience. A specific world of abstract experience, although it is not *in the end* secure from the criticism of philosophical thought, although in the end it must submit to supersession, is nevertheless independent in its character as a homogeneous world. It is impossible to make an historical judgment outside the world of historical experience; an historical judgment cannot be the conclusion of any save an historical inference. But where there is no determinate world of experience, no principle of homogeneity, there is nothing to hinder the concrete totality of experience from taking possession, there is nothing to render philosophical thought or criticism irrelevant. An indeterminate arrest in experience is not perhaps less abstract than an arrest which constitutes a determinate world of experience, but its abstraction is less secure: its abstractness is left unformulated. It is impossible to pass at once to the concrete totality of experience from an abstract world of experience, because that world as a world must first be broken down and dissolved. But the passage from a merely indeterminate arrest in experience to the concrete totality of experience is not so revolutionary, not because the distance is less, but because there is less to abolish, less merely to deny. There is no tight, exclusive formulation to be resolved. Or again, an abstract world of ideas demands (we have seen) to be judged as a complete assertion of reality, but this demand is only implicit; it demands equally to be recognized as a homogeneous (if incomplete) world of experience, and thus contradicts itself. But a merely indeterminate arrest in experience, a mere unformulated failure to realize the concrete whole of experience, has but one demand—to be judged as an attempt to achieve what it has failed to accomplish. And for this reason, such a modification of experience is 'philosophical' in a sense in which any specific world of abstract experience is not 'philosophical': it is, in fact, nothing if not philosophical.

One further point may be remarked. I have insisted already that the notion of a 'floating' idea, of experience which belongs to no determinate world of experience, is an absurd and contradictory notion. Such an experience contradicts the character of experience. Consequently, experience which belongs to an indeterminate arrest in experience, whatever else its character, is certainly not a 'floating' idea, an idea without a world. The world here is the concrete totality of experience, the world of philosophic ideas. And the difference, in this respect, between a pseudo-philosophical idea and a philosophical idea is not that they belong to different worlds, but that while the one is ignorant of its world, the other recognizes it. We have seen already that in order to supersede and convert an indeterminate arrest in experience, there is no alien world to be broken down or dissolved, for none exists. What is required is that the arrest should recognize the whole to which it explicitly as well as implicitly belongs. The failure, the defect of such an arrest is a failure to know the world to which it belongs; and it is in respect of this failure that it is abstract. Every experience belongs to a world of experience; and every experience which does not belong to some determinate and homogeneous, but abstract world, belongs directly to the world of concrete experience. But not every experience which belongs to this world is known as belonging to it. Error and defect is not excluded from this world, any more than it is excluded from the worlds of history, science or practice; it merely becomes error of a certain kind, philosophical error. And wherever there is error and defect in the world of philosophical ideas there is an arrest in experience.

Now, it is not my intention here to consider fully all instances of indeterminate arrest in experience, any more than it was my intention in earlier chapters to consider all instances of determinate arrest. Indeed, beyond what I have said about the general character of these indeterminate arrests in experience, I have nothing to offer except a single illustration. Ethical thought, as I understand it, is an indeterminate arrest in experience within the meaning of the view I have indicated, it is philosophical error; and I shall use it for the purpose of illustrating what I take to be the general character of all pseudo-philosophical experience.[1] In doing so I shall be obliged to touch upon many difficult questions; but I must be excused from pursuing them, for I am engaged merely in illustrating a general mode of experience and not in writing an introduction to ethics. My view is, briefly, that ethical thought is an arrest in experience; it is a modification of experience without being a determinate and homogeneous world of experience. Its *raison d'être* lies in its philosophical or concrete character, but it falls short of the full realization of that character. Ethical thought is nothing if not philosophical, but in so far as it remains 'ethical' it is a modification of philosophical thought. Its defect is not that it belongs to an abstract world of experience, but that it fails to recognize and to realize its membership of the world of concrete experience. And in order to substantiate this view, I have to show that ethical thought does not belong to any of the worlds of abstract experience which I have already considered; that it is incapable of constituting itself a self-determined, homogeneous world of its own; that nevertheless it involves an arrest in experience; and that because this arrest is indeterminate, the world of experience to which ethical judgments belong is the world of concrete or philosophical experience.

The distinction between ethical thought and the worlds of abstract experience which I have already considered is partly, though not merely, a matter of designation. Ethics I take, in general, to be thinking about the world of values, the consideration of judgments of value. And it is, of course, possible to think about judgments of value historically, scientifically and practically—so long as we do not attempt it simultaneously. But the view I wish to suggest is that it is also

[1] The name 'Moral Philosophy' indicates, I think, the character of ethical thought. It is philosophical thought, but qualified and limited philosophical thought. And where philosophical thought is qualified and limited, it at once falls short of its philosophical character. The same general character belongs to Theology, to so-called Political Philosophy, and (I think) to Psychology.

possible to think about judgments of value from a standpoint different from, and therefore exclusive of that involved in any of these modes of experience, and that it belongs to the character of ethical thought to be different from historical, scientific or practical thought.

We may dismiss at once the view that ethics must be identified with the history of value judgments or the history of moral ideas. Such a history is, in a sense, possible; but the view that ethics is this or nothing is not one worth considering. And further, if ethical thought is not historical thought about judgments of value, then a history of such judgments, and indeed any conclusions which historical thought may have to offer on the subject, will be wholly irrelevant to ethical thought. History, we have seen, is a propaedeutic for nothing save more history; and where the mode of thought we follow is not historical, it cannot be said to depend upon history or to owe anything whatever to history. We may dismiss, also, the view that ethics must be identified with a science of moral ideas; it is at once clearly possible to think about value judgments without recourse to the scientific mode of thought, and clearly impossible to construct a science of such judgments. In so far as, for example, moral ideas were to become the subject of scientific thought, they would at once lose their distinctively moral character. There can be a science only of quantitative ideas as such. And this, we have seen, is not less true of psychology (where psychology is conceived as a science) than of any other science. A psychological treatment of moral ideas is, in a superficial sense, possible; but, since what is significant in psychology is not the moral character of the ideas, the adjective remains merely as a perfunctory method of designating an arbitrary subject-matter. Ethical thought is, then, a consideration of judgments of value, but its standpoint is neither that of history nor that of science.

But, such is the confusion of mind upon this point, it is a more difficult matter to establish the difference between ethical and practical experience. To deny that, because practical experience is concerned with judgments of value, all thought which is concerned with judgments of value must be practical; and to attempt to explain away the fact that, for the most part, the history of thought about judgments of value has been the history of practical thought, would appear to be foolish adventures. And yet, the first, the view that it is impossible to consider practical judgments except from the standpoint of practice, is a piece of mere stupidity, akin (for example) to requiring that a theory of humour should itself be a joke: and the second is a mere indication of the interests and prejudices of the majority of mankind. Nevertheless, although the view that the moral philosopher is a man who delivers judgments of value, the view that ethical thought is itself practical has, since the time of Aristotle, become almost traditional, we ought not to accept it without considering where it will lead us.

The view we have to consider is that ethical judgments are themselves judgments of value; that ethics is itself the construction of a world of values; that ethical experience is itself normative experience. The business of ethics, it is said, is to tell us what is intrinsically good and to indicate the means by which it may be attained; it is to tell us what we ought to do and to furnish us with a practical criterion of right action; it is to determine what is valuable and to set about its realization. Courage is a virtue; it is right to keep our promises; pleasure is good, are ethical judgments. Ethics, in short, is an attempt to decide what we shall do and how we shall live. And casuistry may be said to be the goal of ethical investigation. And if we turn to the books on the subject we shall find much to substantiate this view. We shall find lists of virtues and vices; we shall be told that pleasure and a virtuous disposition are intrinsically good. But we shall find also another view of the business of ethical thought. We shall find the view that ethics is the attempt to *define* the notions of 'value', of 'good', of 'right' and of 'ought'; that it is not the construction of a world of values or the attempt to realize what is seen to be valuable, but the consideration of valuation and practical judgment from the standpoint of the totality of experience. We shall be told that the questions for ethics to answer are, What do we mean when we say that this action is right and that wrong, when we say that this thing is good and that bad? What do we mean when we say that something is valuable, or that it ought to be? What is the relation between what is good and what is right and what ought to be? Instead of (or as well as) an attempt to organize and integrate our moral and practical judgments, we shall find an attempt to consider the character and validity of these judgments from the standpoint of the totality of experience, an attempt to consider their relation to reality.

Now it will be observed, first, that these two attempts are exclusive of one another; they belong to different and exclusive worlds of ideas. The arguments which will satisfy the one attempt will not satisfy the other; and the satisfaction of either of these attempts does not involve, is indeed irrelevant to the satisfaction of the other. We have seen already that practical thought is characterized by the acceptance of certain categories, certain postulates and a principle of homogeneity which are exclusive of those of all other modes of experience. Practical experience is practical in virtue of being limited to a world of experience of a certain character; it neither has use for, nor recognizes judgments which are not themselves specifically practical. If thinking is to issue in valid practical conclusions it must be exclusively practical thinking and must set on one side all interests and arguments not determined by the categories of practical experience. And it is clear that the second pursuit, the pursuit of a definition of moral and practical concepts, involves a non-practical world of ideas. Agreement that certain things are good, or that certain actions are right involves neither agreement nor disagreement about the ultimate reason why some things are considered good and others bad, some actions right and others wrong. These two sets of judgments are entirely irrelevant to one another. The organization of the practical world, the determination of what things are valuable, of how we shall live and what we shall do, must be carried out without recourse to what is finally satisfactory in experience: a satisfactory life does not depend upon philosophical knowledge; indeed, such knowledge is irrelevant to it. And if we engage upon the other pursuit, the attempt to see the world of practice from the standpoint of the totality of experience, it will be a matter of complete indifference to us what in particular we (in our practical mood) consider to be good and bad, right and wrong. The actual beliefs and opinions and judgments by which we rule our lives are irrelevant to a view of practical experience from the standpoint of the totality of experience. For a view of that sort must explain, not a particular world of value judgments, but the valuation itself. It must explain equally what lies at the back of our moral opinions and what is involved in, and is the ultimate character of the moral opinions of those whose morality is different and opposed to ours. My first observation is, then, that ethics as we find it is composed of two mutually exclusive worlds of ideas.

It will be observed, secondly, that if ethics is to establish itself as a coherent form of thought, it must resign one or other of these mutually exclusive pursuits. So long as we have writers who pretend to tell us what we ought to do and what things are good on the ground of some conclusions they have reached about the character of valuation and practical judgment from the standpoint of the totality of experience, and writers who pretend to have derived a view of the ultimate character of valuation and moral judgment from certain beliefs about what is valuable and what is good, ethics will remain a hybrid and nondescript mode of thought without legitimate issue or valid conclusion. Who serves two masters, serves none; and a way of thinking which confesses allegiance to two different modes of thought cannot avoid *ignoratio elenchi* at every step.

And I venture to conclude that there is no doubt which of these mutually exclusive pursuits assigned to it by a ruinous convention ethical thought should resign. Ethics, in order to avoid ambiguity and inconsequence, must set on one side this attempt to discover what we really think about moral questions, this attempt to organize, integrate and complete our world of values and to apply its conclusions to our conduct of life. For, if it pursues this end, it must abandon the other, of attempting to view our world of practical experience from the standpoint of the totality of experience; and if it abandons this, it must abandon also its connexion with philosophy—it must abandon, in short, what is strong and disciplined in the ethical tradition for what is merely popular and pedantic. For, while nowhere but in ethics has there been a serious and continuous attempt to ascertain the character of practical experience from the standpoint of the totality of experience, the attempt connected with ethical writers to establish and elucidate a world of values, to determine a way of life has been disfigured by pedantry and (for the most part) vitiated by lack of practical knowledge. I mean, then, by ethical thought the consideration of the world of practical experience from the standpoint of the totality of experience, the attempt to define, to discover the ultimate character of moral and practical concepts, the attempt to ascertain the relation of practical judgment to reality. And if this be the character of ethics, we must expect from it no guidance whatever in our practical life, no practical conclusions at all; and, on the other side, an ethical theory will be morally neutral, will neither be derived from nor depend upon specific practical judgments. "The moral convictions of thoughtful and well-educated people" are not the "data of ethics" in any more explicit sense than that they may suggest genuine ethical problems; and an ethical theory which recommends certain things as valuable or good, and certain actions as right or obligatory will stand convicted of irrelevance.

Ethical thought is, then, neither historical, nor scientific, nor practical; it is a world of ideas different from and exclusive of the worlds of abstract experience which I have already considered. But an attempt has been made to constitute ethics into a homogeneous and self-contained world of experience by itself, to discover it as a determinate arrest in experience. Ethics, it is said, is abstract thought (though it is neither historical, nor scientific nor practical thought), and the world of ethical experience is as independent of the legitimate interference of the concrete totality of experience as any other specific world of abstract ideas. A philosophical ethics is not less a contradiction, an *ignoratio elenchi*, than a philosophical science or a philosophical history, and it is contradictory for the same reason. In short, ethics is taken to be the attempt to define, to discover the ultimate character of the main concepts and categories of the world of practical experience. The questions to be answered by ethical thought are, What is the ultimate character of 'good'? What is the ultimate character of 'right'? What is the relation between goodness, right and moral obligation? and all similar questions. And it is asserted that these questions may be answered, that this ultimate definition of the concepts of the moral world may be achieved, without reference to the totality of experience. These are not philosophical questions. The definition of moral concepts belongs to a self-contained world of ideas by itself. The world of values may (some assert that it *must*) be seen as a whole without reference to the totality of experience.[1]

Now, there are two more or less precise propositions which express, from slightly different standpoints, this view of the business and character of ethical thought. It may be said, on the one hand, that all moral concepts, all the concepts of the practical world are indefinable; or that if any are definable, they are definable only in terms of those which are not definable and never in terms of concepts or categories which do not themselves belong to this world. And on the other hand, it may be said that moral characteristics or concepts

---

[1] Here, as elsewhere, it will be noticed that I write as if all values were moral values. But I do so merely for the sake of convenience. I do not wish to assert either that there are, or that there are not values other than moral values.

are *sui generis*; or that if any of them are not *sui generis*, they belong to the *genus* indicated by some other, or others of the concepts of the moral world. And, in both cases, the concepts in question are taken to be 'good', 'bad', 'right', 'wrong', 'ought' and 'duty' or their equivalents. Both these propositions, however, and the whole view of the nature of ethical thought which they express, are, I believe, misconceived; and the objections to them are, I think, conclusive. From the standpoint of the first proposition, it must be replied that it is nonsensical to speak of any concept whatever as indefinable. Every concept whatever contains a reference to the whole of reality, every judgment whatever is an explicit or implicit assertion of reality, and the definition of a concept, the ultimate meaning of a judgment, is simply the indication of its reference to reality. It is true that certain concepts may be shown to be indefinable if some other view than this of definition is relied upon; but I have already considered the view of definition and the view of experience within which it would be possible to speak of a concept as indefinable, and have given my reasons for dismissing it. All concepts, then, are definable in the sense that all concepts whatever belong to the totality of experience and can be exhibited in terms of that totality, no matter in what abstract world or context they are first presented to us. And further, since the world of practical judgments, the world to which these concepts which it is the business of ethical thought to define belong, is an abstract world, an ultimate definition of these concepts can never be achieved in terms of that world or the categories of that world. We have seen that the moral world is an abstract world, and because it is abstract the act of defining its concepts must involve a transformation of those concepts. To see what is abstract from the standpoint of the totality of experience is, itself, to deprive what is abstract of its abstract character. To define a concept is to exhibit its reference to reality; the reference of a moral concept to reality is always merely implicit; consequently the definition of a moral concept must involve the transformation of its character, the making explicit what is inherently implicit. And these objections hold also against the view that all or some moral concepts are *sui generis*. No concept whatever is merely *sui generis*, for no concept whatever can be permanently divorced from its reference to the totality of experience, its reference to reality as a whole. Its character as *sui generis* is an abstract aspect which is incapable of maintaining itself as the whole. Thus, the view that the first question for ethics to answer is whether or not moral or practical concepts are unique and peculiar, whether or not these concepts are *sui generis*, is misconceived. The concepts of the moral world, these concepts of 'good' and 'right' and 'ought', are, as they stand in the moral world, abstract concepts, they have no power to resist the transforming force of the totality of experience; and definition (the business of ethics) is simply the liberation of this force. Not only, then, is the view false that the world of moral concepts is absolute (nothing is absolute save what is complete and we have seen already that the moral world is abstract and incomplete), but the view that it is absolute for ethical thought is also false, because ethical thought is, by definition, the attempt to see these incomplete and abstract concepts in the light of the totality of experience. If, indeed, ethics were identical with practical experience itself, then the concepts of practice would certainly remain uncriticized by ethical thought, they would be (from that standpoint) irreducible; but if ethics were this, its business would not lie with the definition of moral concepts, but merely with the construction out of them of a homogeneous world.

It appears, then, that the attempt to maintain ethical thought as the elucidation and definition of the concepts of the moral and practical world, and to maintain it, at the same time, as a self-contained, homogeneous, exclusive world of abstract ideas, immune from the relevant interference of the concrete totality of experience, must fail. It involves a self-contradiction. If ethics be the definition of practical experience, its concepts and its categories, then an unphilosophical ethics is a contradiction; for philosophy is definition, the consideration of everything from the standpoint of the totality of experience. And any other view must, in my opinion, rely upon a false view of the character of experience. When ethics resigns the attempt to create a world of values, to tell us what is good and what we ought to do (an attempt which has always been extraneous to, and contradictory of its real character), and when it confines itself to the task of defining the categories and concepts of the practical world, then it is unable to avoid philosophy, it is unable to avoid the transformation of the abstract concepts of the practical world which a definition of them in terms of the totality of experience involves. In short, ethics is the consideration of valuation and practical judgment from the standpoint of the totality of experience, and since valuation and practical judgment are abstract and defective from this standpoint, it is impossible to explain them without explaining them, as such, away.

Of course, the mere determination to supersede the abstractness of moral categories and concepts, though it will save ethical thought from some of the more elementary errors into which it may fall, will not of itself produce a satisfactory ethical theory. And ethical theories are not difficult to find which have avoided these more elementary errors (often by good fortune rather than intentionally), but which remain nevertheless unsatisfactory. This, indeed, is the character not only of such perfunctory attempts to define the categories of the moral world as are represented by Naturalism and Hedonism, but also of many of the more thorough-going attempts to work out a genuinely philosophical ethics. But the defects of these ethical theories need not be considered here. What is important, and all that is important, is for us to understand that ethical thought cannot be a self-contained abstract world of ideas similar to (but separate from) the worlds of history, science and practice. Ethics is nothing if not philosophical; whereas a history, a science, or practical experience which is philosophical has ceased to be a history, a science or practical experience. The world to which ethical ideas belong is the world of concrete experience; ethical thought is simply the application of the solvent force of the totality of experience to the abstract world of practical experience.

Nevertheless, the view I am defending is not that ethical thought is philosophical thought, but that it is pseudo-philosophical thought. And I mean by 'pseudo-philosophical thought', thought which belongs to the world of concrete experience, because it belongs to no other world and because its explicit purpose is the achievement of what is ultimately satisfactory in experience, but which nevertheless falls short of the totality of experience. Pseudo-philosophical thought is an indeterminate arrest in experience. We have seen that the world to which ethical thought belongs is the world of concrete experience; ethics is nothing if not philosophical. But we have seen also that ethical thought is limited and incomplete from the standpoint of the totality of experience, for it is not the attempt to find and maintain a world of experience wholly satisfactory in experience, but merely the attempt to see one particular mode of experience—practical experience—from the standpoint of the totality of experience. And consequently, in spite of its philosophical character, ethical thought must be held to constitute an arrest in experience. A complete ethics would fall short of the concrete totality of experience. Ethical thought is the world of philosophical ideas from a single, abstract and incomplete point of view. It is philosophical because it belongs explicitly to the world of philosophical experience; it is abstract because it fails to provide what is completely satisfactory in philosophical experience.

Now, whatever the defects of this illustration, it will have served its purpose if it has made clear what I mean by an indeterminate arrest in experience, and made clear also the difference between such an arrest and what I have called a specific world of abstract ideas. My view is, then, that when we sail outside this archipelago of abstract worlds of experience, when we desert these tight, exclusive, insular but incomplete modes of experience, and find ourselves in the open sea of experience, what we achieve may still fall short of the totality of experience. For in experience what is satisfactory is only the whole of reality as a whole, a complete and completely coherent world of experience; and even when we put behind us all merely modal experience, we may still fall short of a whole which is seen as a whole and complete. And examples of such failure, such falling short and arrest in experience are to be found in ethical and theological thought. It is true that in these there is nothing for philosophical thought actually to destroy; there are no abstract worlds which, as worlds, must be broken up, no explicit and alien formulations to be resolved. But the totality of experience depends nevertheless upon the supersession of every arrest in experience, whether determinate or indeterminate. Ethics is no more a 'part' of philosophy than science is a 'part' of experience; neither has the capacity to maintain itself unaltered in the face of concrete experience, and consequently neither can be said to have any specific contribution to make to the totality of experience. Abstract experience, of whatever kind or degree, requires wholly to be transformed. Nor, as we have observed already, is any mode or arrest or world of abstract experience necessary. All *might* be avoided, and all *must* be overcome and superseded.

§ 3

Experience, having superseded, put behind itself or merely avoided whatever is abstract and incomplete, having freed itself from whatever is seen to hinder the full realization of its character, becomes philosophical experience. And I wish, in conclusion, to consider briefly some further implications of this view of the character of experience and of philosophy.

The view that philosophical experience is concrete experience, and that complete experience is philosophical does not, of course, involve the belief that everything which sets itself up as philosophy provides what is finally satisfactory in experience. What distinguishes philosophy from all other experience is the explicit attempt to achieve what is finally satisfactory in experience. If it fails to achieve this, then it fails to achieve anything it can recognize as an achievement. And this at once differentiates it from an abstract world of experience such as the world of history, of science or of practice. These, though they fail to achieve what is satisfactory in experience, fail because they achieve something else—a specific degree of what is satisfactory. Thus, it is not in virtue of its actual achievement that an experience may be called philosophical; rather, philosophy should be regarded as the determination to be satisfied only with a completely coherent world of experience. For it is not merely its actual achievement which differentiates philosophical from abstract experience, it is its explicit purpose. In all experience whatever there is the pursuit of, the assertion of the real world; but in philosophical experience alone are this pursuit and this assertion explicit and unqualified. Philosophical experience is, then, experience without reservation or arrest, without presupposition or postulate, without limit or category; it is experience which is critical throughout and unencumbered with the extraneous purposes which introduce partiality and abstraction into experience. It is the attempt to realize the character of experience absolutely. And it is satisfied, consequently, with nothing save an absolutely coherent and complete world of experience; it will accept only that which it cannot avoid without contradicting itself.

This view does not claim for philosophy any special source of knowledge hidden from other forms of experience, it does not claim for philosophy immunity from the criterion of experience; philosophy is in no sense an esoteric experience. Indeed, since it recognizes neither 'authorities' nor 'established doctrines' which depend upon something extraneous to themselves for their establishment, but only that which can substantiate itself, stand upon its own feet and defend itself without recourse to witnesses, it must be counted the least esoteric of all forms of experience. Nor is the claim of philosophical experience to be absolute, a merely arbitrary claim. Nothing is absolute save what is complete; and the absoluteness of philosophical experience is a function of its completeness. Indeed, what is complete does not require to claim absoluteness; to admit its completeness involves the admission of its absoluteness. For to be absolute, as I have already remarked, means here merely to be absolved from the defects of partiality and abstraction. Nor again should the view that philosophical experience is complete experience be confused with the erroneous view that philosophy is the sum-total of experiences. Indeed, the notion of a sum-total of experiences is meaningless; it is contradictory of the character of experience. Experiences, from the standpoint of the totality of experience (and no other standpoint is relevant), are not fixed and finished units, merely to be added to, or subtracted from one another, merely to be accepted and used, merely to be incorporated. Experiences can destroy one another, amplify one another, coalesce, suffer change, transformation and supersession. And the experience which is complete and completely coherent is never a merely comprehensive collection of experiences. What is satisfactory in experience is not a great quantity nor a great variety of experiences, but a unity of valid, absolute irreducible experience. And because what is satisfactory in experience is a single, coherent and complete world, philosophy is a unitary whole.[1] There are neither separate parts nor departments in philosophy: to sub-divide philosophy is to destroy it. Logic without metaphysics, metaphysics without logic are alike barren abstractions. And a theory of

---

[1] Neither here, nor anywhere else, am I asserting that in this single whole of experience there is no differentiation. The concrete world is, perhaps, single in, through and by virtue of an intrinsic variety. On that point I have ventured no opinion. What I am asserting is that the differentiation or variety represented in what I have called modes of experience is not and cannot be intrinsic or ultimate in the concrete whole of experience, because these modes are *abstracta* which do not and cannot even appear when our standpoint is that of the totality of experience.

knowledge which is not at the same time a theory of being is an impossibility.

Furthermore, it is implied in this view of the character of philosophical experience that to philosophy place and time are irrelevant. It is often said that no philosophy can escape from its place and time, and that if we are to understand a philosophy we must go to the biography of its author, we must see it in its setting. Now, it is of course true that every philosophy has, in this sense, a place and a time, a setting; but the admission of this truth does not make relevant an appeal to this aspect of its character. It has a place and a date, but these are irrelevant to it as a philosophy. To consider a philosophy with reference to its place and its time is to consider it from a standpoint unknown in philosophy itself. What we must ask about a philosophy is, Can it maintain what it asserts? and its setting will certainly not help us to answer this question. The fact that a philosophy emanates from Oxford, or that it belongs to the nineteenth century is no relevant ground for accepting, or indeed, for rejecting it. From the standpoint of the totality of experience, all we want to know about a philosophy is whether we can accept it or not, whether or not it is valid. Place and time are, indeed, as irrelevant to a philosophical theory as they are to a scientific observation. Each scientific observation has, of course, a date and a place, but these are not relevant to its scientific character. As a specifically scientific observation it has neither date nor place. And a reference to date or place in scientific argument is just one more example of the *ignoratio elenchi* inherent in every passage from the world of history to that of science. What is true or false for the one world is neither true nor false for the other, but meaningless and beside the point.

And finally, although it is true to speak of philosophical experience as the goal or realization of experience, it is false to think of it as the historical end of experience. Philosophical experience does not follow and abolish all abstract and partial experience. It is the concrete and complete whole implied and involved in every modification of experience. The notion that some day, when men are wiser than they are at present, all experience will be philosophical experience and men will forget the past when their minds were still clouded with abstractions, is a notion foreign to the view of philosophy I am defending. It is possible that such modes of experience as science and history may actually be abolished. The world lived long enough and happily enough before they appeared. But it is not philosophy which will abolish them, for it is not philosophy which can take their place. But it is impossible to conceive of the modification of experience I have called Practice ever disappearing. It is an arrest in experience, but it is indispensable to life. It is not a necessary mode of experience (no mode is necessary), but we cannot do without it. Philosophical experience supersedes all modifications of experience, not historically, but logically. It judges them from the standpoint of experience as a whole and for its own sake, and it convicts them of abstraction and failure; but it has no power to abolish them. It may eclipse, but it cannot remove them. For philosophical experience is not a merely ideal end or goal in experience, something which cannot come into existence until the half-gods of abstraction have perished. It is the actual, operative test and criterion of every experience. It is implied in every failure in experience; for failure in experience is never absolute. It is the actual life and nourishment of every abstraction, every modification of experience. It is not something to come; it is the ground, not the hope of experience; it is not merely the end, but also the beginning. Philosophy is simply experience itself without modification or arrest; and consequently it is the final test and criterion of every world of experience. In the world of philosophical experience there is nothing of the character of an unknowable. Indeed, in the end all that is fully knowable is that world.

There are, of course, other views of the character of philosophy than this view, and some of them I have already considered. It is not, however, part of my plan to consider all views which lie to one side of my own, but only those which, either explicitly or by implication, may be seen to stand in relation to it. There is the view, for example, that philosophy, so far from being less abstract than other forms of experience, is more so, is indeed the most abstract of all experience. Philosophy is just one mode of experience among others; an alternative standpoint, of interest only to those who have nothing better to interest them. And this, I suppose, is a possible view; though what the actual content of philosophical experience would in these circumstances be, it is difficult to say. But if this view advances (as is usually the case) beyond the mere assertion of philosophy as one abstraction among others, to the assertion that in experience there is no concrete whole whatever, then at once it becomes nonsensical. Where there is abstraction there must also be a concrete whole; where there is incompleteness, completeness is implied. And if the attempt to free experience from incompleteness, to disencumber it from any limit, qualification or modification whatever, the attempt to recognize no arrest in experience, is not philosophy, then we must find for it some other name. What is certain, however, is that such an attempt, and such a concrete whole of experience, is implied in every experience whatever. And the scepticism which asserts inherent and necessary failure in experience is merely self-contradictory. There is, then, a concrete whole of experience; it alone is the criterion of the validity of every experience; and this for me is philosophical experience. Philosophy, in my view, is not a kind of experience, it is experience itself undistracted and unhindered. And again, there is the view that the world of philosophical experience is this concrete whole of experience, but that it is a mere sum of abstractions. The defect of this view, however, is that it mistakes the character of abstraction. For an abstraction is not something to be accepted in experience, is not, as such, an element or part of the totality of experience, but something as such to be denied and superseded. A mere collection of abstractions could never be more than an abstraction itself. And a composite whole of abstract experiences, because it must fall short of the totality of experience, must fail also to satisfy philosophy.

But besides these and other views of the character of philosophy which stand in contrast to the view I have been defending, others still are to be found which (though incomplete in themselves) may be seen to present single aspects of my view. The view, for example, that it is the business of philosophy to "correct the inadvertencies of man's ordinary thinking" is a view of this kind. It is true, but it is not in my opinion the whole truth. For what is important is to understand whence philosophy derives the capacity to correct our ordinary ways of thinking. Philosophy is the determination to assert reality absolutely, and it is in virtue of this character that it finds itself in a position to correct or supersede the errors of less complete experience. Thus, the business of philosophy is not to correct common errors; that is merely incidental to its character. And moreover, what is required (as we have seen) is not the mere correction of these errors, for they are never mere errors, but the exhibition of the degree of truth they contain. Philosophy does not aim at the abolition of all abstract points of view, but at the demonstration of their abstract character, their incapacity to provide what is completely satisfactory in experience. And because none of these abstract points of view is necessary, it is a perfunctory and incomplete view of philosophy which sees it as beginning from these and as the attempt to correct them. Another view of this kind is that for which the business of philosophy is to hold the ring. Philosophy has no specific content; it has no actual part to play in the game of experience; its position is that of umpire or referee. And this also is true, but not the whole truth. For here again, philosophical experience derives its capacity to hold the ring from its completeness. Its function as critic of the modes of experience is derived from its character as experience without modification or limit. And to see philosophy as the mere referee of the disputes of the various modifications of experience is to see it as less than it is, and to that extent as other than it is. Philosophical experience, in the view I have recommended, by no means stands above the battle of experience: it is experience itself. It is at once the field and the battle, the strength and what remains undefeated in every combatant, the promise and the criterion of victory. And finally, the view of philosophy as self-conscious experience, as experience turned back upon itself, must be considered a view of this kind also. Without being wholly false, it falls short of the complete truth. Philosophy is self-conscious experience. But it is this because it is more than this. It is able to turn back upon itself, not on account of any acrobatic trick of thought, but merely because it has gone the whole circle. It is self-conscious merely because it is unqualified and complete, not because it is double-jointed. Its self-consciousness, its ability relevantly to criticize itself, is merely one aspect of its character which, if insisted upon to the exclusion of all other aspects or if insisted upon ignorantly (without the recognition that it is a characteristic derived from its completeness), will lead us astray. These views, then, while they must fail as definitive views of the character of philosophical experience, must nevertheless be considered true so far as they go.

One further topic may be taken up again in this conclusion. I have said that one aspect of what I have attempted is the elucidation of the character of *ignoratio elenchi*, and this aspect is connected in particular with my view of the relations between all abstract worlds of ideas, and the relation between any abstract world of ideas and the totality of experience. Leaving on one side the first of these relationships, of which I have already said all I have to say, the relation of any abstract world of ideas to the world of philosophical ideas may be considered from either of two standpoints. It may be considered from the standpoint of the abstract worlds of experience, or from that of the totality of experience. From the first of these standpoints, I have insisted upon the incapacity of all abstract worlds of ideas to provide what is satisfactory in experience, I have insisted upon their irrelevance so far as philosophy is concerned. The notion, for example, that philosophy has anything to learn from the methods of scientific thought, or that the conclusions of philosophy "must be in harmony with the results of the special sciences", is altogether false. And I have tried to show why it must be considered false. And again, what is true of science is true also of historical experience. History has nothing to offer which can be recognized or accepted by the totality of experience. And lastly, in these days when practical usefulness appears to be the only criterion recognized, it is particularly necessary to insist upon the irrelevance of practical experience to a world of philosophical ideas.

But what requires equal emphasis is the standpoint of the world of concrete experience. It is my business to insist equally upon the incapacity of philosophy to take the place of any abstract world of experience, and in particular its incapacity to take the place of historical, scientific or practical experience. With regard to history and science it requires the surrender of only the most elementary prejudices in order to accept the view that, so long as they keep within the limits of their postulates they lie beyond the competence of philosophy. A philosophical science and a philosophical history are alike monstrosities. But, such is the weight of prejudice in favour of a philosophic life, it requires a greater effort to accept this view with regard to practical experience. For, because nobody has ears now for what is not practically useful and because it seems impossible to deny to philosophic experience some significance, instead of rejecting philosophy altogether, writers come forward to justify its existence by showing that it is not without its practical value. But, in the view I have recommended, a philosophic life is not less a monstrosity than a philosophic science or a philosophic history. Philosophy can and must supersede practical experience; but it cannot take its place. And to judge practical life by the criterion of philosophy is to commit an *ignoratio elenchi*. A philosophy of life is a meaningless contradiction.

Philosophy is the surrender of all abstract points of view, and among the abstractions which it is most necessary to set on one side is practical life. "He who regards life as other than an illusion that annihilates itself, is still entangled in life", says Novalis; and the existence of philosophic thought depends upon its being unencumbered with the abstractions of practice. But, for philosophy, it is not necessary for the illusoriness of life to be felt emotionally. Indeed, to feel it emotionally is to experience it practically; and the practical apprehension of the futility of living is something quite different from this philosophic disillusion. The one carries with it melancholy, and may lead to suicide. But the other is itself a disengagement from life to which suicide could add nothing relevant. And again, philosophy may be, as Nietzsche and others have suggested, an escape, a mere refuge from life; and this is enough to condemn it in the eyes of practical men. Indeed, the pursuit of philosophical truth is something which *must* be condemned by practice as inimical to life. Philosophy is born an outcast, useless to men of business and troublesome to men of pleasure. But then, the pursuit of what affords unlimited satisfaction in experience for its own sake is something irrelevant to practical life, is an escape from living; and a philosophy which pretended to offer something practically useful would be a philosophy living beyond its means. To turn philosophy into a way of life is at once to have abandoned life and philosophy. Philosophy is not the enhancement of life, it is the denial of life. We must conclude, then, that all attempts whatever to find some practical justification for philosophical thought and the pursuit of philosophical truth, all attempts to replace life with philosophy by subjecting life to the criticism of philosophy, must be set on one side as misguided. We should listen to philosophers only when they talk philosophy.

We come back in the end, then, to what was suggested at the beginning: the view of philosophical thought as the pursuit, for its own sake, of an unlimited, unmodified experience, and at the same time as a mood, a turn of mind. There is perhaps something decadent, something even depraved, in an attempt to achieve a completely coherent world of experience; for such a pursuit requires us to renounce for the time being everything which can be called good or evil, everything which can be valued or rejected as valueless. And no matter how far we go with it, we shall not easily forget the sweet delight which lies in the empty kisses of abstraction. Indeed, the attempt to find what is completely satisfactory in experience is so difficult and dubious an undertaking, leading us so far aside from the ways of ordinary thought, that those may be pardoned who prefer the embraces of abstraction. For, if these give but little satisfaction, and give that little not for long, it is at least a tangible and certain satisfaction while it lasts and one not to be despised.

# INDEX